SHARED VISION

TRANSFORMATIONAL LEADERSHIP IN AMERICAN COMMUNITY COLLEGES

JOHN E. ROUECHE

GEORGE A. BAKER III

AND ROBERT R. ROSE

The Community College Press
American Association of Community and Junior Colleges

National Center for Higher Education
One Dupont Circle, N.W., Suite 410
Washington, D.C. 20036
(202) 293-7050

Copyright April 1989
Printed in the U.S.A.

Published by The Community College Press, a
division of the American Association of Community
and Junior Colleges. No part of this book can be
duplicated without written permission by the publishers.

ISBN 0-87117-190-2

CONTENTS

i

PREFACE

Although leadership and leaders are critical and vital to our society, as concepts they remain elusive—neither well understood nor appropriately delineated. Leadership is not a phenomenon associated only with power, prerogatives, and prestige, nor is it defined by management tasks of planning, organizing, staffing, directing, and evaluating. Leadership is much more. Parnell writes:

NOTHING is more important for an effective leader than to clarify the mission of the organization that he or she represents. The Good Book says, "Without a vision, the people will perish." Communicating vision is a fundamental task of leadership. Mission clarification and goal setting, therefore, are priority tasks for an effective leader. We live best by living on our hopes rather than on our fears; by looking to the future, not the past. A leader sets the tone, the motivation, and the positive attitudes about the future of an organization or the group that he or she is leading and articulates these clearly as part of the mission and goals of the organization (1988, p. 1).

Clearly, there is a tremendous need for leadership and an expanding opportunity for leaders to make a difference to their institutions. The AACJC Futures Commission states that in the building of the community, **stronger** presidential leadership is required. Community college presidents must be not only effective day-to-day administrators, but also leaders inspired by and able to convey a larger educational mission (1988). Leaders in the community colleges of America will always face new educational and external challenges. Their preparation and their understanding of the values and qualities of effective leadership will empower them and their followers to face those challenges with dynamic and resourceful skills.

In this study of selected leaders of American public community colleges, we were challenged by the idea that leadership was neither an inherited trait nor a product of the "great man" theory. In the teachings of the great philosophers, such as Lao-Tsu and Plato, we found confirmation of our idea that leadership can be learned. From the modern theorists we learned that contemporary studies of leadership focus on the qualities and behaviors of the leaders. We emphasized the interrelationships among the leader, the followers, and the institutions. From our research data we developed a group of themes and behavioral attributes common to transformational leaders; we then employed these themes and attributes to study a number of selected leaders in American community colleges in depth.

We knew that studying *all* 1,220 presidents of junior and community colleges in America would be impossible. Our research design reflected this reality and set our direction: we looked for leaders who demonstrated the transformational characteristics defined by Burns (1978), Bass (1985a), and Tichy and Devanna (1986). Accordingly, we invited all AACJC member colleges to nominate Chief Executive Officers (CEOs) in their state or region who demonstrated the ability to influence the values, attitudes, beliefs, and behaviors of faculty and staff by working with and through them to accomplish the college's mission and purpose.

From that original population, 296 community college CEOs were identified and asked to respond to the first phase of our data gathering; 256 presidents responded. The information from these CEOs provided us with first-hand experiential data of leadership qualities. We then asked each of the 256 to identify two outstanding CEOs with whom they had worked. This nominating process and our decision process yielded 50 presidents (from 30 states) who were interviewed in depth by our research team. Ideally, we would have interviewed all 256 nominees, but time and resources dictated a more feasible research protocol.

In order to examine the concept of leadership, we studied a group of exceptional leaders. All research efforts have limitations, and we acknowledge ours; given the task we set for ourselves—to identify and study transformational presidents—we have succeeded in focusing this study on successful and exemplary leaders in American community colleges.

We believe that CEOs are not necessarily the only group to choose who best meets the criteria of transformational leader, and many will argue that institutional members would have provided better information. We chose to ask CEOs, and we are satisfied with that decision. In addition, we eliminated from the study those who chose not to respond to our request for information or were unable to do so because they were unavailable. In retrospect, we are sure that there exist many CEOs who are transformational leaders who were not intervewed. We believe that although others could have been recognized, additional data would not have altered the outcomes of this study. *We stress, though, that the absence of a particular CEO's name from the discussion of leadership in this book in no way implies that he or she is not an outstanding college leader.*

By identifying the behaviors of these exemplary leaders, we have begun a process of identifying leadership skills for both present and future CEOs. *Shared Vision: Transformational Leadership in the Community College* identifies the qualities and attributes of transformational leaders. We have dispelled the idea that leadership is an innate trait or personality variable. Leadership is not inherent. It can be developed, taught, and learned; and *Shared Vision* points the way. The community college as an open-door institution will always require unique leadership which is innovative and motivational, but excellent leadership will never "just happen."

Excellent leaders are those who have been trained and are motivated to be leaders. Obviously, there are both professional and cognitive dimensions of leadership. Just as we earn degrees and attend educational institutions to become physicians and lawyers and computer scientists, so should we be educated to lead. Leadership preparation is a fundamental obligation of graduate schools in association with the AACJC, the Presidents' Academy, and other state and regional agencies; new leadership training programs must be initiated to prepare new generations of community college leaders. Moreover, present executive leaders and administrators can profit from ongoing leadership training and development. Self-assessment and evaluation should be a top priority for existing leaders; professional development can and should be continuous and self-renewing. The goal of leaders is to motivate and inspire others to fulfill the community college mission of open access and academic excellence. *Shared Vision* points out the attributes of a transformational leader and thus provides an opportunity for self-evaluation by all leaders, to better meet the demanding challenges of the future of community colleges in America.

It is critical that the challenges of leadership in the community college be met. *Shared Vision* consists of the following chapters:

Chapter 1 provides the overview for the study, emphasizes the importance of leadership, and identifies the five themes of transformational leaders.

Chapter 2 summarizes leadership theory and culminates in a discussion of transformational leadership and its place in a rapidly changing society.

Chapters 3, 4, and 5 describe and discuss the study. Chapter 3 describes our approach to the study, including the selection process. Chapter 4 details the demographic findings and compares them to previous studies. Chapter 5 describes our research findings and the theoretical framework that evolved from the statistical data.

Chapters 6 through 10 discuss each of the five themes generated from our research findings. Chapter 6 details the concept of shared vision, which we found to be the key element of transformational leadership. Chapter 7 emphasizes teamwork and collaborative decision-making. Chapter 8 discusses climate and the relationship between the institution and the individuals, including students, within it. Chapter 9 explains the importance of motivation as a means of achieving followers' acceptance of the shared vision. Chapter 10 focuses on personal values, with emphasis on integrity and commitment to learning.

Chapter 11 examines the role of women in community college leadership roles. Chapter 12 presents a summary of the research, a discussion of the problems faced by minority leaders, and a review of study implications.

In a study as comprehensive and detailed as this, it is impossible to acknowledge every individual who made significant contributions. However, we would like to thank those without whose help this study could not have been completed.

First, we thank the many community college presidents, chancellors, and state directors who nominated their colleagues as outstanding leaders. We especially appreciate the 256 CEOs who sent us valuable research information and their personal statements of educational philosophy. For contributions beyond the call of duty, we acknowledge the fifty "blue chippers," who took time from their busy schedules to participate in extensive in-depth interviews, to answer our questionnaires, and to provide us with the names of the members of their college leadership teams. We thankfully recognize the executive assistants/secretaries of these leaders for providing a communication link between the research team and the leadership teams. We are grateful to the leadership team members, whose responses enabled us to make unique comparisons between the CEOs and their teams.

Rosemary Gillett-Karam developed Chapter 11 from her dissertation. She and Mary Ann Roe served admirably as senior research assistants on the project. They have augmented the study through their data collection, analysis efforts, and their contributions to the final manuscript. Dr. Gillett-Karam is currently chairperson of the Social and Behavioral Sciences Division at Austin Community College, and she is also a Kellogg Postdoctoral Fellow at the University of Texas at Austin. Ms. Roe is currently completing her doctoral program at the University of Texas, where she is doing research with Professor George Kozmetsky on the role of the community college and technology transfer at the Innovation, Creativity, and Capital (IC²) Institute.

We owe special thanks to Robert Pred, Research Associate at the University of Texas, for his unique ability to assist us in the development of research questions and statistical methodology to answer them. We are grateful to Jill Bailey-Duckworth, who painstakingly assisted with data collection and interpretation and who produced the many tables, charts, and graphs included in the final manuscript.

We acknowledge the efforts of Suanne Roueche, senior lecturer and Director, NISOD, the University of Texas, who read, reread, and edited each chapter; Frank Wright, a research postdoctoral fellow at the University of Texas, who assisted with the CEO interview process; Reid Watson, who helped with typing of the final manuscript; Libby Lord, who provided continued assistance to us throughout the year-long research project; and Susan Burneson, who generously assisted us by the routine loan of her office, her computer, and her super laser-printer. We are grateful also to every member of the Community College Leadership Staff, all of whom had birthday parties, if not birthdays, during the months we were completing this manscript.

We thank Ann Parish, a high school English teacher with the Austin Independent School District and our senior editor, who has assisted us on a number of earlier studies and whose ability to work with words has made this study both clear and powerful. She has read and edited countless versions of each chapter, with meticulous attention to detail and great concern for accuracy.

We acknowledge our senior Kellogg Postdoctoral Fellow, Robert Rose, who has been involved with this project from Day One, as we sat in our office more than a year ago to discuss leadership needs and opportunities and conceptualized a national study that would provide an in-depth investigation of leader attributes and qualities. Dr. Rose has been the Dean of Students at Mt. Royal College, Calgary, Alberta, Canada, and has had a long career as instructor, head basketball coach, and successful college administrator. We could never properly acknowledge the tremendous contributions of time, talent, and boundless energy that he brought to this project. And we most gratefully acknowledge the on-going support of Mr. Valleau Wilkie, Executive Director of the Sid Richardson Foundation, Fort Worth, Texas. The Richardson Foundation has provided financial support for all of our research efforts and continues to be generous with its funding of our varied activities.

Finally, we extend our thanks to AACJC and the Community College Press for publishing *Shared Vision*. Readers should be aware, however, that responsibility for the study reported here lies solely with the authors. AACJC neither funded nor endorsed it. The opinions expressed on the following pages do not necessarily reflect the views of AACJC or its Board of Directors.

John E. Roueche
George A. Baker
Austin, Texas
January, 1989

CHAPTER 1

LEADERSHIP IN THE COMMUNITY COLLEGE

66 *The most successful leader of all
is one who sees another picture not yet
actualized. The leader sees the things which
belong in the present picture but which
are not yet there... Above all, the leader
should make co-workers see that it is not
his or her purpose which is to be
achieved, but a common purpose born of the
desires and the activities of the group.* *99*

MARY PARKER FOLLETT, *Dynamic Administration*

COMMUNITY COLLEGES AND THE FUTURE

THE SITUATION

THE CHALLENGE

TRANSFORMATIONAL LEADERS

THE NEW STUDY

LEADERSHIP IN THE COMMUNITY COLLEGE

INTRODUCTION

Shared Vision examines successful community college leaders and the behaviors by which they transform the future direction of their institutions through their visions and their dreams. They understand that the community college is guided by the vision they are able to share and communicate with their students, faculty, staff, board, and community. The explosion of community colleges into American higher education is directly related to the framework of values that such **leaders** bring to their institutions as they influence, motivate, and empower others toward greater performance. This book examines the achievements of many successful community college CEOs who understand the interrelationships between themselves and the groups who comprise their colleges. We believe, as Plato and Socrates did, that leadership can be learned and that the vehicle for that process emanates from education. The knowledge gained from the study of these leaders is applicable to the development of future leaders.

Early researchers believed that the leader's role, or the potential to influence the quality of performance of others, was inherent—either you had it or you didn't. Subsequent research has moved away from the idea that leadership is an accidental trait of birth and destiny. Contemporary research supports the idea of leadership grounded in contingency theory—leadership is examined as a function of the behavior of leaders and the quality and duration of their attempts to influence others.

Research demonstrated that leaders who attempt to influence or lead others are engaging in different patterns of behavior based on *task* (goal achievement or planning), *consideration* (people orientation), and *situation* (position with respect to circumstances and conditions). Situational leadership came to be defined as the extent to which the leader varied emphases on behaviors to fit the situation (Blake and Mouton, 1964; Fiedler, 1967; Hersey and Blanchard, 1982).

The leadership exercised by the CEO of the American community college is indeed situational. The research we reviewed and our own led us to one clear, unequivocal conclusion: the American community college is unique. Its uniqueness rests on a foundation of egalitarian education and democratic ideals. It has provided educational access and opportunity to thousands of Americans.

Unique organizations call for unique leaders. Excellence in any situation can be achieved by studying those who excel in performance in a given setting. Studies such as this one provide a strategic path that may enable others to acquire the skills of the exceptional performer. One does not become excellent through the acquisition of knowledge or in the use of knowledge in a simulated environment. One becomes excellent as skills and knowledge are developed in the *process* of actually performing on the job.

We are convinced that the leadership skills of exceptional CEOs can be taught and acquired on the job. The secret, we believe, lies in leaders' recognition that leadership style is developmental. When leadership potential is seen as situational and developmental, a leader's goal is to apply and polish a full range of skills and attributes in a performance repertoire. Those who wish to lead must be willing to risk developing new leadership skills and, after evaluating their own performances, discover what works and what does not.

What remains is for research to continue the quest to identify and understand exceptional CEOs. We have discovered that if leaders lack a vision for themselves, it is difficult to orchestrate the other skills necessary to lead. We believe that we have identified many of the most effective and visionary community college CEOs in America. This study is about them and what they do.

COMMUNITY COLLEGES AND THE FUTURE

THE undergraduate college in America, with its long and vener-
able tradition, has a unique mission to fulfill, one that will en-
rich and, at its best, transform. Why else make it the prerequi-
site to professional study? Why else provide college for those who
otherwise could be trained on the job or in a corporate classroom?
It can only be because of the conviction that something in the
undergraduate experience will lead to a more competent, more
concerned, more complete human being (Boyer, 1987, p. 1).

Community colleges are vital to the future of this nation. It will be the community college that will keep America working. It will be the community college that will be able to transfer the technology, developed in partnerships between the American corporation and the American university, into operational reality. The diversity of needs of individual communities throughout America is constantly being identified and uniquely addressed by their community colleges. We suggest that the totality of this effort nationwide has established the community college as an essential institution, vital to the health and well-being of this country. We further suggest that the leaders of this movement have definition of role and definition of mission. Within this role and mission it is imperative to understand that the myriad needs of individual communities are constantly changing, requiring a variety of responses. The challenges confronting American society, now more than ever, must be met by exceptional leaders who can deal with change and revitalize the institutions of America.

THE SITUATION

We understand that successful organizations are led by successful leaders. And successful leaders have followers. Together they address the twin goals of an open-door policy and educational excellence. Many community college CEOs are confronted with the challenges not only of these dual and often conflicting goals, but also with the myriad problems that accompany them. Yet throughout the country, America's outstanding community college leaders are in the forefront of change, working with strong leadership teams and informed followers to confront and solve these problems. The following examples illustrate some CEO behaviors:

NATIONAL statistics show that college students fail or withdraw from 40 percent of their classes each semester. At Jefferson Community College, the rate is only 27 percent, due to a strong program of faculty counseling and in-class involvement. The CEO was committed to student access and success.

WHEN secretaries in central administration opposed a switch from one word-processing system to another, the CEO of De Anza College invited in experts from both systems. He then asked the secretaries for a recommendation, rather than forcing compliance. To make this change, the CEO sought and valued the opinions of others.

THE Criminal Justice and Public Safety Training Center at Monroe Community College needed more space, forcing one department to move into rental space off-campus. The CEO arranged space at low cost and asked for volunteers to make the move. The Criminal Justice Center volunteered and now has 30,000 feet of excellent space and a highly supportive law enforcement and public safety community. At Monroe Community College, the CEO was able to cause followers to share the vision of the future.

TULSA Junior College received funding to construct a third campus. However, due to statewide economic problems, no operational funds were available when the campus was ready to open. The CEO asked the staff to assume additional responsibilities, delaying the opening for one semester while cash was raised for operations. The campus opened to serve its students and the community because the CEO empowered others by delegating authority and responsibility.

THE Board of Trustees of Tyler Junior College was reluctant to make commitments to a long-term building plan. The CEO worked with all members of the college and the community to develop a master plan through the year 2000. Three new buildings have been completed, and a fourth is planned. The CEO was a risk-taker and change agent.

A predicted enrollment decline at Greenville Technical College failed to shake the complacency of many administrators, although a decline would have been disastrous for the college. The CEO's commitment, enthusiasm, and bias for action resulted the next year in the highest student enrollment in the college's history, while many surrounding institutions did, in fact, experience decline.

AT Macomb Community College, hostile negotiations between the college and the faculty union resulted in a four-day strike in 1983. In 1985, the CEO reached a tentative economic settlement before formal negotiations began. As the bargaining teams cooperated on the details, they built considerable respect and trust. The CEO demonstrated respect for individual differences and motivated followers through clarification of expectations.

WHEN Sandhills Community College needed new buildings, the CEO got the staff and faculty involved in a massive "voter campaign." The bond issue passed by 51 percent, and three major buildings are under construction. The CEO was able to motivate followers to commitment and action.

WHEN area businesses turned to private vocational schools to get training for their employees, the CEO of Los Rios Community College District led the institution into making major changes in the way job training classes were handled. Today a customized curriculum is offered throughout the community on a demand-schedule at employee work sites. The CEO was able to involve others appropriately in decision-making.

THE *theater faculty at the College of DuPage decided to present a controversial play. After the college was picketed by religious groups, the CEO met with the bishop and the press to discuss academic freedom. The play was presented, with discussion groups following each showing. The objectors were satisfied that their voices were heard, and the faculty was pleased with the CEO's support. The CEO built openness and trust through personal and professional behavior.*

WHEN *a new CEO came to St. Louis Community College, he brought several members of his previous management team, creating tensions between the "old guard" and the "new guard." The CEO openly confronted this tension, actively encouraged open communication, and intermingled old and new people on ad hoc committees. The two groups quickly became one team. He was able to cause followers to work together to solve problems.*

WHEN *Brevard Community College needed $2.5 million to fund the operation budget for its Performing Arts Center, a professional fundraiser said there was only $1 million available in the community. The CEO organized, solicited, and assigned nonprofessional group leaders to the task. Long before the deadline, the group had raised $2.6 million—and monies were still coming in! This CEO was able to conceptualize a specific future and inspire others to extra effort through praise and direction.*

SAN *Juan College in New Mexico works with many government organizations, civic groups, and educational resources. The CEO of San Juan College wanted the college to be a catalyst in focusing the efforts of these diverse groups. The new Business Assistance Center has been instrumental in bringing new economic development to the county as well as allowing groups to work together on economic matters. The CEO articulated a sense of mission and was able to build an effective communication network.*

*AN employee in the Foothill-De Anza Community College Dis-
trict was not granted an interview for a promotional position.
After considerable discussion about whether internal applicants
had the right of "first consideration," the CEO made a forceful
and emotional speech about the college "family" and morale. As
a result, it became district policy that all internal applicants would
be given interviews. The CEO understood the character, sentiment, and moral values of the followers.*

From these examples, we have learned that the community college
CEO faces many issues which require a tremendous amount of time,
energy, and money. These issues should be addressed within the context of the educational institution. Baldridge identified several characteristics that, translated to the community college setting (in Baker,
1984), are unique to colleges:

1. Serving clients with disparate, complicated needs is difficult.

2. Decision-making authority is highly diffuse and decentralized,
   causing the process to become fragmented, unstructured, and
   often partisan.

3. Colleges and universities are vulnerable because of external influences, both in their funding sources and in government
   regulations.

4. Educational goals are not product-oriented; they are often ambiguous, and they are highly contested, often by those assigned
   to execute the goals.

These characteristics of the community college, combined with current issues and problems, have focused critical scrutiny on community
colleges and their promises. Obviously, internal and external examination must occur; revitalization of efforts demands a constant re-
examination of role and mission. We believe what is needed to enhance
the quality and clarity of the community college mission is excellent
leadership; that is, colleges need leaders who can perceive and integrate the global picture of community needs with existing institutional

resources and future potential. Moreover, such outstanding leaders must be able to translate this vision into understanding for followers, empowering them to utilize their skills to achieve the "shared vision." The leaders of the 1960s and early 1970s, the first generation of community college CEOs (Vaughan, 1986), were pioneers who established the college within the community. No longer do they face the demands of rapid expansion, but no longer do they enjoy the blessings of abundant funding. Over the course of the past two decades, the ground rules have changed dramatically. Today's leaders, the second generation, must be strong enough to cope with problems of the existing organization and the challenges it faces. We have entered into a new era of leadership in which presidents must develop and communicate their vision, mobilize people in new directions, and convert followers into leaders. These leaders must be able to empower others to meet the dual demands of access and excellence, for they are the keys to successful change.

Such is the critical challenge facing community colleges as they move into the decade of the 1990s and beyond. Community colleges—through excellent leadership—must be adaptable, flexible, and responsive to match the needs of their communities.

THE CHALLENGE

The first step in the challenge is to identify leaders who can integrate changes in the college to respond to changes in the community. The ability to recognize and accomplish this integration requires individuals who possess the conceptual framework of holistic leadership. In the context of leadership, these presidents anticipate and create a vision of what the college can become, while in the context of management they "define and do" to help this vision come true (Keyser, 1985). Parnell indicated that management talent and leadership talent are not the same, but it is a "blessing when these two attributes are combined in the same person" (1988, p. 1).

Collaboration of vision is not accomplished in isolation. We strongly believe that an important element of leadership—perhaps the most important element—is the relationship between leaders and followers. We believe that the most successful community colleges are led by those who have the ability to change the values as well as the behaviors of the followers and to focus the entire college community toward a commonly accepted vision of the future.

TRANSFORMATIONAL LEADERS

This transformation—or change—is accomplished, in part, through the development of a leadership team—a cohesive group of people working and moving together in the same direction. The cohesion of these teams is due to the acceptance of the CEO's influence. Through this acceptance, followers are transformed into leaders, infusing the shared vision into all parts of the college. This vision is then made real by utilizing the skills of competent managers, faculty, and support staff.

We have defined transformational leadership in the community college as "the ability of the community college CEO to influence the values, attitudes, beliefs, and behaviors of others by working with and through them in order to accomplish the college's mission and purpose." We have also defined management as "the ability to integrate the skills of people with the components of technology for the purpose of organizing those elements necessary to accomplish the college's mission and purpose." Thus, leadership is related to influencing human behavior, and management is related to integrating human skills with technology. Both are critical, but leadership is paramount.

Community college leaders who are most successful are those who are committed to actions necessary to bring about appropriate change. They understand that changing the institution necessitates a process of changing people by influencing their values, attitudes, beliefs, and behaviors. Transforming leaders accept that change produces resistance and recognize that commitment for long-term results will not be accomplished through demands for new processes and methods. Followers must be given an opportunity to work through the psychological implications of the change process and, in so doing, to explore the personal impact of change in their working environment. It is essential that followers understand and appreciate the need for change, since new paths require new direction, coaching, and development. Transformational leaders understand that relinquishing familar patterns of behavior is difficult and that the process requires time and careful attention. They also know that well-developed teams desire freedom to perform and yet require vision and direction.

The challenge and responsibility of community college leadership is to create a vision for excellence within the context of institutional problems and characteristics. The challenge continues in the attempt to effect change for successful outcomes through maximizing human potential. A significant number of community college leaders believe that our future is not an amorphous mystery; it is a matter of choice and will and work. These leaders believe, with Chancellor Tom Fryer of Foothill-

De Anza Community College District, that by choosing a vision of the future and working for it, "we can win. We can win the right things for the right reasons. We can win, and we will win—if we choose to do so."

THE NEW STUDY

We have conducted a new national research project to study transformational leadership at America's community college. We wanted, first, to identify a group of leaders who exemplify our definition of transformational leadership: "the ability to influence, shape, and embed values, attitudes, beliefs, and behaviors consistent with increased staff and faculty commitment to the unique mission of the community college." Second, we wanted to illustrate what they believe and what they do as they empower others to lead their colleges toward excellence.

Using our definition of transformational leadership, we asked over 950 community college CEOs—chancellors, presidents, and state directors—to nominate individuals who exhibited such leadership qualities. We thought it important to ask the people who actually work with these leaders—their colleagues and directors—to nominate them. Over 80 percent of the CEOs responded, identifying 256 such leaders. We were pleased to see not only the names of well-known leaders previously acknowledged in other national studies, but also new names of outstanding leaders in small or rural colleges or in new positions. Since 21 of the nominees were women, we also decided to examine possible gender differences in CEO behaviors.

We also asked the 256 nominees to name the very best leaders they knew; as a result, we developed a list of 50 CEOs. Using the themes we had formulated earlier, we interviewed these 50 "blue chippers," because we believe that followers are a critical part of leadership, we also interviewed members of their leadership teams. The interviews resulted in informative and enthusiastic descriptions of the beliefs and attributes of these 50 leaders. These collective descriptions are the basis of this study.

From our CEOs' statements and research on leadership, we generated five themes that we believe are common to transformational leaders: influence, people orientation, motivation, values, and, most important, vision.

TRANSFORMATIONAL leaders believe in teamwork and shared decision-making. They have a bias for action, and they empower others to act. They try to develop a collaborative situation that is not dependent on any one individual for success.

THEY value people, both as members of the team and as individuals. They respect individual differences and value the opinions of others. They reward work well done. Students are a focal point of their efforts.

THEY understand motivation. They have high expectations of others and inspire them to develop their creative and problem-solving skills.

THEY have a strong personal value system. They value consistency, integrity, commitment to student learning, and openness. They model the conduct they expect of others.

TRANSFORMATIONAL leaders have a vision of what their college can become. They are willing to take risks and commit their colleges to new directions that incorporate the needs of their communities.

The purpose of this book is to examine the practices of the group of community college presidents identified in our research study. We will hear from these presidents about how they orchestrated their particular systems to achieve the changes they desired to meet the unique needs of their colleges. The CEOS we studied encouraged experimentation within the key themes. They tried different ways of promoting change, while remaining focused on the important themes; they were not distracted by managerial problems. They were, in fact, focused on that which must be done. They had tremendous vision. Vision, or the ability to see what the future should be, is the *sine qua non* of the transformational leader. While many attributes must be present to bring about appropriate change, the theme of vision remains central and paramount. The transformational leader must have a vision of the changing college and must be able to transform the beliefs of others into a commitment to **shared vision**.

CHAPTER 2

LEADERSHIP

" *Good managers get things done.*
Great managers are able to accomplish
impressive and monumental tasks.
Leaders, on the other hand, tend to alter
dramatically the attitudes of their followers
who, in turn, through conviction,
make significant things happen. **"**

GEORGE R. CONGER, President, Aims Community College

INFLUENCE ORIENTATION: Demonstrated Competencies

LEADERSHIP: WHAT DOES IT MEAN?

LEADERSHIP: A HISTORICAL PERSPECTIVE

LEADERS AND THEIR ENVIRONMENTS

TRANSACTIONAL LEADERSHIP

TRANSFORMATIONAL LEADERSHIP

LEADERSHIP: HERE AND NOW

LEADERSHIP

INTRODUCTION

L eaders make a difference. We know that the leader is a critical factor in the effectiveness of any organization. Leadership has been
analyzed from many different perspectives over the years in an
attempt to determine the elements of success, and the research has
generated a number of theoretical approaches to leadership qualities.

New times have mandated new leadership approaches. As we trace
development from the earliest trait theories, we have come to recognize the need for a new approach described as transformational
leadership—an approach to leadership in which the leader transforms
the institution by enabling those who serve the institution to participate actively in the process. Leaders can no longer be viewed as entities in isolation; rather they must possess the ability to empower their
followers to *be* and to *do*. In order to understand this evolution and
its implications for the present, we need to reflect on the past to create
a perspective for the future.

This chapter will examine leadership: its meaning, its history, current theories about it, and its relationship to organizational culture.
We will also discuss the importance of both organizational and individual dynamics to the transformational process.

LEADERSHIP: WHAT DOES IT MEAN?

Leadership has received much attention over the years, yet there is considerable confusion surrounding its very definition. As noted by Hoy and Miskel (1987, p. 270), leadership is an elusive topic; there are as many different definitions proposed as there are researchers engaged in the study. In reviewing many of the definitions found in the literature, we can generate several key concepts. "Leadership is principally an action-oriented interpersonal process" (Cribbin, 1981, p. v). "Leadership is, by definition, an interpersonal relationship in which power and influence are unevenly distributed so that one person is able to direct and control the actions and behaviors of others to a greater extent than they direct and control his" (Fiedler, 1967, p. 11). "Leadership is the ability to influence or motivate an individual or a group of individuals to work willingly toward a given goal or objective under a specific set of circumstances" (Tucker, 1984, p. 41). Reddin (1970) concludes that leadership is the process by which the leader influences his followers to achieve group objectives.

Arthur Jago (1984) proposes a comprehensive definition that incorporates important aspects from several predecessors: "Leadership is both a *process* and a *property* of the individual. The process of leadership is the use of noncoercive influence to direct and coordinate the activities of the member of an organized group toward the accomplishment of group objectives. As a property, leadership is the set of qualities or characteristics attributed to those who are perceived to successfully employ such influence" (p. 2). Jago further notes it is important to recognize that leadership is not only some quality or characteristic that one possesses or is perceived to possess, but also something that one does. It, therefore, can describe an act as well as a person; it is demonstrated through the interaction between people and thus implies "followership."

As we reflect on the implications of these definitions of leadership as they may be applied to the community college setting, it behooves us to add yet another definition of leadership—one that we feel characterizes and captures the essence of what is happening on community college campuses across America:

LEADERSHIP is the ability to influence, shape, and embed values, attitudes, beliefs, and behaviors consistent with increased staff and faculty commitment to the unique mission of the community college.

This definition is also consistent with the characteristics inherent in the term attributed to James MacGregor Burns—"transformational leadership." Transformational leadership "occurs when one or more persons engage with others in such a way that leaders and followers raise one another to higher levels of motivation and morality (fundamental wants, needs, aspirations, and values of the followers)" (Burns, 1978, p. 8). Thus, for one to influence, another must permit himself to be influenced.

Community college presidents have the unique opportunity to use such influence. Their position enables them to play a pivotal role in leading their colleges to be responsive and progressive in meeting the challenges of the external environment they serve. At the same time, they can provide an internal environment that delegates and empowers those within the organization to address such external challenges creatively.

To accomplish this sense of harmony in the community college, the president and follower(s) need both to understand and to have agreement on the purpose or mission of the unique college in which they serve. Therefore, the leader-follower relationship is critical to our definition of leadership in the community college. Leadership is an evolving, dynamic process in which, at different times, leaders become followers and followers become leaders.

Most of the research has examined the concept of leadership in work settings, rather than in higher education. The evolution of leadership research enables us to focus on current theories and thus to focus on the implication of the concept of leadership in the community college setting. It is important to understand fully how we arrived at where we are.

LEADERSHIP: A HISTORICAL PERSPECTIVE

Empirical investigations of leaders have been conducted by hundreds of researchers over the past fifty years, and still we have no clear and unequivocal understanding of what distinguishes leaders from non-leaders, effective leaders from ineffective leaders, and effective organizations from ineffective organizations. In the past, researchers have attempted to structure the concept of leadership by dissecting the term to reflect the fads, fashions, political tides, and academic trends of the time. For example, leadership articles in the AACJC's *Community, Technical, and Junior College Journal* for the past decade have closely reflected the notions of leadership espoused in publications in other fields. When the profit sector researchers have touted management by objectives, quality circles, or strong aggressive leadership, the literature in our field has followed suit.

An early attempt to explain leadership took the "great person" approach. Numerous researchers sought to determine the unique characteristics or traits that differentiated leaders from followers. They assumed the existence of a finite number of identifiable traits—traits that could be used to differentiate between successful and unsuccessful leaders. Studies were designed to identify and measure physical traits, mental traits, and personality traits, without regard to situational factors. The contention was that if a leader was separated from the masses by superior qualities, studies should reveal what those qualities were. But the results of the studies were inconclusive. Patterns of traits appeared in combinations, and different patterns were appropriate for different situations. These complexities created a problem regarding leadership traits and led to the question, What traits set what leaders apart from followers, and which will vary from situation to situation? Because of the obvious influence of situational factors on leadership traits, this approach failed to answer the critical empirical "difference" question.

After the trait ("great person") approach, the study of leadership concentrated on how leaders behaved. This new focus, which examined what leaders did rather than how they appeared to others, gained support and popularity during the 1950's (Hollander, 1978). This approach recognized that individual traits were significantly influenced by varying situations and that leaders took different actions in varied situations. Not only were leaders responding to task, but they were also responding to other elements of a given situation—e.g., organizational structure, cultural environment, rules and regulations, situational resources, or follower sentiments. Although this approach to leadership was developed as a result of the failure to find one best way to lead, it also failed to answer the critical question: "What is effective leadership?" Such a view of leadership did not adequately consider such factors as the follower personality or motivation, technology, the nature of the group, or the position power of the leader. The greatest failure of the situational approach surfaced when the "path-goal" researchers pointed out that the focus of leadership must be on the follower and not the leader, given that what the follower chose to do or not to do was the true measure of leadership effectiveness. In attempting to address the shortcomings of situational leadership, a third approach to leadership emerged—one which examined the concept of contingency leadership theory.

Contingency theory is the most comprehensive of the leadership theories to date. Underlying this approach is the idea that, to be effective, the leader must cause the internal functioning of the college to be consistent with the demands of the college mission, technology, or external environment, and to meet the needs of its various groups and members. Lorsch and Lawrence (1970) believe that rather than searching for the best way to organize under all conditions, one should examine the goals in relationship to the needs of its particular members and the impact of external pressures. The result is the development of a "contingency" theory of organizations: the appropriate internal states and processes of the organization are contingent upon external requirements and member needs.

Fiedler's work (1967) has resulted in the development of perhaps the most familiar contingency model. He examined the relationship between personal traits and situations, attempting to specify precisely the conditions in which a given style would make the greatest contribution to group effectiveness. He carefully distinguished between style and behavior: behavior differs from situation to situation; style is an underlying and constant attitude towards people which motivates behavior. Fiedler leads us to ask the question, Do we focus more on the leader or on the situation? For example, does the community college environment demand behavior different from that of the profit sector?

Although Fiedler's efforts contributed significantly to the field, others have helped shape this theoretical concept. Several contingency leadership models have focused on followers as individuals rather than as groups. Perhaps the most notable is the "path-goal" model, developed from the expectancy theory of House and Mitchell (1971). This theory attempts to explain ways in which a leader can influence the perceptions of followers towards work and personal goals and to clarify the linkages or paths between these two sets of goals. It proposes that the motivational functions of the leader consist of (1) increasing the numbers and kinds of personal payoffs to followers for work goal attainment and (2) improving the paths to these payoffs by identifying them, reducing road blocks and pitfalls, and increasing the opportunities for personal satisfaction en route (House and Mitchell, 1971).

The situational and contingent nature of leadership styles has been characterized well by Tannenbaum and Schmidt (1958) in their concept of a leadership continuum. They see leadership as involving a variety of styles, ranging from highly leader-centered to highly follower-centered. These vary with the degree of authority that leaders grant to their subordinates. Instead of a choice between the two styles of leadership, authoritarian or democratic, this continuum offers a range of acceptable styles. The concept of the continuum recognizes that an appropriate style of leadership depends on many factors—in particular, situations and personalities. It also assumes that a leader who seeks to influence the behavior of others is wise enough to evaluate the situation before a strategy is implemented.

Finally, we recognize the contribution of Hersey and Blanchard (1969) to leadership theory development. These researchers developed a situational theory of leadership effectiveness that utilized the Ohio State Leadership Behavior concepts of "consideration of others" and "initiating structure," and they explicitly recognized that "a variety of styles may be effective or ineffective depending on the situation" (p. 76). It is a tri-dimensional leadership theory in which their third dimension—effectiveness—is related to the other two more common variables—task and relationship. The Hersey and Blanchard view of leadership provides an excellent foundation for transformational leadership: influence is more powerful in situations where followers (1) are expected to act contingent on their maturity and (2) are then empowered to lead others within a framework provided by those above them in the organizational hierarchy.

LEADERS AND THEIR ENVIRONMENTS

One of the intangibles facing all leaders, and particularly leaders new to an organization, is their sense of the existing organizational culture. A key part of every culture is a set of assumptions about what is "real." While we have come to realize and have begun to appreciate the uniqueness of the community college culture, do we truly understand the different underlying assumptions of the sub-groups within that culture? Earlier work documented the fact that each sub-group in a community college (e.g., faculty, support staff, administration) sees or perceives the prevailing climate or culture differently (Roueche and Baker, 1987). Have we attempted to identify the patterns by which the members of a group perceive situations and relationships? If not, we may not fully understand how the group's culture is affecting our working environment.

The word "culture" has many connotations, and when combined with the word "organization," creates a special confusion. Although there are many definitions of organizational culture, we choose to use Edgar H. Schein's: "Culture is a pattern of basic assumptions—invented, discovered, or developed by a given group as it learns to cope with its problems of external adaptation and internal integration—that has worked well enough to be considered valid and therefore, to be taught to new members as the correct way to perceive, think, and feel in relation to those problems" (1985, p. 9). Schein believes that organizational culture must be better understood because:

• The phenomenon of culture is real and has an impact, and a phenomenon so real should be better understood.

• Individual and organizational performance, and the feelings that people in the college have about the college, cannot be understood unless one takes into account the college's culture.

• The concept of organizational culture is often confused and misunderstood; and if we are to get any benefit from the concept, we must first build a common frame of reference for analysis and then use it in an appropriate manner (p. 24).

Schein's beliefs are further supported by literature in the fields of organizational theory, strategy, and organizational development. His research concludes that an examination of cultural issues at the organizational level is absolutely essential to a basic understanding of what goes on in organizations, how they are run, and how they are improved. Indeed, if leadership is the ability to influence, shape, and embed values, attitudes, beliefs, and behaviors consistent with increased staff and faculty commitment to the unique mission of the community college, then the significance of organizational culture on effective leadership— transformational leadership—is clear. Exceptional leaders can deftly embed and transform institutional philosophy and values that complement the college mission and in doing so, transform themselves, their followers, and their institutions.

In a world where knowledge is doubling every five to six years, change has become the rule rather than the exception, a force of great magnitude that has become interwoven into our way of life. The mandate now is to accept change and learn how to use it, or it will consume us as individuals and as a society. Now, perhaps as never before, we need leaders who can understand the concepts of change, who can relate a specific change to the situation, who can appreciate the implications for the existing culture, and who can utilize this change to affect organizational outcomes through the leadership of others.

Leadership over human beings is exercised when persons with certain motives and purposes mobilize in competition or conflict with others—utilizing institutional, political, psychological, and other resources—so as to arouse, engage, and satisfy the motives of followers.

This is done in order to realize goals mutually held by both leaders and followers (Burns, 1978, p. 18). Burns believes that the leader-follower relationship is the interaction of individuals who not only function with the same purpose in mind and pursue common goals, but also operate with varying degrees of motivation and power potential. He sees this interaction following two paths: transactional leadership and transformational leadership (1978, pp. 19–20).

TRANSACTIONAL LEADERSHIP

Burns (1978) typifies transactional leadership as one person taking the initiative in making contact with others for the purpose of an exchange of valued things, such as paying wages to employees for their efforts and skills. Bass (1985a) indicates that transactional leadership is contingent reinforcement. An agreement is reached between the leader and the follower on the need to attain a specific goal, objectives are developed to reach the goal, and an understanding occurs about the reward for successful completion of the task or punishment for non-completion of the task. Thus, transactional leadership is one of exchange, a positive or negative payoff from the leader to the follower for a task completed or not completed as defined. Once the exchange is completed, there is no further need to interact unless another process of contingent reward is introduced. This leadership style is structured, concerned only with efficient ideas and what will work, thus using the power of the position to reinforce.

In the contingent reward-path-goal style of leadership, follower effort and performance are affected in varying degrees, depending on individual needs and expectations of the follower with regard to motivation for reward and behaviors exhibited by the leader. Klimoski and Hayes (1980) identified six observable behaviors of transactional leaders: explicitness, communication, involvement, support, review, and consistency. These behaviors, or the lack of them, appear to have a significant effect on the success or failure of the follower through the continued clarification of the reward to be expected.

The reward aspect of this interaction between leader and follower appears to be the place where most difficulty arises in the transaction. Extrinsic rewards are frequently the payoffs in an exchange and occur generally in the forms of praise, recognition, promotion, and increases in pay; if handled correctly, these rewards can lead to personal satisfaction and enhanced self-esteem for the follower. If the transactional leader can establish this kind of a relationship with the follower, a flow often results in which the follower is rewarded for the task. This re-warding arrangement often motivates followers to attempt another exchange with the leader. In reality, however, these contingent exchanges with positive rewards are underutilized (Bass, 1985a). Rather, the form that is pursued is one of negative reinforcement through intervention, generating negative feedback or disciplinary action. Often transactional leaders feel no motivation to reward or to intervene if matters are proceeding in the correct way. They will function as leaders or controllers only if the follower strays from the path. The use of contingent disapproval rather than contingent approval may depend on the leader's values. Disapproval is more likely if rationality, objectivity, and certainty are regarded as more important than affiliation. Quinn and Hall (1983) indicate that a leader oriented toward contingent disapproval searches for homogeneity, regularity, standardization, safety, and consolidation.

TRANSFORMATIONAL LEADERSHIP

Burns' transactional leader pursues a cost-to-benefit exchange (which may or may not be economic) to meet the follower's current material and psychic needs in return for "contracted" services rendered by the follower. Burns' transformational leader recognizes these existing needs in potential followers, but goes further, seeking to arouse and satisfy higher needs, to engage the full person of the follower. Transformational leaders can attempt and succeed in elevating those influenced from a lower to a higher level of need according to Maslow's hierarchy of needs (Bass, 1985a).

In Maslow's hierarchy, human needs—physiological needs, safety, love, esteem, and self-actualization—are arranged in a hierarchy of prepotency. In effect, physiological needs have prime influence until they are potentially satisfied. The physiological needs of hunger, thirst, and air drive our actions until these needs are met; their satisfaction reduces their power to motivate. Then successively higher needs—from safety to self-actualization—assume motivational power. Satisfaction at each level activates a new higher-level need. Once lower-level needs are satisfied, people want meaning, dignity, self-esteem, the esteem of others, and opportunities to cultivate and express abilities (Hampton, Summer, and Webber, 1987).

In his study of self-actualizing people, Maslow (1950) indicates that most or even all value dichotomies or polarities disappear or resolve in self-actualizers. Maslow identifies self-actualizing people as those who *must* become what they can become; that is, a person's desire for self-fulfullment is achieved when he or she actualizes his or her potential. Dichotomies do not apply to these people; they are neither selfish nor unselfish, neither self-interested nor other-interested, neither intro-verted nor extroverted. They have very different perceptions of the physical world, the social world, and the private psychological world; they accept the nature of self, social, and physical realities. Moreover, these "acceptance values" account for a high percentage of the total of their individual value judgments. The result is an attitude that les-sens or eliminates conflict and ambivalence over choices. Based upon these observations, one is encouraged to believe that people can grow and change from the inside out, reinforcing Maslow's statement, "What a person can be, he ought to be!" (McHolland, 1977).

This, then, is the arena for the transformational leader. Increased awareness and the arousal of higher-level needs which transcend self-interest can produce extraordinary effort, beyond expectations derived from earlier lack of consciousness, lower-level needs, and self-interest. It is the transformational leader who raises consciousness about higher considerations through articulation and role modeling (Bass, 1985a). To better appreciate the implications of this idea, it is important to review the recent findings of Bennis and Nanus (1985) and Bass (1985a).

In a qualitative study of 90 CEOs, Bennis and Nanus (1985) identi-fied four major themes embodied in each of the successful transfor-mational leaders they interviewed. The themes associated with strate-gies for successful outcomes were:

- attention through vision

- meaning through communication

- trust through positioning

- the deployment of self through positive self-regard

A vision is necessary to articulate a possible and desirable state for the organization. By providing this vision, the transformational leader is in a position to assist individuals in deriving rewards from their roles in the organization, as the organization finds its rewards from identifying a niche in society. Through an understanding of so-cietal improvement, individuals learn to believe that their effort "makes a difference" (Bennis and Nanus, 1985). Expanding populations, cou-pled with assembly line operations in various aspects of the workplace and in conjunction with major change in our world, have served to re-duce the individual, in most cases, to a social security number or a place in line. Personal identity often is lost along with the intrinsic human motivation to "make a difference." Transformational leaders are able to convey the reward of individual recognition through attention to vision, while helping people in the organization to know pride and satisfaction in their work. In fact, Bennis and Nanus suggest that the visions of the transformational leader are magnetic and pull people toward the visions through intensity coupled with commitment. This is not coercive power, but rather the result of an intensity of such magnitude that others are drawn in. Conversely, the transformational leader pays attention to the values and concepts of the followers with the same intensity, creating unity through the movement of transactional energy rather than by unilateral functioning.

Meaning through communication is based upon the premise that organizations depend on the existence of shared meanings and interpretations of reality which facilitate coordinated action. Thus, an essential factor in leadership is the capacity to influence and organize meaning for members of the organization. The transformational leader accomplishes this through the articulation and definition of what has previously remained implicit by inventing images, metaphors, and models that provide a focus for new attention (Bennis and Nanus, 1985).

"Trust is the lubrication that makes it possible for organizations to work," observe Bennis and Nanus (1985, p. 43). The transformational leader understands that it is through consistency and constancy that trust is achieved. Without trust the vision is lost. Within the framework of trust rests the need for organizational identity—that is, a sense of what the organization is and what it is to do. With the establishment of identity, the transformational leader gains the trust of the followership through strategic positioning of the organization in its established environment. Bennis and Nanus (1985) suggest that positioning is the least understood aspect in the management of trust. They indicate that positioning is the organizational reciprocal of vision, that which inspirits and animates the leader's vision.

Leadership is a human business, and transformational leaders well know both themselves and their places in the world. They have clear self-concepts and an unusual degree of self-confidence. This competency is essential if the leader is to raise the consciousness level of others and to encourage them to feel good about themselves. Positive self-regard, related to an inner sense of self and emotional wisdom, seems to exert its force by creating in others a sense of confidence and high expectations. The effective transformational leader is self-actualized, able to accept others as they are while extending trust; capable of working in the present rather than the past; courteous and aware of those who are close; and able to do without constant approval and recognition from others (Bennis and Nanus, 1985).

Bass (1985a) conducted a number of studies on leadership over the past several years, using his Multifactor Leadership Questionnaire (MLQ), to distinguish more clearly the relationship between transactional and transformational leadership attributes. He concluded through these quantitative studies that five factors are required to understand transactional and transformational leadership. He further noted that it is possible to measure each of these factors with high reliability and to construct a leadership profile. This profile, produced on an individual leader, then can be substantiated by respondents describing the same leader using a parallel form of the questionnaire.

The three transformational factors identified by the questionnaire are described by Bass (1985a) as charismatic leadership, individualized consideration, and intellectual stimulation. Charismatic leaders enjoy a high degree of esteem, value, and popularity. Bass suggests that leaders with charisma attain a generalized influence which is transformational, transcending the immediate situation and ordinary exchanges of compliance with promises of rational reward. In an organizational setting, they paint for their followers an attractive vision of what the outcomes of their efforts could be, providing followers with more meaning for their work. Admiration for charismatic leaders and the desire to identify and emulate them are powerful influences on followers. A leader will be held in high esteem by followers, particularly in times of trouble, as a consequence of his/her self-confidence, absence of inner conflict, self-determination, and requisite abilities (Bass, 1985a).

Consideration for others has been found to be an important aspect of leader-follower relations, contributing to follower satisfaction with the leader and in many cases leading to follower satisfaction with productivity. Also, consideration for others is central to participative management to the extent that it focuses on follower needs for growth and participation in decisions affecting work and career. Results of the MLQ suggest that transformational leaders tend to be benevolent to followers as well as friendly, informal, helpful, and supportive while encouraging self-development. Individualized consideration is viewed as promoting familiarity and contact; communicating informally rather than formally; fulfilling individual follower desire for information; paying attention to differences among followers; offering individual counseling; and mentoring. Not all transformational leaders, however, display individual consideration; some depend upon their charisma and/or intellectual stimulation to achieve their shared views (Bass, 1985b).

The third major thematic attribute that Bass identified was intellectual stimulation. This does not necessarily imply scholarly intellectualism, but rather arousal and change in the follower's attention to awareness of problems and how they may be solved. It is not the call to immediate action aroused by emotional stimulation, but a stirring of the imagination generating thoughts and insights. Intellectual stimulation by transformational leaders is viewed as a discrete leap from the problems they face to their solutions. The location and innovation of alternative strategies as well as their evaluation may contribute to the transformation of the organization and its leadership. Meaning through communication is based upon the premise that organizations depend on the existence of shared meanings and interpretations of reality which facilitate coordinated action. Thus, an essential factor in leadership is the capacity to influence and organize meaning for members of the organization. Intellectual stimulation correlates positively with the charismatic leader who has an extraordinary power of vision about the organization and the ability to communicate it (Bass, 1985b).

Bass further identified contingent reinforcement and management-by-exception as the transactional factors of the questionnaire. Contingent reward is found in praise for work well done and recommendations for pay increases and promotion. Commendations for effort and public recognition for outstanding service are also forms of contingent reward. On the other hand, contingent punishment occurs as a reaction to a deviation from norms, such as quality or production falling below acceptable or agreed-upon levels. Negative feedback, coupled with clarification of expected standards and/or penalties, is a form of contingent punishment. If managers choose to intervene only when failures, breakdowns, and deviations occur, management-by-exception is the result. Bass concludes from his studies that a steady diet of management-by-exception can be counter-productive, but that contingent rewards yield a fairly good return in terms of subordinate effort and performance.

Additional research offers positive conclusions regarding various aspects of transformational leadership. Singer and Singer (1986) designed a study to explore the possible links between subordinates' personality traits and leadership preferences as they pertained to transformational vs. transactional leadership. The subjects were asked to imagine an "ideal leader" in a situation and—through the use of the MLQ Form 4—to describe the behavior of this ideal leader. Subjects also completed the Affiliation, Achievement, and Succorance subscales of the Edwards Personal Preference Schedule as well as a conformity rating scale. Affiliation correlated significantly with charisma, individualized consideration, and the overall transformational leadership measure. The personality traits of conformity/nonconformity also correlated significantly with intellectual stimulation, indicating the "nonconformers" prefer leaders who provide intellectual stimulation. High achievers also tended to favor such leaders. None of the other ratings of subordinates' personality traits correlated significantly with ratings of ideal leadership. The results, however, showed that the subjects in the study preferred working with leaders who are oriented more toward transformational than transactional styles.

Bass (1985a) relates further confidence in the factorial structure of the Multifactor Leadership Questionnaire (MLQ) based upon the parallel structures he has drawn between the factors and Zaleznik's (1977) differentiation of managers and leaders. Bass indicates that Zaleznik's managers displayed qualities of transactional leadership while his leaders demonstrated characteristics of transformational leadership. Paralleling Bass' first factor of charisma, Zaleznik wrote that leaders—but not managers—attract strong feelings of identity and intense feelings of love and hate. Leaders send clear messages of purpose and mission, not ambiguous signals. Zaleznik noted that leaders—but not managers—generate excitement at work and heighten expectations through the images and meanings they provide. Paralleling the third factor of individualized consideration, Zaleznik wrote that leaders—but not managers—cultivate, establish, and break off intensive one-to-one relationships as necessary. They reveal empathy for individuals and understand what different events mean to different individuals. On the other hand, managers see themselves as role players engaged in an activity whose meaning lies in itself as a process. Paralleling the fifth factor of intellectual stimulation, Zaleznik wrote that leaders—but not managers—were less concerned with process than with ideas, ideas which the leaders can articulate and project into images.

Conversely, and consistent with Bass' analysis, Zaleznik's managers engaged more often in transactional activities than did his leaders. With the second factor of contingent reward, Zaleznik's managers—but not his leaders—made flexible use of rewards and punishments. Similar to the fourth factor of management-by-exception, Zaleznik observed that managers—but not leaders—tried to maintain (not change) a controlled, rational, equitable system. Zaleznik indicated that his leaders were likely to be more active than managers; his managers were likely to be more passive than leaders. While managers tolerate the mundane, leaders react to it "as to an affliction" (1977, p. 72).

Bass indicates that he may be risking premature closure about the fundamental structure of transformational and transactional leadership.

However, his quantitative analyses and Zaleznik's clinical support provide some confidence about the validity of these five factors: the transformational factors of charismatic leadership, individualized consideration, and intellectual stimulation, and the transactional factors of contingent reward and management-by-exception (Bass, 1985b).

Bass (1985a) states that leaders do not function at all times as transformational leaders; instead, they move back and forth between transformational and transactional strategies to achieve the highest results. Zaleznik (1977) suggests the importance of personal influence through one-to-one mentoring relationships for the development of leaders, indicating that a bureaucratic society which breeds managers may stifle young leaders who need mentors and emotional interchange for their own development. It would seem that while identification of transformational and transactional styles indicates a new era in the knowledge of leadership, findings of further research must direct the movement from theory to application. Indeed, quantitative studies, such as those cited in this chapter, play an important role in the search for the parameters of leadership. A review of the major themes in the transformational literature is appropriate prior to moving on toward a chapter that will provide further clarification of the elusive concept of leadership.

LEADERSHIP: HERE AND NOW

L*eadership*, by James MacGregor Burns, lays the blueprint for the concept of transformational leadership. He deliberately chooses to distinguish between the terms "transactional leadership" and "transformational leadership." He defines "leadership" as leaders inducing followers to act for certain goals that represent the values and the motivation—the wants and needs, the aspirations and expectations—of both leaders and followers. Similarly, Bennis and Nanus (1985) say that the genius of leadership lies in the manner in which leaders see and act on their own and their followers' values and motivation. They further state that transforming leadership occurs when one or more persons engage with others in such a way that leaders and followers raise one another to higher levels of motivation and morality, contrasting with "transactional leadership," which occurs when one person takes the initiative in making contact with others for the purpose of an exchange of valued things. The distinction between "transactional leadership" and "transformational leadership" is significant as we examine the problems facing the modern community college leader.

The transformational leader of today must possess the synergy to create something new out of something old; out of an old vision, these leaders must develop and communicate a new vision and get others not only to see the vision, but also to commit to it themselves. Where transactional leaders make only minor adjustments in the organization's mission, structure, and human resource management, transformational leaders make major changes in these areas and promote fundamental changes in the basic political and cultural components of the organization (Tichy and Ulrich, 1984). Transformational leaders are also sensitive to the fact that change has a dramatic impact on both the college and the individuals within it. Thus, successful transformational leaders attend to myriad organizational and individual needs when initiating change.

In our adaptation of the Tichy/Devanna model (see Figure 2.1), we show how the transformational leader must attend to three stages or acts in the drama of change process. In each of these three stages, the leader must deal with both organizational and individual dynamics. In the first stage, the leader, in this case the community college president, recognizes the need for change and new directions. Thus, the leader indicates a need for "transformation" in the organization and at the same time recognizes a need for "closure" in the individual followers. When, in the second stage, the leader tries to create a new vision, he or she must not only motivate the members of the organization toward a collaborative commitment but also aid in individual transitions toward that vision. Finally, as the leader institutionalizes the change, he or she must change social structures as well as aid individuals in making their new roles permanent.

Since change is an ongoing process, especially in the community college, proactive community college presidents are constantly moving through different phases of the change process. While in one area, a change is being implemented or completed, in another area the trigger for change is just being recognized. Thus, these transformational leaders frequently must cycle back through the process and enable their followers to meet the challenge of change.

SUMMARY

We know that effective leadership is necessary for effective organizations, but absolute definitions of leadership vary across the literature. After careful study of the variations on this theme, we have created our own definition of leadership, specifically

Figure 2.1

The Proactive Community College President

Triggers for Change

Act I: Recognizing the Need for Revitalization and New Direction Around the Mission

Organizational Dynamics

Need for Transformation

—Felt need for change supported by value base
—Strategies to deal with resistance to change
—Action to change organization forms

Individual Dynamics

Closure

—Review of past performance
—Reflection on security of past
—Identified need for change

Act II: Creating a New Vision

Organizational Dynamics

A Motivating Vision

—Participative creation of vision
—Mobilization of commitment
—Movement toward collaboration

Individual Dynamics

Transitions

—Development of new behavior and relationships
—Speculation about ramifications of new visions

Act III: Institutionalizing Change to Accomplish the Mission

Organizational Dynamics

Social Architecture

—Creating realignment
—Reweaving new expectations
—Motivating and rewarding based on accomplishment of the mission

Individual Dynamics

New Beginnings

—Inner realignment
—New relationships
—New solutions
—Renewed energy

The Evolving Community College Mission and Its Evaluation

Adapted from the Tichy/Devanna Transformational Leader Model related to the community college setting: leadership is the ability to influence, shape, and embed values, attitudes, beliefs, and behaviors consistent with increased commitment to the unique mission of the community college. This definition is also consistent with Burns' "transformational leadership," which "occurs when one or more persons engage with others in such a way that leaders and followers raise one another to higher levels of motivation and morality" (1978, p. 20).

Theories about educational leadership have followed closely the theories about leadership in other settings. One of the early attempts, "trait theory," attempted to identify leaders and specific traits that leaders have in common. However, this theory did not take into account the variables of different situations. "Situational leadership theory" attempted to investigate leader behavior in context, rather than inherent characteristics. Then "contingency theory" looked at followers as well as leaders—the leadership of the internal organization was "contingent" upon the situation, the external requirements of the organization, and the needs of its members. Fiedler, one of the most familiar of the contingency theorists, also carefully distinguished between leadership style and leadership behavior. House and Mitchell (1971) developed a contingency theory based on a "path-goal model," in which leaders help followers to identify and clarify the paths to desired goals. Tannenbaum and Schmidt (1958) also devised a continuum of leadership styles, ranging from leader-centered to follower-centered, observing that a leader often varies his leadership style to accommodate different situations and personalities. Hersey and Blanchard (1971) developed a tri-dimensional theory based on consideration of others, initiating structure, and effectiveness—thus, laying the foundation for "transformational leadership theory."

Leaders work in environments. They are affected by the organizational culture and the sub-groups of followers; in turn, leaders affect the culture. Exceptional leaders can change the organizational values and thus change, or transform, themselves, their followers, and the institution itself.

We live in a time of rapid social change. The ability to change appropriately, in fact to determine the nature of the change, is one mark of a successful organization—and a successful leader. Burns distinguishes between transactional leaders and transformational leaders. Transactional leaders initiate exchanges, material or otherwise; they offer positive or negative payoffs in exchange for tasks completed or not completed. Transactional leaders are concerned with the task; often they accept completion of the task as the norm and thus intervene only when the task is NOT completed appropriately.

Burns' transformational leader, on the other hand, goes beyond these existing needs in followers and seeks to engage the whole person. Using Maslow's terms, this leader seeks to raise followers from one level on the hierarchy of needs to another, so that ultimately these followers become, like the leader, self-actualized.

Bennis and Nanus (1985) determined four themes common to transformational leaders. First, these leaders have a vision of what the organization can become, and they are able to show followers ways to share and support the vision, so that followers are recognized for their value in the organization. Second, these leaders are able to articulate their ideas and thus convey meaning that others can share. Third, transformational leaders trust their followers, who in turn are willing to take responsibility for and ownership of the vision. Finally, these leaders know themselves well and have a high self-regard; they are themselves self-actualized. They are able to convey to followers this sense of self-confidence and ability to make a difference.

Bass (1985a) identified three characteristics of transformational leaders: charismatic leadership, individualized consideration, and intellectual stimulation. These characteristics correspond in many ways with the Bannis and Nanus themes. Bass further identified two characteristics of transactional leaders—contingent reinforcement and management-by-exception. Also, he suggests that successful leaders select both transactional and transformational strategies, varying their styles to fit the situation. Zaleznik's distinctions between managers and leaders also correspond closely to Bass' distinctions between transactional and transformational leaders.

Burns (1978) laid the foundation for the concept of transformational leaders, who can create a vision for change, communicate it to others, and then help those others to accomplish that vision through their own commitment to it. Thus, while transactional leaders manage and maintain, transformational leaders promote fundamental change in the organization, helping the organization adjust to the varying needs of today's rapidly changing society.

CHAPTER 3

APPROACH TO THE STUDY

66 *To have a strategy is to put your own intelligence, foresight, and will in charge instead of outside forces and disordered concerns. Strategy means agreeing on some aims and having a plan to arrive at a destination through the effective use of resources.* 99

GEORGE KELLER

THE STUDY

RATIONALE

PHASE I: SELECTION PROCESS

PHASE II: SELECTION PROCESS

PHASE III: AN IN-DEPTH ANALYSIS

APPROACH TO THE STUDY

RATIONALE

Over the last several years, leadership has taken on renewed importance. It has become the central theme for those of us who have studied excellence and how it is achieved. Since Peters and Waterman's *In Search of Excellence* swept the marketplace, scholars and practitioners (sometimes the same individuals) have taken up the tasks of identifying and articulating "excellent leadership." In our own field, George Vaughan, Jim Fisher, and other individuals and organizations recently have written about concepts of leadership and the roles of the community college president. However, when we consider the significance of effective leadership, we find there is indeed a shortage of relevant research associated with the topic. This shortage seems especially important since the leadership of a college is affected by the behaviors exhibited by the college president.

Changing times have generated a multitude of questions and concerns for community college CEOs. Issues and critical challenges that need to be addressed include the management of diminishing resources, shrinking student enrollments, aging faculty, and decreasing student skills in the face of demands for increasing job skills. O'Banion and Roueche observe:

NO institution of higher education has ever undertaken a more challenging and difficult educational mission than the open-door college. The open-admissions policy admits the most heterogeneous and diverse student body to be found in any educational setting in the world. Providing quality educational programs and excellent instruction to students who need the most structured support, while at the same time maintaining strong academic programs for well-qualified students and responding effectively to the needs of local communities, is the leadership challenge of the 1990's for community college executives (1988a, p. 2).

Founding CEOs were the great pioneers who established the concepts and practices that form today's community college base. They were visionaries who responded to expanding opportunities for higher education by translating their ideas and dreams into programs and buildings (O'Banion and Roueche, 1988b). These early times demanded builders, political persuaders, organizers, and master plan developers— individuals with a vision that matched the horizon of the time.

Vaughan (1986) writes that community colleges are well into their second generation of presidents and concludes that the "typical" president is no longer the founder and builder of colleges. This second generation of presidents, generally now in their fifties, has been strongly influenced by the first generation while adapting to the new challenges that they face. Not only are they builders, political persuaders, organizers, and master plan developers, but they are practitioners skillful in establishing a more participative, coalition-building environment. These CEOs have been successful at envisioning and nurturing change toward access and excellence. They have been able to communicate vision and direction and to empower followers to live the dream and make it a reality. These leaders demonstrate the ability to influence, shape, and embed values, attitudes, beliefs, and behaviors consistent with increased staff and faculty commitment to the unique mission of the community college. By doing so, they are able to instill and inspire their followers to take on institutional challenges with renewed vigor.

This study identifies and describes what these transformational leaders in the American community college movement are doing.

In preparation for our study, we attempted to identify writings associated with the leadership styles and qualities of community/two-year college presidents and chancellors over the past twenty-plus years. We hoped our efforts would provide a rich base of valuable information. Our search focused on ERIC as well as a number of professional journals associated with the community college movement, doctoral dissertations, and other selected publications we felt might generate useful information. The results were disappointing but not completely unexpected. Much had been written about community, technical, and junior colleges, about leadership styles and qualities, and about college presidents. However, when we focused on the leadership styles and qualities of community and two-year college presidents, the literature was sadly deficient.

We conducted this study to identify and describe a group of transformational community college leaders. We hoped to generate findings that would increase the fund of knowledge about community college leadership—particularly at the CEO level. We sought a descriptive study that would (1) obtain general information about the CEOs and how they utilized their time, (2) ask a general open-ended question in order to determine the CEOs' educational philosophy regarding leadership, and (3) determine specific behavioral responses to critical incidents through an in-depth interview of selected leaders. We felt that this broad-based approach would enable us to acquire rich information from a relatively large sampling.

PHASE I: SELECTION PROCESS

We sought to design a systematic strategy to identify and examine transformational leadership in the community college, linking leadership theory with practice. In order to examine the breadth and complexity of leadership in this arena, we decided to examine the behavioral attributes of a group of *outstanding* community college CEOs. Specifically, we wanted to describe the leadership attributes (refined characteristics of individual behavior) which college CEOs possessed that enabled them to be identified by colleagues as transformational leaders.

We hoped to demonstrate a relationship between the literature on leadership theory and our current study in order to explain and illustrate the concept of transformational leadership. The data gathered from our group of recognized leaders would enable us to develop a theoretical framework.

In undertaking a project of this magnitude, one of the first questions to be addressed was how CEO nominations might be collected so as to ensure the broadest possible sampling. We wanted to establish a format that would enable us to identify outstanding individuals who might be less renowned nationally and/or from small rural institutions.

Thus, we ruled out employing a "panel of experts" in the nomination process and decided to invite all presidents of public two-year institutions who were members of AACJC in 1987 to participate in Phase I. We realized that this approach also had shortcomings. For example, the more senior presidents would be better known and thus were more likely to receive nominations, and presidents new to a system might be at a disadvantage. However, this approach did provide a comprehensive nomination base.

To accomplish one of our goals—the development of a rich and comprehensive database—we invited 912 presidents from public community and technical colleges to participate (see Appendix 1). They were asked to identify those community college presidents in their states (or from their geographic regions, in the case of states containing less than ten community colleges) who they felt demonstrated the ability to influence, shape, and embed values, attitudes, beliefs, and behaviors consistent with increased faculty and staff commitment to both access and excellence. Each participant was asked to identify no more than five presidential nominees on a self-addressed postcard that had been enclosed in the letter (see Appendix 2).

The response was excellent. Seven hundred and thirty presidents (approximately 80 percent of the total number) participated in the nomination process. We then asked each state director to identify two presidents who were transformational leaders from his/her state (see Appendix 1a). Thirty-nine (or 78 percent of the total number) state directors responded. These two nomination processes resulted in the nomination of 296 CEOs. We were pleased not only with the number of responses received, but also with the rich demographic and geographical base represented by the nominations. CEOs from 44 states were nominated, representing large and small colleges in urban and rural settings. The titles of those nominated included Chancellor, Superintendent, and President. All were the Chief Executive Officers of a group of community colleges, a single campus, or district. We have decided to refer to these community college leaders as "CEOs." Table 3.1 lists the CEOs nominated in Phase I who chose to participate in the study.

Table 3.1 **List of State and National Nominees**

College	Nominee
ALABAMA	
Wallace-Hanceville	James Bailey
Alexander City	Byron Causey
John C. Calhoun	James Chasteen
S.D. Bishop State	Yvonne Kennedy
Jefferson	Judy Merritt
Enterprise	Joseph Talmadge
Walker	Harold Wade
ARIZONA	
Scottsdale	Arthur DeCabooter
Maricopa County CCD	Paul Elsner
Rio Salado	Charles Green
Mesa	Wallace Simpson
Northland Pioneer	Marvin Vasher
Yavapai	Paul Walker
ARKANSAS	
East AR	Bob Burns
Phillips County	John Easley
CALIFORNIA	
Solano	Marjorie Blaha
College of San Mateo	Lois Callahan
Contra Costa CCD	John Carhart
Foothill	Thomas Clements
De Anza	Robert DeHart
Lake Tahoe	James Duke
Napa Valley	William Feddersen
Foothill-De Anza CCD	Thomas Fryer
College of Sequoias	Lincoln Hall
Merced	Tom Harris
LA Harbor	James Heinselman
Lassen	Virginia Holton
Rancho Santiago	Robert Jensen
Riverside City	Charles Kane
N. Orange Cnty CCD	James Kellerman
Santa Barbara City	Peter MacDougall
Los Rios CCD	David Mertes
Santa Rosa	Roy Mikalson
Santa Monica	Richard Moore
San Diego CCD	Garland Peed
Diablo Valley	Phyllis Peterson
Mt. San Antonio	John Randall
College of Siskiyous	Eugene Schumacher
State Center Dist.	William Stewart
Rio Hondo	Herbert Sussman

Table 3.1   (Continued)

College	Nominee
Yosemite CCD	Tom Van Groningen
Grossmont CCD	Donald Walker
LA Pierce	David Wolf
Kern CCD	James Young
COLORADO	
CO Northwestern	James Bos
Aims	George Conger
Pikes Peak	Cecil Groves
CC of Denver	Byron McClenney
Otero	William McDivitt
Arapahoe	James Weber
Northeastern	Marvin Weiss
Pueblo	Tony Zeiss
CONNECTICUT	
Housatonic	Vincent Darnowski
Mohegan	John Hurd
Quinebaug Valley	Robert Miller
DELAWARE	
DE Tech	John Kotula
FLORIDA	
South Florida	Catherine Cornelius
Palm Beach	Edward Eissey
Valencia	Paul Gianini
Brevard	Maxwell King
Manatee	Stephen Korcheck
St. Petersburg	Carl Kuttler
Miami-Dade	Robert McCabe
Hillsborough	Andreas Paloumpis
Okaloosa-Walton	James Richburg
Sante Fe	Alan Robertson
Edison	David Robinson
FL CC-Jacksonville	Charles Spence
Gulf Coast	Lawrence Tyree
GEORGIA	
DeKalb	Marvin Cole
Waycross	James Dye
Dalton	Derrell Roberts
Brunswick	John Teel
Albany	B.R. Tilley
Gainesville	Foster Watkins
ILLINOIS	
Southeastern IL	Harry Abell
Truman	Wallace Appelson

Table 3.1 (Continued)

College	Nominee
Elgin	Searle Charles
Moraine Valley	Fred Gaskin
Elgin	Paul Heath
Kishwaukee	Norman Jenkins
Danville Area	Ronald Lingle
College of Du Page	Harold McAninch
Highland	Joseph Piland
Lincoln Land	Robert Poorman
Parkland	William Staerkel (deceased)
IL Valley	Alfred Wisgoski
INDIANA	
Vincennes	Phillip Summers
IOWA	
North IA Area	David Buettner
IA Western	Carl Heinrich
IA Valley CCD	John Prihoda
KANSAS	
Johnson County	Charles Carlsen
Highland	Larry Devane
Fort Scott	Richard Hedges
Colby	James Tangeman
KENTUCKY	
Southeast	Bruce Ayers
Prestonsburg	Henry Campbell
Somerset	Richard Carpenter
Jefferson	Ronald Horvath
Hazard	Edward Hughes
Henderson	Patrick Lake
Hopkinsville	Thomas Riley
U of KY CC System	Charles Wethington
MARYLAND	
Howard	Dwight Burrill
CC of Baltimore	Joseph Durham
Anne Arundel	Thomas Florestano
Cecil	Robert Gell
Catonsville	John Kingsmore
Montgomery	Robert Parilla
Essex	John Ravekes
MASSACHUSETTS	
Holyoke	David Bartley
Cape Cod	Philip Day
Bristol	Eileen Farley
Quinsigamond	Clifford Peterson

Table 3.1   (Continued)

College	Nominee
Bunker Hill	Harold Shively*
North Shore	George Traicoff
Roxbury	Brunetta Wolfman
MICHIGAN	
Grand Rapids	Richard Calkins
Alpena	Charles Donnelly
Jackson	Clyde Letarte
Macomb	Albert Lorenzo
Schoolcraft	Richard McDowell
Lake MI	Anne Mulder
Washtenaw	Gunder Myran
Oakland	Stephen Nicholson
Kalamazoo Valley	Marilyn Schlack
Glen Oaks	Philip Ward
MINNESOTA	
Minneapolis	Earl Bowman
Anoka-Ramsey	Neil Christenson
Rochester	Geraldine Evans
North Hennepin	John Helling
Lakewood	Jerry Owens
MISSISSIPPI	
MS Gulf Coast	Barry Mellinger
Meridian	William Scaggs
East Central	Eddie Smith
Copiah-Lincoln	Billy Thames
MISSOURI	
St. Louis	Michael Crawford
Crowder	Kent Farnsworth
Jefferson	Ray Henry
St. Charles County	Donald Shook
MONTANA	
Dawson	Donald Kettner
NEBRASKA	
Metropolitan Tech	Richard Gilliland
Western Tech CC Area	John Harms
Mid Plains Tech	Williams Hasemeyer
Central	Joseph Pruesser
NEW JERSEY	
Middlesex County	Flora Mancuso Edwards
Somerset County	Charles Irace
Camden County	Otto Mauke
Union County	Derek Nunney

Table 3.1   (Continued)

College	Nominee
Cumberland County	Philip Phelon
Ocean County	Milton Shaw
NEW MEXICO	
East NM U-Clovis	Jay Gurley
San Juan	James Henderson
Sante Fe	William Witter
NEW YORK	
Ulster County	Robert Brown
Schenectady County	Peter Burnham
Fashion Inst. of Tech	Marvin Feldman
Nassau	Sean Fanelli
Westchester	Joseph Hankin
LaGuardia	Joseph Shenker
Genessee	Stuart Steiner
Monroe	Peter Spina
NORTH CAROLINA	
Fayetteville Tech	Craig Allen
Davidson County	Bryan Brook
Rowan Tech	Richard Brownell
College of Albemarle	Jesse Chesson
Vance-Granville	Ben Currin
Wilkes	David Daniel
Forsyth Tech	Bob Greene
Asheville-Buncombe	Harvey Haynes
Coastal Carolina	James Henderson
Wake Tech	Bruce Howell
Lenoir	Jesse McDaniel
Nash Tech	Reid Parrott
Surry	Swanson Richards
Central Piedmont	Ruth Shaw
Sandhills	Raymond Stone
Durham Tech	Phail Wynn
OHIO	
Lima Tech	James Biddle
Cuyahoga CCD	Nolen Ellison
Columbus Tech	Harold Nestor
Lakeland	Omar Olsen
Sinclair	David Ponitz
Cincinnati Tech	Frederick Schlimm
OKLAHOMA	
El Reno	Bill Cole
Rogers State	Richard Mosier
Tulsa	Alfred Philips

Table 3.1   (Continued)

College	Nominee
Northern OK	Edwin Vineyard
Carl Albert	Joe White
Northeastern OK A&M	Bobby Wright
OREGON	
Southwest OR	Robert Barber
Linn-Benton	Thomas Gonzales
Clackamas	John Keyser
Chemeketa	William Segura
PENNSYLVANIA	
CC of Philadelphia	Judith Eaton
Northampton County	Robert Kopecek
CC of Allegheny Cnty	John Kraft
Butler County	Frederick Woodward
RHODE ISLAND	
CC of Rhode Island	Edward Liston
SOUTH CAROLINA	
Greenville Tech	Thomas Barton
Trident Tech	Charles Branch
Florence-Darlington	Fred Fore*
Tri-County Tech	Don Garrison
Orangeburg-Calhoun	Rudy Groomes
Midlands Tech	James Hudgins
Horry-Georgetown	Kent Sharples
Piedmont Tech	Lex Walters
TENNESSEE	
Dyersburg State	Karen Bowyer
Walters State	Jack Campbell
Roane State	Cuyler Dunbar
Cleveland State	James Ford
STI at Memphis	Charles Temple
Chattanooga St. Tech	Harry Wagner
TEXAS	
Alvin	Rodney Allbright
Austin	Dan Angel
Temple	Marvin Felder
Brookhaven	Patsy Fulton
Southwest TX	Jimmy Goodson
Tyler	Raymond Hawkins
Wharton County	Elbert Hutchins
Cooke County	Bud Joyner
Dallas Cnty CCD	Jan LeCroy*
Kilgore	Stewart McLaurin
Paris	Dennis Michaelis

Table 3.1 (Continued)

College	Nominee
Richland	Stephen Mittelstet
Texarkana	Carl Nelson
Midland	Jess Parrish
Galveston	John Pickleman
Howard County JCD	Bob Riley
Tarrant County JCD	Joe Rushing
San Jacinto CD	Thomas Sewell
Odessa	Philip Speegle
North Harris	Nellie Thorogood
Houston CC System	J.B. Whiteley
Grayson County	Jim Williams
VERMONT	
CC of VT	Kenneth Kalb
VIRGINIA	
Southside VA	John Caven
New River	Randall Edwards
Northern VA	Richard Ernst
Mountain Empire	Victor Ficker
VA CC System	J. F. Hockaday
Southwest VA	Charles King
Piedmont VA	George Vaughan
WASHINGTON	
Shoreline	Ronald Bell
Skagit Valley	James Ford
Highline	Shirley Gordon
Clark	Earl Johnson
Pierce	Brent Knight
Grays Harbor	Joseph Malik
Edmonds	Thomas Nielsen
Seattle CCD	Donald Phelps
Bellevue	Paul Thompson
Walla Walla	Steven Van Ausdle
WEST VIRGINIA	
WV Northern	Barbara Guthrie-Morse
WISCONSIN	
Blackhawk Tech Inst	James Catania
WYOMING	
Laramie County	Timothy Davies

[* retired during the course of the study]

PHASE II: SELECTION PROCESS

I n the second phase of our study, we wanted to determine what these outstanding CEOs nominated by colleagues and state directors did that resulted in their multiple nominations. We invited the 296 nominated CEOs to share with us, in writing, their personal philosophies regarding educational leadership (see Appendix 3). They were asked to respond to an open-ended question which required them to articulate and reflect on their personal philosophies of leadership (see Appendix 4). Next, we asked them to provide examples of their thinking and behavior that might help us better understand their community context. They also were encouraged to include any supporting documents of their own development that supported their leadership philosophy. This was a tall order, and we realized that it might discourage the nominees from continuing to participate. Indeed, we did receive many comments from presidents about the arduous task we had given them. Yet one CEO succinctly noted that the educational leadership philosophy statement had created the need for considerable introspection, an activity in which he was not regularly engaged. He had, however, found the results of the task to be meaningful. He titled his statements "Harold's Educational Leadership Philosophy," which provided a highly appropriate acronym—"H.E.L.P."

In addition to the open-ended educational leadership philosophical statements, the participants were asked to provide general information about themselves and how they utilized their time (see Appendix 5), to provide a personal vita, and to nominate one or two persons who they felt were exceptional transformational CEOs (see Appendix 6). The guideline for these nominations was the definition of leadership used in Phase I of the study (that is, the ability to influence, shape, and embed values, attitudes, beliefs, and behaviors consistent with increased staff and faculty commitment to the unique mission of the community college), but two additional criteria were added: first, the CEOs could be nominated from anywhere in the nation, but the individuals nominating them must have had direct personal and/or professional experience with the nominees within the past five years; second, the nominees must have been active CEOs within the past twelve months. Two hundred and fifty-six of the 296 presidents (86 percent) responded in Phase II.

The data generated in this phase of the study were most interesting. The comprehensiveness of the written statements and supporting documents regarding educational leadership philosophy was both inspirational and powerful. Global themes were generated from the education leadership philosophy statements submitted by the nominees. Philosophical concepts were then extracted from the descriptions provided within the global themes. (The philosophical statements and attributes are presented in Chapter 5.) The next step in the process resulted in the translation of the global themes and philosophical concepts into transformational attributes. Around each of these attributes, and consistent with the philosophical concepts, was the development of specific attribute descriptors designed to determine what a community college transformational leader valued (see Appendix 7a). It was in this component of Phase II that we linked the theories of transformational leadership found in the literature to the statements generated from the presidents' philosophical statements.

The nominating process associated with Phase II of the study generated a refined list of nationally-respected community college CEOs—a group of 50 "blue chippers." By definition, these "blue chip" CEOs had been recognized by their colleagues as being the top nominees from within their states (or geographic regions) and/or had each received at least five national nominations in Phase II. In addition, the nominees were required to have submitted the requested information, as the database of the study was entirely generated from participants' responses. Thus, if a CEO met our criteria for recognition in either Phase I or Phase II of the study but did not participate, he or she was not listed in either Table 3.1 or Table 3.2. We realized that outstanding CEOs who had been nominated by this process would then be denied recognition by choosing not to participate in Phase II of the study. In some cases, the CEOs were out on sabbatical or were otherwise not available to participate in this research study. However, given that the study was dependent upon the data received in Phase II of the process, we were compelled to proceed with the decision rules listed.

While our decision rules eliminated some excellent CEOs from recognition in this study, they also identified many outstanding leaders (Table 3.2). These leaders and their organizations are capable of accomplishing the dream of balance between open access and excellence.

Table 3.2 **"Blue Chippers" List**

College	Nominee
ALABAMA	
Jefferson	Judy Merritt
John C. Calhoun	James Chasteen

Table 3.2   (Continued)

College	Nominee
ARIZONA	
Maricopa County CCD	Paul Elsner
ARKANSAS	
Phillips County	John Easley
CALIFORNIA	
De Anza	Robert DeHart
Foothill-De Anza CCD	Thomas Fryer
Los Rios CCD	David Mertes
Rancho Santiago	Robert Jensen
Santa Barbara City	Peter MacDougall
Yosemite CCD	Tom Van Groningen
COLORADO	
CC of Denver	Byron McClenney
CONNECTICUT	
Quinebaug Valley	Robert Miller
DELAWARE	
DE Tech	John Kotula
FLORIDA	
Brevard	Maxwell King
Gulf Coast	Lawrence Tyree
Miami-Dade	Robert McCabe
GEORGIA	
Dalton	Derrell Roberts
ILLINOIS	
College of Du Page	Harold McAninch
Danville Area	Ronald Lingle
IOWA	
North IA Area	David Buettner
KANSAS	
Johnson County	Charles Carlsen
KENTUCKY	
Jefferson	Ronald Horvath
MARYLAND	
Montgomery	Robert Parilla
MASSACHUSETTS	
Bristol	Eileen Farley
MICHIGAN	
Macomb	Albert Lorenzo
Schoolcraft	Richard McDowell

Table 3.2   (Continued)

College	Nominee
Washtenaw	Gunder Myran
MISSISSIPPI	
Meridian	William Scaggs
MISSOURI	
St. Louis	Michael Crawford
NEBRASKA	
Metropolitan Tech	Richard Gilliland
NEW MEXICO	
San Juan	James Henderson
NEW YORK	
Monroe	Peter Spina
Westchester	Joseph Hankin
NORTH CAROLINA	
Central Piedmont	Ruth Shaw
Sandhills	Raymond Stone
OHIO	
Cuyahoga CCD	Nolen Ellison
Sinclair	David Ponitz
OKLAHOMA	
Tulsa	Alfred Philips
OREGON	
Clackamas	John Keyser
PENNSYLVANIA	
CC of Philadelphia	Judith Eaton
RHODE ISLAND	
CC of Rhode Island	Edward Liston
SOUTH CAROLINA	
Greenville Tech	Thomas Barton
Midlands Tech	James Hudgins
TENNESSEE	
Chattanooga State Tech	Harry Wagner
TEXAS	
Dallas Cnty CCD	Jan LeCroy*
Kilgore	Stewart McLaurin
Midland	Jess Parrish
Tyler	Raymond Hawkins
VIRGINIA	
Northern VA	Richard Ernst

Table 3.2   (Continued)

College	Nominee
Piedmont VA	George Vaughan
WASHINGTON	
Grays Harbor	Joseph Malik

[* retired during the course of the study]

In addition to identifying 50 outstanding CEOs, we chose to examine the relevance of gender differences in effective leadership.
Women have been an essential element of the community college movement and have been assuming leadership roles in growing numbers.
We assumed a null hypothesis: that there was no gender difference
among men and women when it came to being a good leader. Our research verified that some behavioral differences did exist between male
and female CEOs.

Chapter 11 discusses in detail the research on gender comparison.
Twenty-one (100 percent response) of the nominated women were compared to 21 men on the basis of two primary factors—demography and
experience.

PHASE III: AN IN-DEPTH ANALYSIS

I n the third and final phase of our research, we chose to study the
50 CEO leaders, in depth. We developed specific questions around
the transformational leadership themes, generated from the collective
contributions of the nominated participants. Each question had two
parts: Part A was general in nature; Part B asked the CEOs to relate
a critical incident that pertained to Part A of the question.

These questions were used to guide a structured oral interview conducted with each of the 50 CEOs (see Appendix 7). The purpose of
the interview was to obtain further in-depth descriptions of the characteristics of transformational leadership. Also, the degree to which our
outstanding CEOs articulated the strength of their transformational
behaviors was assessed. As noted earlier, this instrument was developed
directly from the behavioral attributes introduced by the CEOs. The
CEOs' responses were then scored using a code book developed from
the literature and from behavioral statements generated from the

participants' educational leadership philosophies. These behavioral statements also provided the basis for the development of the 34-item Multifactor College Leadership Questionnaire (see Appendix 8). Our questionnaire differed from that of Bass' "Multifactor Leadership Questionnaire, Form 5 Revised" (1985a) in that we did not include both transformational and transactional behaviors; we narrowed the focus to transformational behaviors only. We also limited our focus to the CEOs' behaviors that related only to the leadership team (not to the entire followership).

Finally, each of the top 50 CEOs and members of their immediate decision-making teams were asked to complete our Multifactor College Leadership Questionnaire. Form A of this instrument was used to acquire the CEO's perception of his/her leadership behavior (see Appendix 8). Form B, a parallel form of this instrument, was used to correlate the perceptions of each individual member of the decision-making team with those of his or her CEO (see Appendix 9). This instrument was sent to 373 administrative team members identified by their respective presidents, generating 290 responses (see Appendix 10).

SUMMARY

Our study has been an attempt to identify and describe a group of transformational leaders of the American community college movement. We wanted to obtain general information about CEOs, to find out how they used their time, to determine their own beliefs about educational leadership, and to identify the behaviors that led to their recognition as leaders. We believe the successful community college leader today is a transformational leader, one who can and does empower followers to become leaders themselves.

To ensure a broad sample, in Phase I we asked 912 community college CEOs and 50 state directors to identify those college CEOs in their areas who they felt demonstrated "the ability to influence, shape, and embed values, attitudes, beliefs, and behaviors consistent with increased faculty and staff commitment to both access and excellence." The 296 nominees comprised Group I of the study.

In Phase II we asked these 296 nominees to describe, in writing, their personal philosophies of educational leadership; to answer some questions about themselves and how they used their time; and finally to nominate one or two outstanding transformational leaders. Of the 296 nominees in Phase I, 256 responded in Phase II. These 256 leaders, previously identified as excellent, supplied both (1) the information we used to develop themes and attributes for later use in the study and (2) our list of 50 "blue chippers." During Phase II we also compared men and women to determine if there was a gender difference in reference to leadership attributes; there was not.

In Phase III, we focused our study on the 50 "blue chip" leaders. Using the data supplied by the 256 nominees, we conducted structured oral interviews with these 50 outstanding leaders. From these interviews we developed a questionnaire, the Multifactor College Leadership Questionnaire. We then sent one form of this questionnaire to each of the 50 "blue chippers" and an alternate form of this questionnaire to the leadership teams on each of these 50 campuses, so that we were able to compare the leaders' responses with those of their followers. From the data generated by these questionnaires, we were able to identify philosophical themes and leadership attributes common to transformational leaders. These themes and attributes comprise the heart of our study of transformational leaders—those who have the vision to change and the skill to empower others to help that vision become a reality.

CHAPTER 4

THE DEMOGRAPHICS
OF THE COMMUNITY COLLEGE
TRANSFORMATIONAL LEADERS

66 *Why study the community college presidency?
Attempting to understand the community college
without understanding its most important leaders, is,
at the risk of engaging in a bit of hyperbole, tantamount
to trying to understand the American revolution
without studying Jefferson and Washington. To expect
the community college to provide effective leadership in
the years ahead without a better concept of how its
leaders function, would be like asking Machiavelli to
write* The Prince *while ignoring Cesare Borgia.* **99**

GEORGE VAUGHAN, The Community College Presidency

PRESIDENTIAL INFORMATION QUESTIONNAIRE

*OTHER STUDIES
THE CURRENT STUDY
PERSONAL DATA
BACKGROUND AND EXPERIENCE
DEGREES
TIME UTILIZATION
TIME SPENT WITH OTHERS
CONSTITUENT GROUPS
ROLES PLAYED BY COLLEGE LEADERS
COMPARISONS WITH THE VAUGHAN STUDY*

THE DEMOGRAPHICS
OF THE COMMUNITY COLLEGE
TRANSFORMATIONAL LEADERS

INTRODUCTION

The major working hypothesis of the study of exceptional community college CEOs is that if we wish to understand exceptional performance, we must study exceptional performers. To understand exceptional community college CEOs, we must discover something of who they are, where they have been, how they achieved their executive posts, and how they spend their time.

Several researchers and practitioners have examined the role of the college president in this decade (Carbone, 1981; Benezet, Katz, and Magnusson, 1981; Kamm, 1982; Fisher, 1984; Vaughan, 1986; Cohen and March, 1986). George B. Vaughan, former President of Piedmont Virginia Community College, Charlottesville, Virginia, in his study of almost 600 community colleges nationwide (1986), describes the changing nature of the community college president:

THE time to take a closer look at the community college president is at hand. The position of the community college president is well into its second generation: over 50 percent of the presidents have been in their current level for five years or less. Thus the "typical" president is no longer the founder and builder of colleges so typical of the 1960s when so many community colleges opened.

THE path to the presidency is also changing. Serendipity often played a major role in deciding who became a president during the period of rapid growth. Today, however, the presidency is often viewed as the culminating point of a career that has been years in the making (p. 9).

Vaughan's purpose for his study of the community college presidency was to examine the individuals who currently occupy that position. From his perspective as a community college president with a single set of experiences, Vaughan wondered: Who are today's presidents? Where did they come from? Where are they going? With whom do they socialize? And what is their relationship with the middle class American phenomenon—the social club? He answers these and many other crucial questions about the leaders of American community colleges. Reviewers have found his work "vividly detailed, grounded in both extensive research and first-hand personal experience as a distinguished community college president. . . the most far-reaching study of its kind ever attempted" (Vaughan, 1986, p. viii).

OTHER STUDIES

Leadership and Ambiguity (Cohen and March) was originally published in 1974 and updated and republished in 1986. Both versions examine some general ideas about leadership and ambiguity in the context of the American college president. Since the research for the book was completed, several thousand college presidents have been appointed to their posts, replacing several thousand who have left. That turnover of presidents is reflected in the sample of colleges and universities in the Cohen and March study. In the 14 years from 1970 to 1984, 53 new presidents were appointed to office in the 41 colleges and universities in the sample. Of the 41 college presidents on which the Cohen and March study was based, only six were still in the same presidency in April of 1985, some 15 years after the original study. By 1984, Cohen and March were able to study a new generation of presidents. But their general conclusions did not change. They explain:

SINCE the book was completed, there has been a new generation of presidents. The world of colleges and universities has also changed. The political activism and revolutionary rhetoric have been replaced by financial exigencies and other problems and other solutions. The changing role of women has affected the characteristics of students, faculty and administrators in ways that are dramatic with respect to the conditions at the time the original research was done. The demographics of birth cohorts and population movements, changes in the family, and the changing market for educated people have changed colleges and their curricula. New technologies have been introduced, and although contentiousness of campuses appears to have declined, lawyers, litigation and regulation play a more important part in university administrative life. The years of the 1980s are different from the 1970s, and it would be extraordinary if these changes did not bring important changes in the college presidency. College presidents attend to somewhat different agendas, use somewhat different staffs, and have somewhat different relations with their various constituencies than they did 14 years ago. The problems and solutions they confront are perceptibly different. It is reasonable to ask whether these changes so transform the presidency as to make a book published in 1974 hopelessly archaic. It may not be surprising that we believe they do not (1986, pp. xi–xiii).

Although Cohen and March studied senior college and university presidents and although their analyses focus mainly on presidents as managers (transactional leaders), their study of presidents' use of time is an important one and will be used in this study as a basis for examination of and comparison with a group of the best transformational leaders of community colleges.

During 1987, the American Council on Education (ACE) surveyed the CEOs of 2105 colleges and universities. Their report was thought to be the most comprehensive statistical profile ever completed of CEOs in higher education. The conclusion of the ACE study was that the current generation of college presidents has not changed much in recent years. Ninety percent of the college presidents are men, and 93 percent are white. Academic backgrounds are similar for both men and women with over 40 percent of all degrees earned in Education. Eighty percent of the presidents hold doctoral degrees with the majority of that number earning the Ph.D. degree. The path to the presidency is incremental, with 17 percent of the presidents recruited from previous presidencies and 42 percent from vice-presidents' positions. The ACE report focuses on the "traditional" president:

THE data confirmed many of the impressions widely held by observers and students of the college presidency—the image of who shall occupy the chief executive office is clearly a traditional one. One reason may be that search committees clearly favor presidential candidates who have come from similar kinds of institutions; they look for a particular kind of academic and administrative background which automatically reduces the pool of candidates (Mooney, 1988, p. 14).

William Lex, as a research associate at The University of Texas at Austin, conducted a national research project in 1983 to investigate similarities and differences between a group of highly successful community college CEOs and a group of randomly selected CEOs. Subjects for the Lex study were identified in two phases. Identification of the highly successful CEO group was accomplished through a process of peer nomination by a panel of experts consisting of 46 men and women who were two-year college presidents and were also current or recent members of the Board of Directors of the American Association of Community and Junior Colleges. Ninety-six individuals were nominated by the panel on the basis of their professional qualities and attainments that epitomized the highest standards of success in the profession of community college administration. A randomly selected group of 202 two-year college CEOs was drawn from the remaining population.

Lex's study revealed significant differences between successful CEOs and randomly selected CEOs in the areas of achievement motivation, constructs of work competency, educational backgrounds, number of years between completion of the highest degree and becoming a CEO, years of service as a CEO, and institutional size and complexity. Additional variables included salary and benefits, productivity, self-perceptions, and position satisfaction. The findings validated Lex's peer nomination process and suggested a particularly strong link between CEO success and the prestige of the institution from which the highest degree was earned.

THE CURRENT STUDY

This current study of community college CEOs also examines biographical, demographic, experiential, and time utilization factors derived from the Presidential Information Questionnaire. The PIQ was also compared to previous research. However, the broader design was to engage in a systematic effort to identify and examine transformational leadership exhibited within the community college in a way that would link leadership theory with practice. To achieve our objective, multiple processes were employed to discover the characteristics and behavioral patterns of public community college CEOs. The result was a selection process in which the CEOs and state directors selected some outstanding leaders. The processes used in each phase of the study are defined and explained in the previous chapter.

The response to our invitation to participate in the study was extremely gratifying—over 80 percent in both phases elected to participate—signaling to us the timeliness of the subject as well as the need for further research. These responses, coupled with the data generated, were most valuable and enabled us to acquire an enlightened insight into the comprehensiveness of transformational leadership. The database, developed from demographic information, oral taped interviews, and written statements with supporting documents regarding educational leadership philosophy, was rich from a research perspective.

Initially, we chose to examine the demographic data generated by the total group of 256 respondents that elected to participate in Phase I of the study. We will refer in this chapter to these individuals as the "Phase I group." In continuing the process of Phase II, 50 "blue chippers" were selected by their peers as the participants for the third and final phase of the study. We refer to this group as the "blue chip" group. This division then allowed us to make demographic comparisons between the entire group, the group of "blue chippers," and the remaining group of 206 CEOs. Comparisons also were made with the women presidents of the study. Wherever possible, the demographic data will be related and compared to studies by Vaughan (1986), Mooney (1988), Lex (1984), and others (Carbone, 1981; Benezet, Katz, and Magnusson, 1981; Fisher, 1984).

PERSONAL DATA

The biographical data sheet completed by the 256 CEOs in Phase I of the study included age, place of birth, the population of the cities in which the presidents were born, and some information about their length of residency within the state where they currently reside. These data have been compiled and will be reported in this chapter. We will also report information on the CEOs' background and experience. We will include types of positions held, length of time in the position, number of years served in present positions, and the number of community colleges served while rising to the top. Data will be provided that will allow the reader to examine the entry-level administrative position of the CEOs, the age of the exceptional CEOs when they became educational administrators, and the extent to which these individuals were founding presidents. We will also list the type and source of the highest degree attained.

A major portion of our report will deal with how exceptional CEOs spend their time. We will look at hours spent per week in various activities, and we will look at how exceptional CEOs spend their day. Our primary focus in this chapter will be to provide data collected from the 256 presidents who constituted our Phase I group. In this group of 256, twenty-one women were identified as outstanding presidents, four of whom were selected as "blue chippers." We have used this population of 21 women to conduct research related to gender differences. When we report demographic data from the 50 "blue chip" CEOs, the reader should realize that the "blue chippers" were extracted from the larger group. For clarity, we will refer to the 256 CEOs who were chosen in the initial phase of the study as the Phase I group. The Phase II group will consist of the 50 "blue chip" CEOs, while we will refer directly to the 21 women as the women's group, four of whom were also "blue chippers." The "reference group" will be the remaining 206 presidents and chancellors, male and female, once the "blue chip" presidents are factored out.

The average age of the Phase I group who completed our information sheet was 51.5 years of age. The Phase II group, the "blue chippers," were slightly younger, but only by six months, with an average age of 51.0 years, while the women presidents of the study were the youngest of the three groups, reporting an average age of 48.7 years. All of these groups are younger, on average, than the CEOs who responded to the ACE study (Mooney, 1988) and the Cohen and March study (1986). The ACE study concluded that the typical college president is a (53-year-old) married, white male, with a doctoral degree and previous experience in a high administrative job in academe. Cohen and March found that the presidents they studied in 1974 averaged 51.4 years of age; by 1984 their average age had risen to 53.4.

The members of the reference group were born in almost every state of the union with Texas, New York, and North Carolina leading the list, while the top-50 group recorded New York and Illinois as the states where the largest number of presidents were born. The women of the study most often listed Texas, Alabama, Pennsylvania, and Kentucky as their birthstates. The reference group primarily hailed from rural settings; about 45 percent of this group were born in a rural setting while only 30 percent of the "blue chippers" reported the same. About 29 percent of the women were born in rural areas (populations under 25,000). Thus the reference group listed rural settings as the place of birth considerably more often than did the "blue chippers."

We also asked all CEOs for the number of years they had resided in their present state. The average number of years was 31; that figure for the women was 29. As was the situation with average age, little difference existed between the exceptional CEOs and the remainder of the Phase I group, although some difference was noted for the women of the study. This finding also supports the ACE study in which it was reported that mobility for presidents was found to be limited, with chief executives generally making career moves from the same institution or a similar one. Vaughan reported that almost half of his group of CEOs were currently institutional leaders in the state in which they finished high school (1986, p. 13).

We also ascertained the nature of the family background of the female college presidents, assuming that they were similar to the Vaughan study (1986) and different from the Cohen and March studies (1974, 1986). Like Vaughan's presidents, the women of the study came primarily from working-class backgrounds (about half their fathers were farmers or laborers); both the women and the men were unlike those of the Cohen and March (1974) study where family background of typical presidents are middle-to-upper socioeconomic status and where fathers' occupations tend to be entrepreneurial. Surprisingly, their mothers tended to be more highly educated than their fathers and more highly educated than both the fathers and mothers of the Vaughan study. Only 19 percent of the mothers had less than a high school education, whereas 60 percent of presidents' mothers in Vaughan's study had less than a high school education.

BACKGROUND AND EXPERIENCE

B oth the "Blue Chip" CEOs and their reference group reported that they had experience in teaching at the high school level, at community colleges, and at universities. The average number of years of teaching for the total group, including the "blue chippers," was approximately seven years, with experience typically at all three levels. For the women in the study, the average number of years involved in teaching at the various levels was 15 (we may assume that this difference in number of years spent teaching may account for "age" gaps between women and men as women assume their first administrative position or their first presidency). Most CEOs reported that they had significant administrative experience prior to attaining the presidency. The reference group averaged just over 13 years of administrative experience; the women averaged just over 12 years of administrative experience. The "blue chippers," however, averaged almost 14 years experience, with over 11 years at the community college level prior to attaining the presidency.

We also asked the CEOs to report the number of community colleges with which they had been associated either as an instructor or as an administrator. The majority reported being associated with two community colleges; approximately 37 percent of the total group indicated that they had been associated with three or more community colleges in their careers. These data were almost identical for all three groups (36.2 percent for the total group, 38 percent for the women, and 37.8 percent for the "blue chippers"). Interestingly, when we asked the 256 Phase I CEOs to report their entry-level administrative position in the community college, the data were different from those of the "blue chip" list. The reference group primarily had held positions as dean of the college, dean of administration, and dean of instruction, while the majority of those on the "blue chip" list reported a deanship or vice-presidency in administration or business services to a much larger degree than did their counterparts. The data presented in Figure 4.1 support the belief that the total group of CEOs enjoyed a wonderful opportunity when entering the community college field. Four percent of the CEOs were appointed to the presidency as their first administrative position, while over 17 percent were named dean of the college as their first job.

Figure 4.1 First Administrative Position

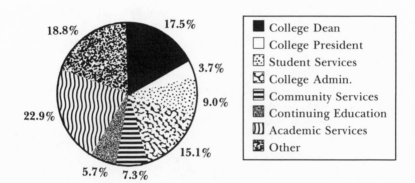

The average age of attainment of the first administrative position was 30 for the reference group, while the average age for the "blue chip" group was 28.8.

These data were very different for the women of the study. Women entered the profession later than did the men, and their entry-level position overwhelmingly tended to be that of college administrator, such as department head or division chair (40 percent). Their next two highest held entry-level positions were public school administrator (20 percent) and college dean (20 percent). None of the women began their careers as college presidents. The difference in age between women and men at the time of their first administrative position is critical and statistically significant. For the total group, it was 30 years; for the "blue chip" group it was 28.8 years; and for the women it was 34.4 years. While we may assume that women defer careers for family and child-raising purposes, we may also assume that the phenomenon of women in positions of leadership is relatively new.

CEOs in both the reference group and the "blue chip" group had been founding presidents. Eighteen percent of the reference group and 32 percent of the "blue chip" group indicated that they had been founding presidents. When the respondents indicated their immediately previous position, 31 percent of the total group indicated a presidency. However, the most common position held prior to achieving a college presidency was that of vice-president and/or dean. Forty-eight percent of our total group of outstanding CEOs had held such a position. Only about 20 percent of the women of the study had held previous positions as college presidents. About one-third of their number had been vice-presidents before assuming the presidency and about one-tenth of their number had been college administrators. None of the groups came to the presidency from the superintendency or other positions in public school administration. Eighty-one percent of the women of the study had held previous positions in community college education, as had 75 percent of the reference group and 88 percent of the "blue chippers."

Vaughan (1986) found that 38 percent of his sample of college presidents had been chief academic officers before they assumed the presidency (their position at the time of the survey) and that 12 percent had previously been vice-presidents of community colleges. Eight percent of his group came to the presidency via the student services route and approximately that same number came from public school administration (down from 24 percent in 1960 and 14 percent in 1970). Ninety percent of the presidents in the Vaughan study held previous positions in community colleges.

Carbone (1981) found that 23 percent of the community college presidents he studied came to the presidency from positions of dean or director and that 23 percent came from positions outside community college education or postsecondary education. In the ACE study, 17 percent of the respondents reported that their previous position had been president of another institution, 42 percent had previously been vice-presidents, and almost 19 percent had been deans or directors.

When the total Phase I group identified their prior organization by type, 76 percent of the reference group indicated that they came from another community college while 87 percent of the "blue chippers" indicated that they had served previously in a community college. Therefore, approximately 24 percent of the reference group and 13 percent of the "blue chip" group entered their presidency from an organization other than a community college. These outside organizations are listed according to the number of times they were named by the CEO: colleges and universities, trade schools, and public school districts.

We were surprised to discover that while the literature records that CEOs have moved frequently, 63 percent of our total group indicated that they have been in their current position for five years or more. In fact, as we look at each five-year component, 26 percent of our total group have held their current positions for six to ten years, 20 percent for 11 to 15 years, and 17 percent for 16 years or more. The women of the study have held their positions for a much shorter period than either of the other groups. Average tenure in their present positions is 4.6 years. The "blue chippers" differ from the total group in all four time divisions: 83 percent of the "blue chippers" have held their positions for six years or more. It is interesting to note that the CEOs who have been identified as transformational leaders appear to be a stable group. This is particularly true of the "blue chippers." This stability, in conjunction with the transformational qualities identified in our study, suggests that these proven leaders provide excellence in modeling for the next generation of community college leaders.

The time-gap factor between women and men was also critical when the presidents reported the age they first became college presidents: for the men of the study that age was 36.1 years, but for the women it was 43.6 years, again demonstrating the traditional seven-year age gap between females and males in the acquisition of their first CEO position (Shakeshaft, 1987).

DEGREES

The typical terminal degree earned by the total group in our study was Doctor of Education. About 50 percent of the reference group and the "blue chip" group held this degree, while about 38 percent of both groups held the Ph.D. Nearly 10 percent of the respondents in the reference group and in the "blue chip" group had a Master's degree, but no Doctorate. The women presidents overwhelmingly had earned Ph.D. degrees (71 percent); only 24 percent had earned Ed.D. degrees, and five percent had earned M.A. degrees. A comparison between the ACE, the Lex, and the current studies reveals that those community college CEOs who were rated as excellent hold a significantly lower number of Ph.D.s than does the total ACE population, since the typical degree held by these exceptional CEOs is the Ed.D. However, Lex's exceptional group held a higher percentage of Ph.D.'s. The comparisons are shown in Table 4.1. In the current study, both the "blue chip" group and the remainder of the reference group were similar in the acquisition of and types of degrees.

Eleven percent of the respondents in the reference group indicated they had received their terminal degree in California, ten percent indicated Texas, and eight percent listed New York. Florida and North Carolina followed at about 7.5 percent each. For the "blue chippers," 17 percent had earned their degrees in Florida while about nine percent listed Texas or California, and almost 6.5 percent listed Illinois or Indiana. This study supports a connection between the institutions where the CEOs earned their degrees and the institutions where the Kellogg Leadership programs were located in the 1960s. Many of these leaders in both the "blue chip" group and the reference group received their

Table 4.1   **Terminal Degree Earned by CEOs**

Highest Degree	Current Study	Women	ACE Study	Lex Study
Bachelor's degree	2.0%	0.0%	N/R	N/R
Master's degree	10.0%	4.7%	11.4%	10.0%
Ph.D.	38.0%	71.0%	55.9%	29.0%
Ed.D.	50.0%	24.3%	22.2%	47.0%

degrees as a result of the Kellogg Leadership Program in one of these aforementioned states. The women presidents received their degrees from Texas (19 percent), California (19 percent), Michigan (19 percent), and Alabama (14 percent). The other states granting doctoral degrees to women were Utah, Florida, Minnesota, Washington, and Arizona. Since many of the current group of women presidents came along after Kellogg funding was completed, few had the opportunity to participate in this exceptional leadership preparation program.

TIME UTILIZATION

College presidents are busy people. The presidents in our study describe their jobs as demanding in terms of both time and energy. The people with whom they interact—students, faculty, administrators, trustees, and external contacts—make a similar assessment. By every report, the CEOs' job is physically demanding and emotionally exhausting. There is not enough time. There are too many people to see. There are too many things to do.

Not only do CEOs report themselves overloaded, they also describe themselves as being unable to attend adequately to the "important" aspects of their jobs. This view is one also held by individuals who report directly to the CEOs and who desire more of their time and attention. However, in spite of the demands of the job, our CEOs make time to address the transformational themes, and they do it exceptionally well.

Studies supported the idea that CEOs typically invested tremendous energy and time in their work. In our survey, we asked CEOs to describe a typical work week and a typical work day, recording total hours per week on campus and total hours per week off campus where the CEO was engaged in college business. We discovered that the typical CEO invested about 60 hours per week in all roles, both on and off campus. This number was supported both by Cohen and March and by the ACE study. The CEOs reported 47 hours per week on campus and supplemented this activity with an additional 14 hours per week off campus conducting college business. Indications are that the typical CEO spent about 75 percent of the work week on campus and about 25 percent of the work week off campus.

CEOs reported that they spent about five hours of work per week at home working on college business. Thirty hours per week (or about 50 percent of their total time) were spent in the office. About nine hours per week (15 percent of their time) were invested on campus but out of the office, and 9.8 hours (16 percent of their time) were spent off campus but within the service area. While we have reported the averages in time utilization, we must also report that the CEOs varied considerably in their responses to us.

In the analysis of the data on time utilization, three statistically significant factors were revealed about use of time for the women of the study. On average, women worked a longer number of hours per week, investing 51 hours per week on campus. Also, women tended to work longer at home than did the other groups. This fact, combined with the hours worked per week at the office and hours worked in college-related activities, demonstrated that women worked a total of 75 hours per week at college activities. Finally, women reported that they spent more hours per week with their faculty than did the other groups—almost 25 percent more time.

TIME SPENT WITH OTHERS

A major thesis of the transformational view of leadership is that certain leaders are more effective than others primarily because they demonstrate a special capacity to influence and organize *meaning* for others. It is difficult to influence people without being in contact with them. Thus, an important aspect of the current study was to determine how CEOs spent their time in the process of influencing others. Analysis of these data indicates that typical CEOs spend about 25 percent of their time alone, 32 percent of their time with one person, and 42.5 percent of their time with more than one person. Figure 4.2 supports the idea that CEOs tend to spend the majority of their time influencing groups. These data do not differ significantly from the research of Cohen and March (1974, 1986). In the Cohen and March study,

CEOs reported 25 percent of the time spent alone, 35 percent with one other person, and 40 percent of their time with two or more other persons. These groups include the leadership team, the board, or other constituent groups. Unlike the variance reported in the time utilization aspect of the survey, the time spent with others was relatively stable. In general, the CEOs did not vary by more than two hours per week in the amount of time they reported spending with others.

Figure 4.2   Time Spent With Others

TIME SPENT WITH OTHERS

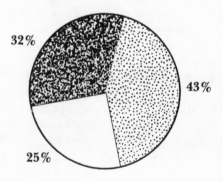

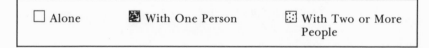

CONSTITUENT GROUPS

Another portion of the time utilization study sought to determine how CEOs invested their time with constituent groups. Summarized data appear in Table 4.2. These groups include trustees, faculty, students, administrative team, classified staff, and outside individuals and agencies. We discovered that the CEOs invest about 42 hours per week with constituent groups, with their administrative team taking up approximately one-third of their total time (36 percent). This percentage was followed by outside individuals with whom the CEOs reported investing about 26 percent of their time. Faculty consumed

14 percent of the CEOs' time. Trustees received about 7 percent and classified staff nearly 10 percent of the CEOs' time. Table 4.2 charts these percentages of allotted time.

Table 4.2   **Time Invested With Constituent Groups**

	Hours Invested by Group	
Constituent Group	Percent of Total	Average Hours
Trustees	7.4	3.1
Faculty	14.1	5.9
Students	6.4	2.7
Administrative Team	35.9	15.1
Classified Staff	9.8	4.1
Outside Individuals and Agencies	26.4	11.1
T O T A L	100.0%	42.0

From our analysis of the CEOs' leadership behavior (to be reported in Chapter 5), we have concluded that the executive leadership team generally desires more face-to-face time with the CEO. Typical CEOs invest about 15 hours per week with their executive leadership teams. This investment (36 percent of their time) far exceeded the time spent with other groups. Obviously, many CEOs invest more than 36 percent of their time, and many invest considerably less; yet in all cases, most members of the CEOs' leadership teams expressed a desire for both more time and more quality time with the CEOs.

ROLES PLAYED BY COLLEGE LEADERS

One line of questions sought to determine how much time CEOs would report in key leadership roles. Based on a study of the literature, we envisioned three major roles that CEOs play in their institutions: (1) leading and influencing others; (2) developing, disseminating, and evaluating information; and (3) planning, making, and evaluating decisions. We were not surprised to discover that the CEOs invested about 43 percent of their time leading and influencing others, a statistic of special interest to the current investigation. Twenty-six percent of the CEOs' time was spent in dealing with information,

and 28 percent of their time in planning, making, and evaluating decisions. Thus, chancellors and presidents spend about half their time leading and influencing others, about a fourth of their time developing
information, and another fourth planning, making, and evaluating
decisions.

Figure 4.3   **Time Spent in Roles Played by the CEO**

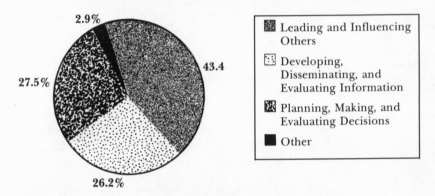

COMPARISONS WITH THE VAUGHAN STUDY

When comparing our findings with those of Vaughan's study,
we note several differences. For example, we find that the
number of years served in the current position held by the
effective CEO is approximately nine years; 83 percent have been in
their positions for five years or longer. In Vaughan's study 50 percent
of the CEOs had been in their current jobs for five years or less. These
data lead us to conclude that the CEOs nominated by their peers are,
generally, seasoned and experienced veterans who have earned their
reputations over a decade or so. Vaughan finds that almost half of the
presidents in his study were presidents of colleges in states where they
finished high school; our study documented that 29 percent met this
criterion. While 71 percent of our group of exceptional presidents have
migrated from the state in which they were raised, our data indicated
that they have resided within the boundaries of their adopted states
for approximately 30 years. We once again conclude that the group
of exceptional leaders is a highly stable group of people, having served
in the communities in which they live for an exceptionally long period
of time.

SUMMARY

I n 1958, Ron Lewis and Rosemary Stewart commented:

WE know more about the motives, habits, and the most intimate arcana of the primitive peoples of New Guinea or elsewhere, than we do of the denizens of the executive suites (p. 17).

In answering Lewis and Stewart's charge, we have developed a new picture of the effective community college CEO. The exceptional community college CEO who responded to our survey is 51 years of age and was most likely born in New York or Texas in a rural or small-town setting. On average, these CEOs have been residents of their current states for a significant part of their lives and have had seven or eight years' experience in high school and college teaching (although the women reported an average of 15 years at this level).

The typical CEO in the study is an experienced administrator, having served about ten years in various community college leadership roles before attaining the presidency. We also see a fairly mobile individual who, on the average, has served at two or more community colleges, often in the same state. Our typical CEO most probably has served as dean or vice-president of administration, instruction, students, or as dean of the college. We find a group of individuals who attained their first administrative position relatively early in their careers, at 29 to 30 years of age, although the women averaged almost 35 years of age when they attained their first administrative positions. We find that some of these CEOs were founding presidents of colleges, which would indicate that, given their current age and their entry level into administration, they were entering the community college movement approximately 20 years ago, when many community colleges were being built and opened at an extraordinary rate. As George Vaughan reports, it is obvious that many of these presidents benefited from the great demand for their services as they were entering the community college movement. None of the women was a founding president, again a reflection of the recent entry of women into positions of executive leadership.

We also find a group of CEOs with considerable experience at the presidential level. In the total group of 256 CEOs, approximately 35 percent have held presidencies at more than one college. When they have moved upward, they have also moved to larger or more urban community college settings. The most likely position held by this group prior to attaining the presidency was vice-president or dean, depending upon the structure of the college involved. Yet several of the older CEOs moved directly into a deanship or vice-presidency with no previous experience in the community college.

In our total group, we find a typical CEO who is less mobile nationally than we had imagined. Yet we find an upwardly mobile group serving an average of three years in their former positions before moving to their present positions. We find a group of degreed individuals, 90 percent of whom hold a doctorate, with the typical degree being an Ed.D. with a major in educational administration. We find that those states that were very active in the Kellogg movement some 20 to 25 years ago—Florida, California, Texas, and Illinois—housed universities that trained many of these CEOs.

CEOs tend to work long hours—about 60 hours a week for men and 75 for women. They spend about 75 percent of their time with others, and about a third of that time is spent with the leadership team, more than with any other group. About half their time is invested in leading and influencing others, both on and off the campus. The other half is used to develop information and to make and evaluate decisions.

The careers of exceptional CEOs provide persistent fascination. Those of us in the university who work in the field of higher education have an understandable interest in the natural life history of a CEO who resides in the community college setting. Our primary justification for looking at CEOs lies in the possible clarification of the ways in which these leaders function within the community college setting and of the special problems associated with leadership in the open-door college.

CHAPTER 5

RESEARCH FINDINGS

66 *As one reads, learns, and gains insight into the subject matter presented, one should eventually come to view statistics as a collection of methods that helps an individual or scientist make reasonable decisions from limited amounts of information.* **99**

LEONARD A. MARASCUILO, Statistical Methods for Behavioral Science Research

THE DEVELOPMENT OF THE THEORETICAL FRAMEWORK

REPORT OF THE FINDINGS

RESEARCH FINDINGS

INTRODUCTION

T he focus of this study is on transformational leadership. The literature reflects that there are no perfect transformational leaders; sometimes leaders have transactional qualities and styles as well as transformational ones. These two phenomena relate to the need and the situation that are present at any particular time. Very little has been written
about transformational leadership as it relates to universities or colleges.
Thus, the specific contribution of this study is to look at the transformational phenomenon as it applies to CEOs in community colleges. Important to our search of the literature were the ideas of James McGregor
Burns in building the foundation for transformational behavior. However, it was the studies of Bass (1985a) and Bennis and Nanus (1985)
that led us to the initial inquiry of how a transformational model might
be developed for community college CEOs. Their research led them to
conclude that transformational leaders had certain behaviors in common, behaviors that were absent in other leaders. We therefore focused
on identifying leadership behaviors in our exemplary presidents.

The CEOs surveyed in this study provided rich data that we have
been able to match to leadership theory. The comprehensiveness of
the CEOs' responses has enabled us to identify transformational themes
and the leadership behaviors. This information, in turn, generated the

Multifactor College Leadership Questionnaire (MCLQ), a self-assessment instrument that gave us additional information about transformational leader behaviors and demonstrated concurrence between
leader and follower responses. The data enabled us to build a theoretical
framework for transformational leadership that is unique to the community college environment. This framework is compared with the writings of other researchers in the field of leadership and forms the basis
of the book. The purpose of this chapter is to provide the reader with
an understanding of how the data were interpreted.

THE DEVELOPMENT OF THE THEORETICAL FRAMEWORK

Our generalized model for transformational leadership in the
community college was developed in several phases. In Chapter 3 we discussed our development of several protocols and
collection devices: the CEOs' written educational and philosophical
statements, the PIQ (the CEOs' biographical sketch on background and
experience), time utilization, and the identification and composition
of the CEOs' leadership teams.

Phase 1

We concentrated our efforts on the analysis of the written philosophical leadership statements generated by the CEOs. We wanted to
capture their perspectives of leadership related to behavioral practices.
A process was developed that enabled us to analyze each philosophical statement: 1) global themes were generated from the educational
philosophy statements written by the nominees; 2) the global themes
and philosophical concepts were translated into transformational attributes; 3) specific attribute descriptors, consistent with the philosophical concepts, were developed. Table 5.1 presents major themes and
attributes that represent the foundation of our model for transformational leadership.

Phase 2

Once the transformational themes and attributes were identified, a
series of open-ended questions was developed and used to guide a structured interview conducted with each of the 50 "blue chip" presidents.
The content of these questions reflected the five themes identified in
Table 5.1, and our interviewing techniques were based upon the Critical

Table 5.1 **Attributes of Transformational Leaders**
Developed from Philosophical Statements

Theme	Attributes
Vision	Possesses a future orientation Demonstrates a positive orientation toward change Takes appropriate risks to bring about change Demonstrates commitment to making appropriate changes Is mission-oriented Perceives a shared vision
Influence Orientation	Places responsibility with authority Is action-oriented Causes followers to feel powerful Employs appropriate decisional style Demonstrates willingness to be influenced by followers Builds a collaborative environment Encourages open communication Is in touch with followers Demonstrates high energy
People Orientation	Understands the organizational ethos Rewards appropriately Demonstrates respect toward others Considers individual needs Is student-centered Values others
Motivational Orientation	Is flexible in dealing with issues and people Encourages creativity Assists in the development of others Helps clarify expectations Attempts to inspire others
Values Orientation	Demonstrates commitment to learning Advocates quality education Demonstrates high standards Demonstrates sound judgment Demonstrates openness and trust Demonstrates sense of humor Leads by example

Incident Technique (CIT) formulated by John C. Flanagan (1954) and the Behavioral Event Interview Technique (BEIT) developed by David C. McClelland (1978). Because the CIT allows the collection of real-world examples of behavior that characterize either very effective or very ineffective performance of some activity and the BEIT identifies the competencies required for various jobs, we chose to incorporate both techniques in this particular study. Part A of each question focused on a particular theme but was general in nature, while Part B asked each of the 50 CEOs to relate a critical incident pertaining to Part A of the question (see Appendix 8). The purpose of the interview was to obtain further in-depth descriptions of the characteristics of transformational leadership. In addition, the interview was used to assess the degree to which the presidents articulated the strength of their transformational attributes. The interviews were designed to encourage CEOs to articulate the thoughts that accompany their behavior, not just the behavior itself (Klemp, Munger, and Spencer, 1977)—a strength of the BEIT. Likewise, structured interview questions, designed to focus on specific transformational themes, further provided us with the real-world examples, the strength of the CIT. Table 5.2 lists the refinement of the five themes and attributes that were elicited from the interview process. The table includes attribute descriptors that the CEOs furnished in the interviews.

The extent to which the CEOs articulated their transformational attributes was assessed by counting the frequency with which they employed the attribute descriptors when responding to the questions. The attribute descriptors were developed from the concepts used in Klemp's 1977 naval study and were designed to identify recurrent patterns of leadership behavior discerned from the interview tapes. After the descriptors were determined, they were tested on pilot tapes, revised, and edited for purposes of this study. The interview data were coded into pre-existing categories of vision, influence, people, motivation, and values. The degree to which a leader emphasized these 34 attributes was measured by frequency of occurrence in the interview.

Phase 3: The Multifactor College Leadership Questionnaire

Once the behaviors and action descriptors were developed and analyzed, we sought to develop an instrument that would allow us to determine the extent to which these CEOs and their followers were able to evaluate CEOs' performance. We used the CEOs' philosophical statements and their interview statements, as well as an adaptation of Bass' Multifactor Leadership Questionnaire, to develop our instrument. The items reflected the themes and the behaviors identified by community college

Table 5.2   **Attributes of Transformational Leaders**
Developed from Oral Interviews

Theme	Attributes	Attribute Descriptors
Vision	Is able to conceptualize a specific future	specific; challenging; conceptualizes
	Believes that he/she can shape the future	expects; believes; shapes
	Takes appropriate risks to bring about change	appropriate; skillful; calculated risks
	Is committed to specific courses of action	planning; strategic action
	Articulates a sense of mission	powerful; strong
	Is able to cause followers to share vision of the future	strong; moral; missionary
	Is committed to student access and success	access; success of students
Influence Orientation	Empowers followers by delegating appropriate authority/ responsibility	appropriate; reasoned; facilitates action
	Is characterized by a bias for action	action-oriented; energy
	Causes followers to feel strong through tasking & consideration of needs	empower; tasking, consideration of others
	Is able to involve others appropriately in decision making	appropriate; shared decision making; collaboration
	Allows followers to influence his/her values	adopts values of others
	Is able to cause followers to work together to solve problems	collaboration; teamwork; problem solving
	Is able to build an effective communication network	inside, outside; networking
	Demonstrates high need to be visible & to stay in touch with followers	model; shape; visibility
	Is highly energetic when the situation demands action	measured response; situationally controlled
People Orientation	Understands the character, sentiment & moral values of followers	knows well; believes in; character/senti- ment/moral values

Table 5.2   (Continued)

Theme	Attributes	Attribute Descriptors
	Rewards others contingent on their effort and performance	earned rewards; contingent
	Demonstrates respect for individual differences	tolerance; shapes
	Is able to accommodate individual needs	accommodation
	Values students and considers their needs	student-centered
	Seeks and values the opinion of others	respects others; believes in them; seeks opinions
Motivational Orientation	Is able to motivate followers to commitment and action	higher commitment to college, students; empowering
	Motivates others to use their creative skills	creative; skills
	Is able to enhance the development of followers	high expectations
	Motivates followers through clarification of expectations	states beliefs; structuring
	Inspires others to extra effort through praise and direction	praise & structure; control; shape
Values Orientation	Demonstrates commitment to intellectual self-development	higher; development of self
	Demonstrates commitment to the quality development of others	quality; development of others
	Is committed to a higher ethical code of personal behavior	ethics; morality
	Demonstrates consistent judgment in professional behavior	model; demonstrates; consistent
	Builds openness and trust through personal and professional behavior	model; believes in self; fairness
	Employs humor to motivate and inspire others	appropriate; sense of self
	Leads others through setting a personal example of expected conduct	modeling for others; demonstrate

CEOs, but differed from the MCLQ (Form 5 Revised) developed by Bass in that it did not include both transformational and transactional behaviors. We focused specifically on transformational behaviors; we limited the focus to the CEOs' behaviors that related to the leadership team and did not seek to measure the extent to which the CEO practiced leadership and influence with other groups beyond the leadership team.

Table 5.3 not only lists the themes and attributes previously developed from the philosophical statements and the interviews but also reflects, in the final column, the 34 MCLQ items developed in conjunction with these attributes. Two versions of the MCLQ were developed. Form A of the instrument was used to record the perceptions each president has of his or her own leadership attributes. Form B, a parallel form of the instrument, was used to determine perceptions that members of the leadership teams share with their presidents. The MCLQ was subsequently sent to the 50 CEOs and to the followers (see Appendix 9 a, b) who were listed in the demographic materials from Phase III of the study. Each of the presidents and each member of the leadership team was asked to complete the MCLQ. The instrument was mailed to 373 leadership team members, as identified by their respective presidents. Of the 373 leadership team members, 290 responded, yielding a 78 percent response rate. The analyses of the responses of the presidents and their leadership teams on the MCLQ are presented later in this chapter.

Finally, Table 5.4 (pp. 90–91) is the presentation of the theoretical framework for transformational leadership that guided our research. Column 1 lists the five transformational leadership themes generated from the data. Column 2 provides an operational definition for each specific theme. Subsequent columns relate the major transformational leadership researchers to the operational definitions and to the themes that we have developed. The reader will notice that our model is strikingly similar to that of Burns, in that he developed five themes that relate closely to those we identified. The frameworks of Bass, Bennis, Tichy, and Zaleznik relate in varying degrees to the overall framework we developed. Therefore, we found it useful to link the theories of transformational leadership found in the literature to the statements generated from the presidents' philosophical statements.

REPORT OF THE FINDINGS

While endless statistical data could be presented to report our findings about transformational leadership, we have selected the following to highlight our study.

(Left)

Table 5.3 MCLQ Items
Developed from Attributes of Transformational Leaders

Theme	Attributes	
Vision	V1.	Is able to conceptualize a specific future
	V2.	Believes that he/she can shape the future
	V3.	Takes appropriate risks to bring about change
	V4.	Is committed to specific courses of action
	V5.	Articulates a sense of mission
	V6.	Is able to cause followers to share vision of the future
	V7.	Committed to student access and success
Influence Orientation	I1.	Empowers followers by delegating appropriate authority/responsibility
	I2.	Is characterized by a bias for action
	I3.	Causes followers to feel strong through tasking & consideration of needs
	I4.	Is able to involve others appropriately in decision making
	I5.	Allows followers to influence his/her values
	I6.	Is able to cause followers to work together to solve problems
	I7.	Is able to build an effective communication network
	I8.	Demonstrates high need to be visible & to stay in touch with followers
	I9.	Is highly energetic when the situation demands action
People Orientation	P1.	Understands the character, sentiment & moral values of followers
	P2.	Rewards others contingent on their effort and performance
	P3.	Demonstrates respect for individual differences
	P4.	Is able to accommodate individual needs
	P5.	Values students and considers their needs
	P6.	Seeks and values the opinion of others

(Right)

Table 5.3 MCLQ Items
Developed from Attributes of Transformational Leaders

MCLQ Item

6. I am able to conceptualize a specific future for the college/district.

23. I believe that I can shape the future as it applies to the college/district.

4. I take appropriate risks to bring about change.

20. I am committed to specific courses of action in order to accomplish selected goals.

32. I am able to communicate to others a sense of mission.

28. I am able to cause my team to share in a vision of the future.

15. I articulate a strong commitment to student access and success.

3. I empower my leadership team by delegating appropriate authority and responsibility.

11. When interacting with my leadership team, I am characterized by a bias for action.

22. I cause my leadership team to feel powerful through tasking and consideration of their needs.

16. I am able to involve my leadership team appropriately in decision-making.

9. My values are influenced by my leadership team.

25. I am able to facilitate high-level problem solving within the leadership team.

33. I am able to build an effective communication network within the leadership team.

19. I demonstrate a high need to be visible and to stay in touch with those I am attempting to influence.

29. In interacting with the leadership team, I am energetic when the situation demands action.

12. I understand the character, sentiment, and moral values of my leadership team.

31. I reward those within my leadership team contingent on their effort and performance.

27. In responding to the needs of my leadership team, I demonstrate a respect for individual differences.

8. Within my leadership team, I am able to accommodate individual needs.

18. Above other concerns, I value students and consider their needs.

5. I seek and value the opinion of my leadership team.

(Left)

Table 5.3 MCLQ Items
Developed from Attributes of Transformational Leaders

Theme	Attributes	
Motivational Orientation	M1.	Is able to motivate followers to commitment and action
	M2.	Motivates others to use their creative skills
	M3.	Is able to enhance the development of followers
	M4.	Motivates followers through clarification of expectations
	M5.	Inspires others to extra effort through praise and direction
Values Orientation	A1.	Demonstrates commitment to intellectual self-development
	A2.	Demonstrates commitment to the quality development of others
	A3.	Is committed to a higher ethical code of personal behavior
	A4.	Demonstrates consistent judgment in professional behavior
	A5.	Builds openness and trust through personal and professional behavior
	A6.	Employs humor to motivate and inspire others
	A7.	Leads others through setting a personal example of expected conduct

Interview Data

In analyzing the structured interview scores for the various presidents, we noticed tremendous variability from one to another in the emphasis of attributes, as measured by the frequency of the attribute descriptors. Our conclusion was that CEOs employed different behavioral patterns. In order to examine these various leadership patterns, we decided to conduct a median split based on the CEOs' overall composite interview scores to form two groups: the upper 25 CEOs (Group 1) and the lower 25 CEOs (Group 2).

Figures 5.1 through 5.6 display the mean responses by the CEOs to the interview questions. Figure 5.1 reports the composite scores associated with each theme, while Figures 5.2 through 5.6 display the specific attributes associated with each theme separately.

(Right)
Table 5.3 MCLQ Items
Developed from Attributes of Transformational Leaders

MCLQ Item

24. I am able to motivate my leadership team to significant levels of commitment and action.

30. I am able to motivate my leadership team to utilize their creative skills.

10. I demonstrate a commitment to the quality development of the leadership team.

14. I motivate my leadership team through clarification of my expectations.

2. I inspire my leadership team to extra effort through appropriate praise and direction.

26. I demonstrate a commitment to the higher intellectual development of the leadership team.

7. I am able to enhance the development of my leadership team.

1. When interacting with the leadership team, I attempt to apply consistent ethical standards of professional behavior.

17. When interacting with the leadership team, I demonstrate consistent judgment.

21. When interacting with the leadership team, I build openness and trust.

34. I employ humor appropriately to motivate and inspire the leadership team.

13. I influence my leadership team by setting a personal example of expected conduct.

In Figure 5.1, the vertical axis of the figure indicates the mean number of times that a CEO expressed one of the five themes in the interview process. The horizontal axis of the figure indicates the five thematic areas, including vision, influence, people, motivational, and values orientation. We expected Group 1 to score higher than Group 2 on many items, since Group 1 consisted of the upper half of the median split. However, we thought that the two groups would overlap somewhat, in that the scroes of the lower 25 would exceed those of the upper 25 in some areas. The results indicated that Group 1 scored consistently higher than Group 2 on all but two items; there was less overlap than we expected. It is clear that for these five thematic areas the Group 1 CEOs differed significantly from Group 2. The mean scores for both groups are displayed at the bottom of Figure 5.1 (p. 92).

(Left)

Table 5.4   Theoretical Framework For Transformational Leadership

Themes of The Current Study	Operational Definition	Burns
Vision	A leader-conceptualized view of the future. While shared with others, the vision is the primary responsibility of the transformational leader.	1. Through shared vision, elevates followers to a higher level of motivation.
Influence Orientation	The process of shared attention to problems and understanding of roles to be played in resolution. Generally results in increased delegation and empowerment, resulting in self-actualization of both leaders and followers.	4. Leader's intention has the effect of raising the needs of both followers and leaders to a higher plane.
People Orientation	The process of leader and follower interaction in which the team is considered a living system, and where the strengths of each team member are maximized. At the same time, there exists a strong focus on the individual.	3. Leader interacts with followers for the purpose of the exchange of valued motivators.
Motivational Orientation	The process whereby the mass of the organization accepts a new vision and mission. Followers are motivated to achieve and are excited through performance and results.	2. Leader induces followers to pursue goals that represent shared values.
Values Orientation	Constitutes the moral fiber of the leader to include: commitment, quality, integrity, trust, and respect through modeling. Viewed as an ethical orientation that is morally accepting to an uplifting for followers.	5. Through a shared vision, the leader and followers create new values and new commitment. The changes sought create a new culture.

(Right)

Table 5.4 Theoretical Framework For Transformational Leadership

Bass	Bennis	Tichy	Zaleznik
1. Charismatic Orientation	1. Attention to Vision 3. Meaning through Communication	1. Creation of Vision 3. Institutionalization of Change	1. Attitude toward Goals 4. Sense of Self
1. Charismatic Orientation 2. Consideration for Others 3. Intellectual Stimulation 4. Contingent Reinforcement 5. Leadership by Exception	4. Deployment of Self	1. Creation of a Vision 2. Mobilization of Commitment 3. Institutionalization of Change	1. Attitude toward Goals
2. Consideration for Others 4. Contingent Reinforcement 5. Leadership by Exception	2. Trust through Positioning 3. Meaning through Communication	2. Mobilization of Commitment	2. Work as an Enabling Process 3. Relations with Others
3. Intellectual Stimulation 4. Contingent Reinforcement	2. Trust through Positioning 3. Meaning through Communication	2. Mobilization of Commitment	2. Work as an Enabling Process
2. Consideration for Others 3. Intellectual Stimulation	2. Trust through Positioning 3. Meaning through Communication 4. Deployment of Self	1. Creation of a Vision 2. Mobilization of Commitment 3. Institutionalization of Change	1. Attitude toward Goals 2. Work as an Enabling Process 3. Relations with Others 4. Sense of Self

Figure 5.1   "Blue Chipper" Median Split
Comparison on Individual Attributes

COMPOSITE

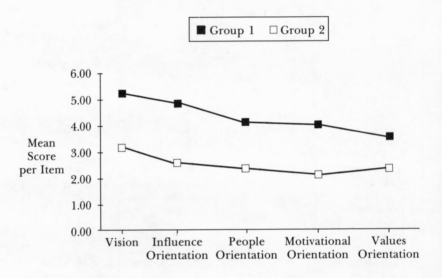

Attribute	Group 1	Group 2
Vision	5.30	3.24
Influence Orientation	4.74	2.53
People Orientation	4.11	2.30
Motivational Orientation	4.08	2.05
Values Orientation	3.49	2.29

Figure 5.2 depicts the CEOs' mean response to each of the attributes associated with vision. The figure displays the mean number of times that the CEO expressed the attribute during the interview process. Again, the vertical axis displays the mean number of times the attribute was expressed, and the horizontal axis displays the specific attributes associated with vision. Figure 5.2 indicates that for both groups the highest sub-score associated with the vision theme was V6, reinforcing the importance that our CEOs placed on the need to develop a shared vision.

Figure 5.2 "Blue Chipper" Median Split Comparison on Individual Attributes

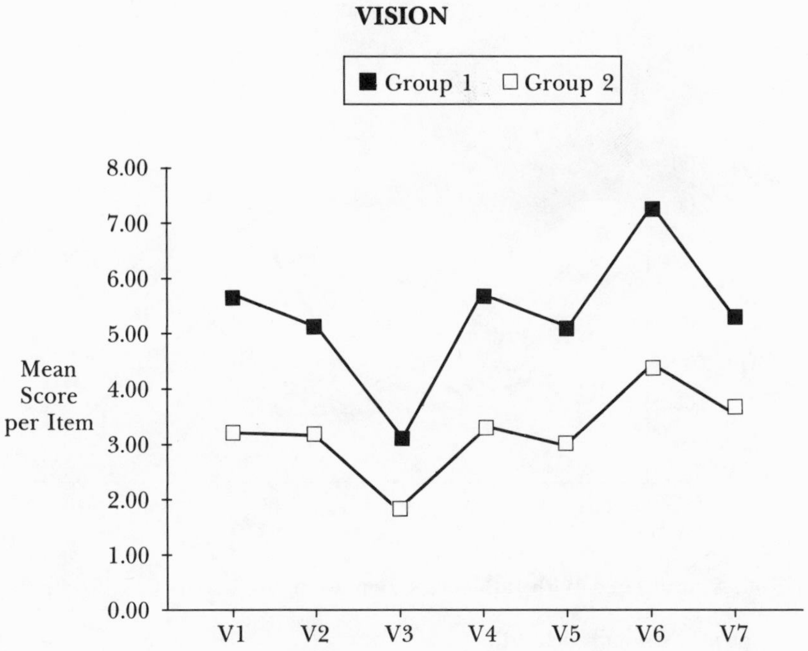

VISION

■ Group 1   □ Group 2

Attributes Associated With Vision	Group 1	Group 2
V1: Has a future orientation	5.56	3.28
V2: Demonstrates positive orientation to change	5.04	3.20
V3: Takes appropriate risks for change	3.12	1.80
V4: Demonstrates commitment to making changes	5.64	3.40
V5: Is mission-oriented	5.04	2.92
V6: Perceives a shared vision	7.44	4.52
V7: Is committed to student access and success	5.24	3.56

Figure 5.3 indicates the CEOs' mean responses associated with the influence theme of the study. Nine attributes were examined. Notice again the difference between Group 1 and Group 2. Item I7, "encouragement of open communication," earned the highest score for both groups.

Figure 5.3 "Blue Chipper" Median Split Comparison on Individual Attributes

INFLUENCE ORIENTATION

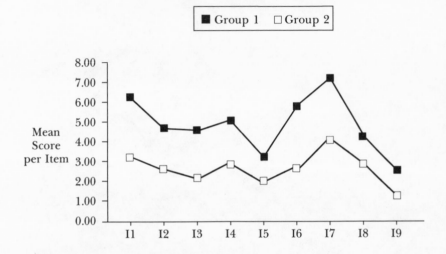

Attributes Associated With Influence Orientation	Group 1	Group 2
I1: Empowers through delegation	6.16	3.20
I2: Is action-oriented	4.64	2.64
I3: Causes followers to feel powerful	4.52	2.08
I4: Employs appropriate decisional style	5.00	2.76
I5: Is willing to be influenced by followers	3.04	1.96
I6: Builds a collaborative environment	5.72	2.56
I7: Encourages open communication	7.04	3.96
I8: Is in touch with followers	4.16	2.68
I9: Demonstrates high energy	2.36	0.96

Figure 5.4 indicates mean responses for the theme of people orientation (includes all constituents directly associated with the institution, e.g., board, faculty, support staff, administrative team, and students). Under this theme there were six attributes. The top CEOs most frequently mentioned items P1, "understanding organizational ethos," and P5, "student-centeredness."

Figure 5.4   "Blue Chipper" Median Split Comparison on Individual Attributes

PEOPLE ORIENTATION

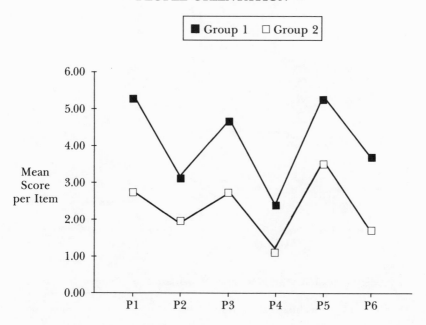

Attributes Associated With People Orientation	Group 1	Group 2
P1: Understands organizational ethos	5.28	2.76
P2: Rewards appropriately	3.20	1.92
P3: Demonstrates respect toward others	4.60	2.72
P4: Considers individual needs	2.40	1.08
P5: Is student-centered	5.44	3.60
P6: Values others	3.72	1.72

Figure 5.5 indicates the CEOs' mean responses associated with their orientation to the theme of motivation. There were five specific attributes associated with this area. M3, "assists in the development of others," was the attribute most emphasized by the CEOs in Group 1 of the study.

Figure 5.5 "Blue Chipper" Median Split Comparison on Individual Attributes

MOTIVATION ORIENTATION

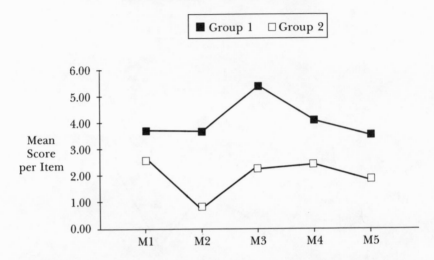

| ■ Group 1 | □ Group 2 |

Attributes Associated With Motivation Orientation	Group 1	Group 2
M1: Is flexible in dealing with issues and people	3.72	2.68
M2: Encourages creativity	3.64	0.88
M3: Assists in the development of others	5.52	2.40
M4: Helps clarify expectations	4.12	2.48
M5: Attempts to inspire others	3.40	1.86

The mean responses to the final theme, values orientation, are indicated in Figure 5.6 (on the next page). There were seven attributes described within this theme. Responses were not significantly different between these two groups, although A1, "demonstrates a commitment to learning," did produce the greatest difference score.

MCLQ Data

As mentioned earlier, the MCLQ was derived from the philosophical statements submitted by the transformational leaders, from the statements in the interviews with the "blue chip" CEOs, and from Bass' leadership instrument. Researchers have seldom attempted to gather information about the followers' perception of their leader's attributes.

Figure 5.6 "Blue Chipper" Median Split Comparison on Individual Attributes

VALUES

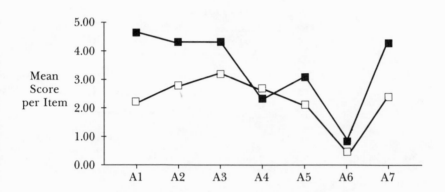

Attributes Associated With Values Orientation	Group 1	Group 2
A1: Demonstrates a commitment to learning	4.76	2.16
A2: Advocates quality education	4.40	2.88
A3: Demonstrates high standards	4.44	3.20
A4: Demonstrates sound judgment	2.44	2.72
A5: Demonstrates openness and trust	3.12	2.12
A6: Demonstrates a sense of humor	0.84	0.48
A7: Leads by example	4.44	2.48

Thus we simultaneously measured the perceptions of the CEOs' strengths from both the followers and the CEOs.

The means for the MCLQ responses were computed for each CEO and leadership team and then compared using T-tests to determine if they were significantly different for each item. The results of the T-tests indicated no significant differences between the presidents' self-ratings on the MCLQ and their respective leadership teams' ratings. Findings were similar for the upper and lower median split CEO groups. Thus, we determined that no significant differences existed in the self-ratings of the CEOs and the ratings by their subordinates for all items developed for the MCLQ. Figure 5.7 shows the composite scores for the five themes, as measured by the MCLQ, for all fifty CEOs and their respective leadership teams.

Figure 5.7   Multifactor College Leadership Questionnaire President-Leadership Team Perceptions

COMPOSITE

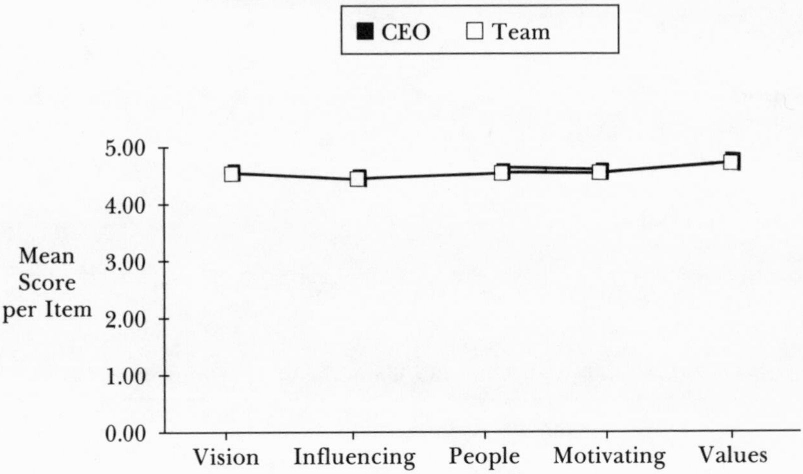

■ CEO   □ Team

Attribute	CEO	Team
Vision	4.52	4.56
Influencing	4.33	4.34
People	4.41	4.36
Motivating	4.37	4.39
Values	4.48	4.46
Overall	4.22	4.22

Next, we determined the reliability of measurement or "internal consistency" of the MCLQ—whether people scored consistently high or low on attributes within the same theme. The Cronbach Alphas for each theme, as well as an overall MCLQ Composite, are shown in Table 5.5 for the CEOs and the leadership teams, respectively. The reliability coefficient ranges from 0.00 (totally unreliable) to 1.00 (perfectly reliable). Table 5.5 indicates that all themes of the MCLQ possess high reliabilities for subordinates with Cronbach Alphas ranging from a low of 0.86 to a high of 0.97. For the CEOs, two themes of the MCLQ show less than exceptional Cronbach Alphas. Those were the people orientation theme at 0.56 and the values orientation theme at 0.63. In other words, the CEOs discriminated more than their administrative teams on separate attributes within these themes, rating themselves high on some attributes and low on others.

Table 5.5   Cronbach Alphas: MCLQ Themes

Alphas	No. of Variables	CEOs	Leadership Team
Vision	7	0.79	0.86
Influence Orientation	9	0.79	0.88
People Orientation	6	0.56	0.88
Motivational Orientation	5	0.80	0.89
Values	7	0.63	0.90
Composite	34	0.92	0.97

Intercorrelations were then computed to determine the statistical relationships among the five leadership themes of the MCLQ. We wanted to know if people who were rated high or who rated themselves high on one theme were consistently rated high on all the others. Tables 5.6 and 5.7 show these correlations for both CEOs and followers, respectively. Among CEOs rating themselves, the correlations among the themes ranged from 0.40 to 0.77 on a scale of −1.00 to +1.00. But the correlations were generally higher among followers, with values ranging from 0.77 to 0.90. All the correlations reveal positive or direct relationships (all significant at the 0.01 level), indicating, for example, that a high endorsement of one theme coincides with a high endorsement of the others. Among followers, the correlations were higher (closer to +1.00) because the followers perceived the five themes as highly interrelated. However, as shown in Table 5.6, the correlations were lower among CEOs. We interpreted these findings as an indication that CEOs discriminated more between themes than did their followers. This suggests, for example, that according to these CEOs, rating oneself highly on the influence orientation theme does not necessarily mean rating oneself highly on people orientation. However, the overall trend among both CEOs and followers is that a high endorsement

Table 5.6 Intercorrelations Among MCLQ Themes and MCLQ Total for CEOs Only

	Vision	Influence Orientation	People Orientation	Motivational Orientation	Values
Influence Orientation	0.5593	—	—	—	—
People Orientation	0.6166	0.4006	—	—	—
Motivational Orientation	0.6278	0.8480	0.5148	—	—
Values	0.4960	0.6824	0.5445	0.7733	—
MCLQ Total	0.7983	0.8580	0.7194	0.9227	0.8378

Table 5.7 Intercorrelations Among MCLQ Themes and MCLQ Total for Leadership Team Only

	Vision	Influence Orientation	People Orientation	Motivational Orientation	Values
Influence Orientation	0.7998	—	—	—	—
People Orientation	0.7669	0.8309	—	—	—
Motivational Orientation	0.7960	0.8833	0.8740	—	—
Values	0.7571	0.8480	0.8978	0.8998	—
MCLQ Total	0.8785	0.9344	0.9400	0.9597	0.9507

of a given theme tends to be associated with a high endorsement in other themes.

Table 5.8 highlights the average MCLQ responses by the participants. The overall means listed at the bottom of Table 5.8 (4.42 for each group) indicate tremendous agreement between CEOs and their followers in observing the same phenomena. In other words, there was absolutely no difference in the composite grand mean score on all 34 items for the 50 CEOs and for the 290 followers. Since there was no difference on the composite scores, we chose not to display all item scores by theme as we did in the previous analysis of the interviews.

Table 5.8 Highest and Lowest MCLQ Item Means by Theme

	LEADERS			FOLLOWERS		
	Theme	Item	Mean	Theme	Item	Mean
HIGHEST	Vision	V3	4.69	Vision	V3	4.73
	Influence	I1	4.79	Influence	I8	4.76
	People	P1	4.81	People	P4	4.55
MEAN	Motivation	M2	4.48	Motivation	M5	4.48
	Values	A1	4.98	Values	A1	4.84
LOWEST	Vision	V1	4.35	Vision	V1	4.33
	Influence	I2	3.81	Influence	I2	3.70
	People	P6	4.02	People	P6	3.98
MEAN	Motivation	M1	4.21	Motivation	M1	4.21
	Values	A2	4.17	Values	A2	4.25
MEAN OVERALL			4.42			4.42

Item with Highest Mean
26. (A1): Demonstrates commitment to intellectual self-development
Item with Lowest Mean
11. (I2): Is characterized by a bias for action

Table 5.8 lists the item numbers having the highest and lowest scores in each theme and the means for each of those items.

Tables 5.9 and 5.10 reflect our tests of whether the size of the institution would be a predictor of performance on the interviews and/or on the MCLQ ratings. We expected large institutions to produce high-scoring leaders. Table 5.9 shows results of a one-way analysis of variance (ANOVA) comparing the scores derived on the MCLQ after presidents were classified into three categories by size of institution. It is important to note that on the MCLQ (Table 5.9), presidents who were in medium institutions, as opposed to small or large ones, scored themselves higher on the MCLQ. The ANOVA indicated a significant difference at the $p < .05$ level for the total instrument, vision, leadership, and motivation, but no significant difference (N/S) for the people or values themes.

Table 5.10 indicates the results of the ANOVA performed on the interview scores, again using institutional size as a factor. The larger the institution, the higher the CEOs' scores generated from the interviewing process. All F-values were significant at the $p < .05$ level or better, showing a statistically significant difference of attributes as a

Table 5.9 **ANOVA: MCLQ Means By Enrollment**

	ENROLLMENT			ANOVA RESULTS	
	(1) Small	(2) Medium	(3) Large	F	* Pairs
MCLQ Total	4.28	4.60	4.39	4.19 $p < 0.05$	(1) – (2) (2) – (3)
Vision	4.39	4.77	4.44	4.51 $p < 0.05$	(1) – (2) (2) – (3)
Influence Orientation	4.15	4.53	4.33	3.46 $p < 0.05$	(1) – (2)
People Orientation	4.38	4.52	4.34	N/S	NONE
Motivational Orientation	4.14	4.61	4.37	4.28 $p < 0.05$	(1) – (2)
Values	4.44	4.57	4.43	N/S	NONE

(1) Small: enrollment of 4,999 or less
(2) Medium: enrollment of 5,000 up to 11,999
(3) Large: enrollment of 12,000 or more

* Groups significantly different in paired contrasts

function of the size of the institution. For example, CEOs in the largest institution had the overall highest means for entire interview at 148.83 hits, which was significant at the $p < .001$ level.

Table 5.11 compares attributes drawn from the interviews. It shows that the theme of *vision* was emphasized by the CEOs to a greater extent than the four other thematic areas. The second most highly emphasized theme was influence orientation, emphasized to a greater degree than all remaining three themes. Statistically speaking, no other comparisons were significant, but people orientation was third, followed by motivation orientation and values.

SUMMARY

This chapter has presented the selected highlights of the research findings from this transformational leadership study. The chapter's major focus has been to present and analyze the five themes associated with transformational leadership in the community college.

Table 5.10 ANOVA: Behavioral Mean Scores By Enrollment

	ENROLLMENT			ANOVA RESULTS	
	(1) Small	(2) Medium	(3) Large	*F	** Pairs
MCLQ Total	89.88	110.80	148.83	8.16 p < 0.001	(1) – (3) (2) – (3)
Vision	22.41	30.27	36.61	6.58 p < 0.01	(1) – (3)
Influence Orientation	25.47	31.27	40.78	5.66 p < 0.001	(1) – (3) (2) – (3)
People Orientation	13.12	18.00	26.00	8.32 p < 0.05	(1) – (3) (2) – (3)
Motivational Orientation	11.06	14.27	20.22	4.63 p < 0.001	(1) – (3) (2) – (3)
Values	17.82	17.00	25.22	3.58 p < 0.05	(1) – (3) (2) – (3)

(1) Small: enrollment of 4,999 or less
(2) Medium: enrollment of 5,000 up to 11,999
(3) Large: enrollment of 12,000 or more

*All tests significant
**Means statistically significant difference in paired contrasts

Table 5.11 Paired Comparisons of Transformational Leadership Themes Among the "Blue Chippers"

Themes Compared		Mean 1	Mean 2	Mean Difference	Paired T-Test
1	2				
Vision vs. Influence		4.27	3.64	0.63	3.16**
Vision vs. People		4.27	3.20	1.07	4.42*
Vision vs. Motivation		4.27	3.06	1.21	6.30*
Vision vs. Values		4.27	2.89	1.38	6.23*
Influence vs. People		3.64	3.20	0.44	2.11***
Influence vs. Motivation		3.64	3.06	0.58	3.18**
Influence vs. Values		3.64	2.89	0.75	3.49*
People vs. Motivation		3.20	3.06	0.14	N/S
People vs. Values		3.20	2.89	0.31	N/S
Motivation vs. Values		3.06	2.89	0.17	N/S

NOTE: —Asterisks indicate level of significance: * to 0.001 level
                                                    ** to 0.01 level
                                                    *** to 0.05 level
—N/S indicates no statistically significant difference.

These themes and accompanying attributes were first gleaned from our analysis of the 256 philosophical statements submitted by CEOs in Phase I. The attributes were further refined through data collected in Phase II from the "blue chippers." The acquisition and development of this information led us to the formation of our theoretical framework which incorporated our own and others' research findings. This theoretical framework, in turn, has led to the development and use of the MCLQ.

This questionnaire is a significant component in our research model. Our analysis of the interviews with the 50 "blue chip" CEOs confirmed the five themes and enabled us to develop 34 attributes, based on these themes, that described the CEOs' behaviors. As a part of the process, we were able to select specific words, termed "attribute descriptors," used by most CEOs when they were discussing the five themes. By measuring the frequency with which each CEO employed these attribute descriptors, we were able to assign a "score" (value) to each interview and assess the leader's verbal commitment to each of the five themes.

We then employed the five themes developed from original philosophical statements, the 34 attributes, and Bass' Multifactor Leadership Questionnaire to develop our own Multifactor College Leadership Questionnaire. Two forms of this instrument were developed: one for the CEOs and one for their followers. Both are self-report paper/pencil forms utilizing a Likert-type scale. Form A provides CEOs with an opportunity to assess their individual transformational attributes; Form B ascertains follower perceptions of the transformational attributes exhibited by their respective CEO.

The findings generated from this study indicated that vision was the most significant theme identified by the "blue chippers." This theme is clearly an essential element of transformational leadership, and the data confirmed that both leaders and their teams regarded vision as the key to successful leadership. Vision appears to be the catalytic component that enables leaders to implement successfully the remaining four transformational themes.

We also found that the "blue chippers" and their leadership teams enjoyed extremely high levels of agreement on the two parallel forms of the MCLQ. In fact, on the 34-item questionnaire, the composite average on all items for each group was 4.42 on a scale of 5.0.

A Cronbach Alpha reliability analysis on the MCLQ determined that the CEOs' perceptions of themselves tended to be more discriminating than those of their leadership teams, both among the attributes within each theme and among the themes themselves. This fact may have resulted from the teams being subconsciously influenced by a halo effect—i.e., the tendency of followers to be influenced by a generally favorable impression of the CEO when responding to the MCLQ.

Finally, we determined that the size of the CEOs' institution was related to the CEO's scores on the interviews and the MCLQ. CEOs from large institutions produced the highest scores on the interviews, while CEOs from medium-sized institutions scored themselves highest on the MCLQ.

The theoretical framework and transformational themes and attributes generated from our research form the basis for the subsequent chapters. These chapters will discuss each theme and report first-hand experiences related to each from the perspective of both CEOs and their leadership teams.

CHAPTER 6

VISION FOR EXCELLENCE

&& *Vision is a key component of leadership; it is that mental journey from the known to the unknown, creating the future from the montage of current facts, hopes, dreams, risks, and opportunities that effective leaders embrace in all walks of life.* **99**

HICKMAN AND SILVA, *Creating Excellence*

VISION FOR THE FUTURE: Demonstrated Competencies

FUTURE ORIENTATION
THE MISSION
SHAPING THE FUTURE
INFLUENCING THE VISION OF OTHERS
PLANNING AND ACTION
RISK-TAKING
COMMITMENT TO ACCESS AND STUDENT SUCCESS

VISION FOR EXCELLENCE

INTRODUCTION

Transformational leaders use influence and various leadership styles that are difficult to categorize neatly. The influence and values of a transformational leader appear to be as much like art as like science. All the writers on transformational leadership, however, identify one central theme that recurs in descriptions of transformational leaders—the role of vision. These researchers corroborate our findings by emphasizing that the powerful leaders of the past and present were dreamers and visionaries. They were people who looked beyond the confines of space and time to transcend the traditional boundaries of either their positions or their organizations.

History reports many examples of such leaders and their visions of the future. Queen Isabella of Spain had a vision of claiming and settling new lands during a time when the known world was steeped in fear and superstition. Isabella's scholarship debunked that of her geographers, who believed that the world was flat; her vision led to the golden age of discovery of the "New World." Thomas Jefferson and James Madison had a vision of a government based on the principles of a democratic republic where power was vested in the people. By creating a constitution that protected the civil liberties of society, they empowered the

common man and guaranteed that no government could abuse that priv-
ilege. Harry Truman had a vision of egalitarian education that would
prevent the denial of higher education on the basis of race, ethnicity,
sex, or handicap. He convinced Congress to promote higher education
for the majority population, thus originating the modern community
college. Lee Iacocca had a vision of rebuilding and reinvigorating a failing auto industry; he set into motion the action necessary not only to
revitalize a dying corporation but also to bring new strength to the sag-
ging role of the United States in the world automobile market.

What these visionaries have in common is a unique vision of a future that they helped shape. Although they carefully planned strategies
for accomplishing their goals and then translated those goals into action, they took huge risks in doing so. While they were dedicated to their
visions, they also informed and influenced others to share in their mission. Finally, these leaders found the necessary resources to ensure the
successful outcome of their vision. That these characteristic attributes
are common with community college transformational leaders is not
coincidental. In our conversations with some outstanding community
college CEOs, we were struck by how often these men and women discuss their own community colleges with a vision of what the college is
and ought to be.

Indeed, vision is the distinguishing characteristic of the transformational leader. Although most community college CEOs have a sense of the
future direction of their colleges, the transformational leader adds depth
and breadth to our understanding of the future of the community college in the United States. Those leaders dream, imagine, and take risks
to prove the worthiness of their dreams. They then communicate their
plans with and for others so that their vision is shared. As Bennis and
Nanus (1985) explain, such leaders have a clear vision that results from
a profound understanding of their organization and its environment.

Judy Merritt, President, Jefferson State Junior College, Alabama,
observes:

---

*I always look at what I do through rose-colored glasses, but my
attempt at this institution has been to establish goals that I work
with from a group goal-orientation; that is, that we share not just
my vision but a common vision. We're able to work out that the
participants who look at the future have a vested interest in making
it occur. I have never been inclined to say this is what I want
to do ten years down the road, or this is where the institution should*

be five years in the future. Instead, what I want is to put our common talents to the best use. I think what I've done is establish the expectation that we will have future goals. I have attempted to bring the resources to the leadership and the faculty that will reflect how outside activities will have an impact on our future.

Without a doubt, it is extremely important that the followers within the institution not only participate but feel they have contributed to and are supported in the development of the shared vision of what the college is striving to become. Vision is more than any one individual's perspective.

President Richard McDowell, Schoolcraft College, Michigan, supports the shared vision idea. He reports:

MANY of the people in our college have been here for a long time, longer than I, and they also have expectations of the college. Since followers have an opportunity to participate in designing the blueprint regarding the college's future direction—a vision of what the college is attempting to achieve—followers feel a greater sense of ownership and commitment in assisting the college to move in its newly prescribed direction.

He expands on this theme:

THROUGH our well-defined planning process, we develop strategies for how we are going to improve our programs; how we are going to better serve students; how we are going to develop ourselves and assist our staff to keep up-to-date on the new technology. The underlying theme is the constant improvement of the college so that we may better serve students. When we deliberately go about establishing our change strategy in this way, people buy into it because it is their college; it is their job; it is their curriculum; it is their program. It is also critically important that the followers receive the necessary support. The consequence

*of this involvement is that people work hard, they have owner-
ship, and it is all of us working in unison, not just someone at
the top giving the orders saying, "This is what we are going to
do today." That makes it work.*

FUTURE ORIENTATION

Bennis and Nanus (1987) note that leadership involves creating a
larger vision and engaging people's imaginations in pursuit of
such a vision. Leaders of the community college movement concur. Says Chancellor Bill Stewart, State Center Community College District, California: "We are entering an era which presents the greatest
challenge to imaginative and creative leadership that community colleges have ever known, in which both individuals and institutions should
move confidently and eagerly into that future." Our interviews with
some outstanding CEOs lead us to believe that they operate on a sym-
bolic as well as a practical level, choosing out of all the options those
that appear to blend most evenly the anticipated needs of the community with the resources of the institution.

Transformational leaders operate integratively, bringing other people in, bridging multiple realities, and reconceptualizing activities to
take account of this new, *shared* reality. But at the same time, these community college CEOs are sensitive to the implications of change.
Rosabeth Moss Kanter, in *The Change Masters* (1983), notes that the art
and architecture of change work through a new medium in institutional
leadership. The success of change efforts must mobilize people around
what is not yet known, not yet experienced. It requires a leap of imagination, a leap of faith that cannot be eliminated by presentation of fore-
casts, figures, and advance guarantees. This success requires leaders and
followers working in concert—with the leader composing and orches-
trating and enabling a quality sound that is achieved by and through
the institutional musicians.

A constant theme generated throughout the interviewing process
was that "the only thing constant about a community college is change"
(President Ed Liston, Community College of Rhode Island, Rhode Island;
Chancellor Michael Crawford, St. Louis Community College, Missouri;
President Richard Ernst, Northern Virginia Community College, Vir-
ginia; and Chancellor Paul Elsner, Maricopa County Community College
District, Arizona). President Paul Magelli, in his inaugural remarks to

his new faculty and staff at Parkland College, Illinois, appropriately noted:

AS we create the future, we must understand the founding and formation of the college. As we collaborate to envision the future, it will be important to me that I share your understanding of the values and dreams of those whose life blood has nurtured the programs and policies of the college. Knowing how big decisions were made in the past, along with an awareness of their consequences, will affect the way we envision possibilities for our shared future.

I think many administrators in transition are too eager to supervise change without truly listening to the history of the institution and the individuals whose collective possibilities they seek to lead to realization. I assume that I want to know the past so that we may envision a splendid future. For many, change is threatening: there are many questions, perhaps anxieties, possibly even fears (notably, the fear of change) that result from transitions. "Resistance to change, in fact, is a hallmark of academia. We in the academic arena so often gravitate to a collective willingness to rationalize our resistance to change."

Magelli refers to the words of Michael Crawford, who alerts us to the need to engage in constant dialogue which moves us beyond our collective resistance to collaborative creativity. Crawford suggests that there is usually only one argument for doing something—the rest are arguments for doing nothing. It is important for us to appreciate the fear of the unknown that exists in the minds of those non-risk takers within the organization, and therefore it behooves "change masters" to ensure both effective communication and steady input from the various college constituents. Society and, in particular, community colleges cannot afford to maintain the "status quo."

The community college movement has established a solid foundation that enables it to continue to seek new and better ways of conducting its business of education. Sensitive to their history and in concert with their mission, excellent community colleges are meeting their challenge to change in innovative ways. Through the joint effort of trustees, faculty, students, staff, and community representatives, these colleges are effectively assessing their strengths and weaknesses, measuring the needs of their particular community, and taking the appropriate steps to bring the optimum college to its constituents. President David Ponitz, Sinclair Community College, Ohio, expresses it well:

A college should be involved in the hopes, in the dreams, in the aspirations, and even in the frustrations of its community. The college must assist in achieving the dreams while at the same time helping deal with the frustrations. The reality of hopes, dreams, and aspirations can only be accomplished through a shared vision on the part of all the key internal and external leaders and their constituents.

President Barbara Guthrie-Morse, West Virginia Northern Community College, West Virginia, speaks to both vision and strategy:

WE try to focus ourselves on the review of national, regional, and local trends that we believe have some implications for the community college and specifically for West Virginia Northern. A key action in thinking about advancing the long-range interests of our institution is a significant amount of reading, talking to, thinking about, and speaking on the future in the generic sense: that is, the larger future and change. We explain the kinds of changes that we are having to make in our society today and the kinds of changes that involve the community college. Then we begin preparing people for those kinds of changes that are critical to our future.

President A. Robert DeHart, De Anza College, California, conceptualizes his vision of excellence as follows:

ALL of us who care about students and care about our college have been engaged consistently over the years not only in "doing things right" but, just as important, in "finding the right things to do" during these turbulent times of changing demographics, economics, and social values. What to keep, what to throw out, what to add, what to enhance, and what to scale down are questions that lie at the heart of a college that is striving to be the best it can be. Certainly excellence is never achieved by drifting into it. We must have a vision of our future and then not leave it to chance, but plan for it. That vision should seek the optimum but must have reality filtered into it because above all we need a working vision—that which can be translated into meaningful action.

The ability to translate future educational needs of a community into concrete plans is consistently exhibited by the CEOs identified in this study. As Max King, President of Brevard Community College, Florida, so appropriately summarizes:

PLANNING is one of the big parts of the job as I see it. We're just completing a Performing Arts Center that started as a plan some ten years ago. You must be aware of the potential needs of the institution and start planning for those needs. You also have to recognize that you don't get instant success in any area. You have to look to the future and have a vision of what the community and the college need. Then you put all those plans into writing. You start talking about them, getting the involvement of all the constituent groups, getting support from the community, and slowly but surely moving the project forward. I think that's true whether you're building a physical plant, a building or a campus, or planning a new college program.

THE MISSION

I t is critical for an organization to know "what business it is in." Peters and Waterman (1982) would advise organizations to "stick to their knitting." Such is the case for exemplary community colleges. Despite some opinions to the contrary, community colleges, for the last two decades, have maintained a clear yet flexible vision of what their business is. While land-grant colleges were the means of increasing educational access in the nineteenth century, community colleges are that means in the twentieth. Gleazer (1980) noted that the following qualities should be considered requisite for the mission of any community college:

1. The college is adaptable. It is capable of change in response to new conditions and demands, or circumstances.
2. The college operates with a continuing awareness of its community.
3. The college has continuing relationships with the learner.
4. The college extends opportunity to the "unserved."
5. The college accommodates diversity.
6. The college has a nexus function in the community's learning system.

Gleazer's synthesized mission statement for the community colleges is "to encourage and facilitate lifelong learning, with community as process and product" (1980, p. 16).

The American Association of Community and Junior Colleges (AACJC) Board states that the mission of the colleges is to "deliver accessible educational opportunities designed to address the needs of the individuals, organizations, and communities forming their constituencies" (1987, p. 2).

In *The Neglected Majority*, Dale Parnell (1985) identifies five elements that form the basis of his philosophy of education supporting excellent community colleges. These elements include the belief that colleges must be community-based; they must be cost-effective for both the student and the taxpayer; they must provide a caring environment in the college; they must have a competent faculty; and they must offer a comprehensive community college program.

What makes the community college unique in the educational setting is its bond to the community. The genius of the community college has been its ability to provide these opportunities in a flexible fashion, within a local community. Clearly, the community college has been the most responsive institution to changing local educational needs. Yet, in spite of the community college's obvious success, many of our presidents feel that the community college is still too insular—that one of the critical challenges facing their particular institution was "what they are all about." Unfortunately, the concerns expressed do not simply focus on the external community, as one might expect. Presidents talk in detail about the importance of internal awareness. For example, retrenchment has resulted in myopic vision, which, in turn, has created the need for presidents to communicate actively to staff and faculty the college's mission in attempting to maintain a broad base of understanding and acceptance of where the college is headed. The degree of success achieved by our CEOs has enabled those internal and external constituents within the college community not only to understand more fully the role of the community college, but also to be positively engaged in the continuing challenge that underlies the responsive mission of the community college.

SHAPING THE FUTURE

While no document can ever capture everyone's vision of the future, De Anza College's planning and strategy document, *Planning for the 80s and Beyond,* has sought facts as a foundation and tempered those facts with an open process that has used the judgment of all segments of the De Anza College staff in arriving at long-term strategies. The collaborative effort of many individuals and groups has gone into the planning. While not everyone was involved in the preparation of the document, everyone was afforded the opportunity to participate in the process. Bob DeHart, De Anza's president, acknowledged those responsible for the creation of the final product: "Their creativity established the framework that others built upon in producing this vision of our future. They always sought the best for the college and its students even when the implications of the trends seemed to lead in directions contrary to the current conventional wisdom."

De Anza's *Planning for the 80s and Beyond* is an example of planning in which many colleges engage and get results in varying degrees of success. This exceptional process requires commitment, dedication, and hard work. It also requires creative risk-taking—an element that is perhaps more conspicuous in its absence than we might care to admit.

Transformational leaders clearly articulate that it is the responsibility of the CEO to create the vision of what the college has a chance to become and to establish the vehicle that facilitates the concrete plans to accomplish such a task. Without exception, it requires input from an array of individuals and organizations—identifying and involving both internal and external constituents. It starts with knowing the needs of one's particular community and staying apprised of changing community needs. President Tom Barton, Greenville Technical College, South Carolina, suggests that:

PROVIDING for the changing needs of the college often requires departure from the norm and what is routine. When action moves the college away from the routine areas and the college begins new learning, the resulting changes ultimately cause people to do new things. When this change occurs, the CEO must be sensitive to the individuals involved and the concerns they might have surrounding new directions. Greenville Technical College is a reflection of the community we are serving. In order for us to meet changing needs of our community, it is important that we assist our people to become flexible enough to keep up with those needs and to adjust to those needs as change occurs in the workplace.

In relating the process utilized by John C. Calhoun State Community College, Alabama, to locate a permanent site for an off-campus educational program, a member of the college leadership team stated:

THE governing board was requested to approve the off-campus site. The Alabama Commission on Higher Education was asked to approve the Board Resolution. The new site was approved, renovated, and is currently utilized for approximately 2,000 students in the Huntsville, Alabama, area. All of this was accomplished by sound budgeting, appropriate planning, and legal approval—all because my CEO used his energies to go about accomplishing a difficult task with vision and singleness of purpose.

For President Byron McClenney, Denver Community College, Colorado, change starts with a strategic plan, which is the agenda that establishes the future for the institution. To accomplish the strategic plan he uses a community advisory group and an internal group that he calls a "Planning Council," which is a representative body of faculty, staff, and students identified by each constituent group. The initial charge of this Council is to conduct both internal and external assessments, which generate information that is used to direct the Council. While creating a vision is critical, McClenney emphasizes that once the vision is established, a climate must be developed that will allow the institution to get moving:

CONTINUING the translation from vision to action is the annual planning process that is put in place. This process helps explain what the institutional priorities are for the year ahead in order to take steps that we have decided are important for our college. Such an approach provides for a clear focus and a strong agreement on where the institution needs to go, both from the perspective of community leaders and the perspective of people on campus. There must be a recognition that contradicting institutional culture can lead to difficulty. On the other hand, the "shared struggle" and intelligent risk-taking are required if the institution is to develop. The other choice is to drift and decay.

Other presidents report that the needs of the community often require an external orientation. David Ponitz notes that "several years ago, it was becoming clear that the economic base of our community had limited growth potential, and what might be required was a change in the mix of jobs." To address this challenge, the president and board of Sinclair Community College, Ohio, spearheaded a joint public venture designed to shape the environment to meet the future economic needs of the community more effectively. The outcome of this process was the development of a research park that joined together business and industry, education, and professional engineers and scientists from the adjacent military base in the establishment of technology transfer.

President Lois Callahan, College of San Mateo, California, met her challenges and, in turn, helped to shape the future of other California community colleges:

SAN Mateo, as well as other community colleges in California, was unable to stay current with our needs for instructional equipment, and there seemed to be no mechanism for replacing or upgrading the equipment. My team and I conducted a state-wide study to identify what our needs were in instructional equipment and wrote a paper on the situation. I made some recommendations for funding both in the immediate time frame and for the future. Ultimately, the governor approved, in a single year, $31 million for instructional equipment for the community colleges.

I think that illustrates tackling a problem which, in my view, could not be solved short-term. As we look towards the future and all of the changes in technology, we realize that unless a

*college can stay current, we will be unable to maintain our pro-
grams in a satisfactory fashion for student progress. And it wasn't
just a problem for one campus—it was a state-wide problem. I
think sometimes it's possible to take what the needs are at your
own institution and discover that they are not unique.*

———

Sinclair Community College and College of San Mateo are solid
examples of how external orientation affects the community college,
and they provide excellent models for other institutions. However, the
importance of external orientation was discussed by most other CEOs
as well. It is perhaps best reinforced by a comment from Chancellor
Mike Crawford: "In my opinion it is the CEO's job to maintain an external perspective and not only keep the community focused on the
institution but, more importantly, ensure the institution keeps focused
on the community."

Individuals have always tried to predict and control future events.
Community college leaders are no exception. These transformational
leaders are involved in shaping the future of their institutions in an-
ticipation of and response to community needs. While their approach
to designing that preferred future may vary, they all rely heavily on
responsible participation of their followers.

INFLUENCING THE VISION OF OTHERS

Community college presidents do not function in a vacuum. They
know that they cannot accomplish their charge alone. Therefore, they consciously work at building internal and external
bridges with the expectation that in so doing, not only will they share
the vision but, reciprocally, others will accept and enhance that vision
for the good of the institution and the community.

Chancellor Donald Walker, Grossmont Community College District, California, believes:

———

*LEADERSHIP is a subtle combination of the act of creating a
vision of what an institution can be and then selling that vision, by personal example and by successful experience in which
it's possible for many people to participate.*

———

President Byron McClenney, Community College of Denver, agrees:

THE shared vision of what an institution can become (desired outcomes) is most likely to emerge through a shared struggle of faculty, staff, and students; and it is the president who must facilitate this shared struggle.

A further example expressed by President Robert DeHart, De Anza College, suggests:

CONSTANT, purposeful innovation is a hallmark of our college, and that has happened because our college leadership has a focused vision of what the college is trying to achieve. We have a fully functioning organization to keep us moving toward that vision, and we have a highly committed staff that generally accomplishes what it sets out to do.

Similarly, the accomplishment of influencing the vision of others is enhanced dramatically in an environment or atmosphere that is open and direct. The "cards are on the table," and yet it is relaxed, flexible, and in tune with the needs of the community.

Most of our CEOs strongly emphasized the importance of the collaborative environment. A president acting in isolation cannot expect to have enough good ideas to keep as complex an organization as the typical community college operating properly. Indeed, the best administrative staff one could possibly assemble could not collectively achieve all that is necessary in accomplishing the community college's mission. Instead, the effective president, working with college trustees, must try to maintain a properly balanced collegiate environment that recognizes the importance of at least four fundamental elements: effective communication; freedom for all constituencies within the college to develop successful approaches to meeting the community's educational needs; respect for the traditions and structures appropriate to the community college; and the constant pursuit of student and professional excellence. These elements do not necessarily come together comfortably—but effective leadership is the art of striking (and restriking) delicate balances among these and other critical elements.

Chancellor Don Walker agrees:

ACADEMIC communities are full of talented people, individuals who creatively respond to a "bubble-up" environment rather than one that denotes a "hammer-down" approach. The key is to conjure up and facilitate superior performance through awareness and understanding rather than by command.

Because of the unique and responsive mission of the community college, attention must be directed toward service to the community. Thus, while influencing the vision of our internal constituents is important, so is continually educating our external constituents. Chancellor Jeff Hockaday, Virginia Community College System, comments:

I believe that communicating and interpreting the community college mission is a primary responsibility of any community college leader. If community colleges are not well understood by many policymakers, and there is ample evidence that they are not, community college leaders must continuously tell the story, mindful always that one is talking to a parade. The job is never done.

Many of our community colleges have a well-deserved reputation of effectively meeting the needs of the community they were created to serve, and Los Rios Community College District, California, is exemplary in this regard. However, mindful of the previous statement that the job of improving community awareness is never done, they undertook to create a strong advocacy group. As former Los Rios Chancellor David Mertes (currently Chancellor of the California Community Colleges) noted:

WE did not have a group that felt so committed that they wanted to step forward and champion our cause. To address this issue, we decided to restructure our foundation and invite into our foundation a number of prominent and influential individuals from our community. They were brought onto the foundation board with a carefully structured orientation meeting that made it clear that we did not want them to participate as fund-raisers but rather as college district liaison representatives with the community, informed advocates acting on behalf of the college district, and evaluators of what it was that the college district was doing. We wanted them to be folks who would know what we were doing, tell us if they felt that we were doing it well, indicate ways that the district might improve what we were attempting to achieve, but also play the role of advocates. That has worked extremely well.

OUT of this group we have set up two subcommittees. One committee is called the governmental affairs committee. It works primarily with the legislators regarding positions the college desires legislatively. The committee makes formal presentations to the legislators regarding what it is that the community college district needs through their dual capacity as advocates of the college district and as interested and concerned community representatives.

THE other committee acts in an advisory role to an institute for business, government, and industry that we established to deliver educational services to business and industry on location, much of it by contract. Also this sub-committee will personally contact new business CEOs to inform them of Los Rios Community College District, the Institute, and the educational services that are available. We see this as an excellent way of improving our networking into the community.

WHAT this community focus has also brought to our attention is the fact that we have directly interacted, in various ways, with over 4,000 people in the community but have never coordinated their interaction. Thus, we are now developing plans that will help us better interact and network with people who have already stepped forward, and then move beyond that to those people in the community who have not yet utilized our services.

Speaking to the issue of community interaction, an administrator on the leadership team at San Juan College, New Mexico, related:

THE Business Assistance Center has been instrumental in assisting with economic development in the county. A Business and Industry Council has been established to bring community leaders together from all over the country to discuss economic matters and positive actions for development. The college has become an effective catalyst for coordination of economic growth activities within the county.

Through their mission, community colleges can responsibly serve the community in the pivotal role of facilitating linkages of existing resources as well as locating new resources. This process not only provides a linkage with the community, but also assists the internal constituents to prepare students better for service to their communities. Planning is the key to the acceptance of such a challenge.

PLANNING AND ACTION

Transformational leaders recognize the need for planning. These leaders cultivate planning teams with the understanding and knowledge that such a process will systematically design and develop pathways to reach institutional objectives as well as providing ownership in the shared vision of the future. Without these pathways, major objectives will not be attained.

President Gunder Myran, Washtenaw Community College, Michigan, tells us again that, unfortunately, the time that we most frequently are reminded that our objective was to drain the swamp is when we are up to our waists in alligators! Myran writes:

IT is hard to spend time on long-term planning and college development when you are under daily pressure to deal with a myriad of crises, deadlines, complaints, projects, and meetings; yet there is a growing sense that a transformation—perhaps one could even call it a revolution—is taking place in community college management. The transformation involves a shift in emphasis from the operational to strategic management, from running a smooth ship to steering the ship (1983, p. 1).

Now, some five years later, we can readily see the evidence of this shift in emphasis from operational to strategic management on the part of transformational community college leaders. Clearly, one of the key issues discussed by the CEOs who participated in Phases II and III of the study was the importance they gave to developing and implementing a specific plan of action. How such activities were accomplished, the timelines that were addressed, and the magnitude of internal and external participation in the development of these planning activities varied extensively. However, the value of establishing a comprehensive course of action was clearly articulated by all. Although they do not fully capture the creative ways such plans were generated, the following examples do suggest the diversity of means of achieving various institutional goals.

President Richard Gilliland, Metropolitan Technical Community College, Nebraska, explains the process he and his college have successfully adapted:

———

THERE are several activities in which we are involved that tend to be future-oriented or set the sense of mission or vision for the institution. One of the first things that I would mention would be what we call comprehensive institutional master planning. On a regular basis, approximately every three years, we have a community-wide large group activity in which we take a look at where we are as an institution in its many manifestations. We look at it and come up with some broad-based recommendations as to where we should go over the next three-year period. Essentially all the constituencies of the college are included—faculty, operations and maintenance, classified, students, administration, board, and community representatives. We initiated this approach in 1982. At that time we talked about the major areas of where we wanted the college to go. We examined student services, facilities, fiscal management, community activities, and community services—all the major areas one would think of in terms of where our community college ought to be. We repeated the process in 1985 and again this spring. We have now clearly established a three-year pattern in which we formally talk about where we are going as an institution. From my perspective the chief planning agent of a community college is its president. Therefore, I take a lot of personal pride in what we do, and I pay a lot of personal attention to the whole issue of the comprehensive master planning activities.

THIS work is updated every year in what would be called strategic planning. We review the master plan and make sure we are pursuing its basic thrusts. We also pull major projects that we are working on or major inputs from the community. We work our way through everything that is significant, so that when we go into a master planning event we have our heads around all the major sources that are possible—they may be ideas that came up in a board meeting, or they may be ideas that have been presented by a faculty member, or through our governance structure, or from the community. Items or issues can come from any source. We try to incorporate all those inputs into the updating of our comprehensive master plan. Then, as I previously mentioned, we do that on an institutional basis every year. Between the master planning events, we also do strategic planning. The individual divisions and departments tend to work very closely from that framework. The process tends to focus us, tends to keep us on target in terms of what we are doing. Master planning is a big deal to us. It helps us stay on target and know what the target is!

From our interviews, it has become clear that it is not enough to simply have great visions for the future if the organization has not developed a mechanism for such creativity to surface. Leaders who generate ideas are usually willing to pursue a clearly articulated vision, even when the line of least effort or resistance would make it easier to give up. They know that good ideas deserve more than mere consideration. This underlying philosophy is essential in any organization that values risk-takers. If such a philosophy does not permeate the organization, faculty and staff will be reluctant to take risks. Effective college leaders and their leadership teams not only know their roles, but also understand and appreciate the importance of enabling other people to contribute to and participate in the design and creation of the college's "big picture." The team concept is based on the premise that leadership in a contemporary organization like the community college "is very complex and involves sensitivities, talents, and expertise beyond that of any one individual. This concept holds in highest priority the human resources within an organization" (Wallace Simpson, President, Mesa Community College, Arizona).

Promoting innovation and risk-taking requires a well-articulated "game plan." President Al Philips, Tulsa Junior College, Oklahoma, notes that "community colleges have life cycles which should be in a constant state of flux—that is, not dormant; they remain open or become closed." And Philips warns, "There is no such thing as a community college standing still."

Byron McClenney continues this thought:

THERE is a need for the CEO to create and/or facilitate and articulate the future of the college. The identification of the critical issues facing the institution, honest debate about alternatives, and pursuit of wise decisions are in the realm of presidential leadership. The tools of planning and evaluation are powerful factors in facilitating movement of an institution if people are appropriately involved.

President Nolan Ellison of Cuyahoga Community College District, Ohio, describes a planning process that has both structured and unstructured elements:

WE have a fairly systematic internal strategic planning process that is ongoing and is connected to the president's office. It is a structured process that provides input into our long-range planning and its relationship to the state's long-range planning for community colleges. It provides an opportunity for input from the broader college community as we think ahead for some three to five years about where the institution is today and where it is trying to go. Connected to this strategic planning process is also the long-range financial planning process. This is a fairly methodical, well-organized, strategic planning program that has been in place since 1976.

ON the unstructured side, we have an annual retreat for the board of trustees, so we can incorporate their ideas about where the college is today and where it is heading in the future. At least once a year, we also hold retreats for the twelve members of the administrative team, plus selected others who are invited to join us in this annual planning process.

In developing comprehensive strategies, colleges must assess not only those trends external to the college but also trends, strengths, and weaknesses internal to the college. The Sloane School of Management of MIT has developed a process that allows organizations to identify and measure Critical Success Factors (CSFs) and the degree to which the organization is able to perform in the identified key areas. De Anza College adapted this process and identified six CSFs seen as key components for the continued success of the college. These CSFs are:

- Attractiveness to students
- Comprehensive, quality programs
- Productive, state-of-the-art staff
- Constant purposeful innovation
- Fiscal soundness
- Reputation

In each area, measures are made to give the degree to which the college is able to perform. Hard data are used where possible, and in those instances where hard data are not available, executive summaries of surveys or annual reports are used.

RISK-TAKING

The taking of appropriate risk is a hazard for the transformational leader. For each change strategy envisioned and attempted, there exists a chance of loss of power and acceptance by those envisioned in the change. Yet the transformational leader must press ahead because without risk, little can be gained.

In the corporate world, Lee Iacocca has been identified as an excellent role model and change agent. He expects nothing more from his people than he is ready to deliver himself. To reinforce the behavior of risk-taking, he openly acknowledges his mistakes and recognizes the lessons in them. He appreciates the value of being able to say, "I took a risk and I made a mistake; however, I also learned from it." By acknowledging his own mistakes to his managers, he encourages them to be risk-takers and to apply what they have learned to future decisions.

Outstanding community college leaders are intuitive risk-takers. At the same time they realize that innovative accomplishments necessitate participation, collaboration, persuasion, and communication. Change and redirection within organizations are accomplished by truly understanding and implementing the collaborative processes required to achieve such undertakings. This concept is analogous to building a structure. The CEO may develop the blueprint, but without the commitment of the entire college team, the building remains only a plan. The involvement of others serves as a check and balance, reshaping the task or project to make it come ever closer to reality. The meaningful involvement of everyone in the college broadens the base of understanding and at the same time enables others to have a vested interest in goal attainment through their involvement in providing information, resources, and support for the project. As a result, all college personnel now have a more active stake in the outcome. What begins as a "risk" where individuals put forth an untried idea and place their credibility on its ultimate success is gradually converted into a joint effort in which risk recedes as participation and involvement grow. Not only did the CEOs in our study reinforce this style of participatory leadership, but also they emphasized the importance of creating an organizational climate that encouraged and sustained risk-taking. Machiavelli cautioned us to remember that risk-taking in the final analysis is the responsibility of the leader. Machiavelli wrote:

———

THERE is nothing more difficult to plan, more doubtful of success, nor more dangerous to manage than the creation of a new system—for the innovator has the enmity of all who would profit by the preservation of the old institutions and has merely lukewarm defenders in those who would gain by the new ones. This coolness is due in part to the hesitation of their adversaries, who have current laws on their side, and in part from the general skepticism of people, who do not really believe in an innovation until experience proves its value. So it happens that whenever his enemies have occasion to attack the innovator, they do so with passion of partisans while his supporters defend him sluggishly, so that both the innovator and his party are vulnerable (The Prince, *1513*).

———

COMMITMENT TO ACCESS AND STUDENT SUCCESS

The egalitarian mission of open access to the community college is the first attempt by any culture to educate great numbers of its populace. Community college employees, students in particular, and Americans in general should feel a deep and abiding pride in this endeavor.

Indeed, an open-door college, if it is to "walk the way it talks, and talk the way it walks," must better serve student learning needs than it has done to date (Robert DeHart, De Anza College).

We know that community colleges dramatically change the lives of many people. David Wolf, former president of Los Angeles Pierce College, California, says it well:

OUR colleges help move people from lesser to greater states: from unformed ambitions to clear career goals; from immigrant status to competent citizen; from financial dependence to economic independence; from high school graduate to third-year university student; from the unskilled to the fully licensed; from the confused to the informed.

President Fred Gaskin, Moraine Valley Community College, Illinois, emphasizes that the key factor with all new initiatives is *ensuring student success.* It is not enough to limit our thinking to the students who presently make up our student body; we must also consider the potential students who currently do not attend. Chancellor Michael Crawford, St. Louis Community College, Missouri, adds that there are so many things that we must do to reach out, in particular to the disadvantaged student, since the traditional ways just don't seem to work. We must develop new paths for those people to get to our institution and make them aware of what we are all about!

Providing for student access is critical. As President Derrell Roberts, Dalton Junior College, Georgia, notes:

APPROXIMATELY fifty years ago this state began providing a free education for its citizens, grades one through twelve. Since that time we have not provided a free public education to our citizens any further. We ought to be providing, or at least looking at providing, two more years of free public education. Some of us are going the opposite way—we are increasing our tuition all the time. We're going in the wrong direction; we ought to be going toward the point where we provide education at the 13th and 14th years, at least, free of tuition charges. In the future, we ought to be looking at a four-year degree provided free of charge. The answers to many of our problems lie in education.

Thus, as our CEOs reflected upon how well they are achieving their perceptions of the community college mission, many of them expressed the importance of becoming even more interested and action-oriented in meeting the needs and wants of the people their respective colleges had been created to serve. Educators associated with higher education, and indeed, even some of us involved in the community college arena, have historically superimposed our wishes, perhaps too strongly, on clients, on communities, on everyone, in our honest attempt to provide an effective postsecondary education. President Al Lorenzo, Macomb Community College, Michigan, demonstrated clear vision when he said: "I think that two keys to meeting our constituents' needs successfully in the future are to commit ourselves to being society's servant and to explore the legitimate wants and needs of the people we have been created to serve."

Providing that opportunity for student access is critical. As president Derrell Roberts of Dalton Junior College notes:

WE feel about 80 percent of the students are forgotten in a current move toward "college degrees for everyone." Students who have not taken a college-preparatory curriculum in high school are penalized rather severely. The problem is that they must have prescribed courses in social science and lab science, and they must have a foreign language. If they don't have the prescribed courses, then we must require that they take college courses without college credit; they must make a C. So a student who has taken the general track in high school might be here for a year before he takes any courses for college credit. That's a problem. We're providing summer experiences for those who want to take these courses then, so that they can start out in the fall with college work.

I would like to see education possible for more people with fewer barriers. At a time when we need more people involved in our kind of education, we are just placing barrier after barrier to keep them out instead of taking them in. I would take down some of those educational barriers.

Indeed, student access is now an extremely important issue, but perhaps even more challenging than the issue of student access is that of student success. "Of all the issues that we continue to face, the need to improve our students' human development success rate is paramount. The cornerstone for all our academic initiatives must continue to focus on this critical issue" (Chancellor Larry Tyree, Dallas County Community College District, Texas). Indeed, many colleges are attempting to address ways and means of assisting students to achieve greater success. Some colleges have had outstanding success in implementing such programs. Miami-Dade is an acknowledged leader in this area. However, other college districts have also been making great strides in addressing this issue—such districts as St. Petersburg, Maricopa, Dallas, Jefferson, and Los Rios, to name but a representative few. Clearly, leadership by outstanding CEOs in the community college movement will cause the goal of student success to be better achieved. It is toward this end of seeking new and better ways of conducting our business of education that we dedicate our collaborative efforts. Our students, the communities that we strive to serve, and our society as a whole can ill-afford to maintain a state of "status quo" in attempting to meet the challenges we face. Community colleges must get better in assuring quality; through transformational leadership, the colleges will continue to improve.

SUMMARY

We began our discussion of the concept of vision by citing some of the great visionaries of our age, individuals who demonstrated the strength of conviction and the confidence to dare visualize what was yet to be! As a result of their early creative conceptualizations, we are the better. So it can also be said of our outstanding community college CEOs. They, too, possess the tools that enable one to be a transformational leader. They are creative and interactive; they have intellectual, conceptual, and cultural dimensions and attributes that enable them to have an impact on the internal and external communities that they serve. These college leaders deal in visions, shared understandings, and symbols. They are able to generate institutional "ownership" as they achieve successful implementation. They have developed the ability to deal with ambiguity while at the same time rallying their internal and external constituents to participate and share in their vision of the future, a future full of optimism and challenge, channeled both to anticipate and to meet the needs of the communities their colleges serve.

R. Stephen Nicholson, President, Oakland Community College, Michigan, summarizes our attempt to define vision in his "ode" to the future of the community college movement:

Upon the desert floor
Beneath the mountains
Listening to the echoes
From the daring Spanish quest
Here
Across the wind-blown wagon tracks
Of pioneers
Who loved these meadows
We build a college.

No easy task or simple plan
To form a place where mind meets mind
And time meets tomorrow.
Of all man's accomplishments
The motion of ideas from mind to mind
Is most complex—
Most fragile and easily flawed
By distractions large or small.

As fragile as a dew-laden spider's web
As essential as air or water
As clear as dawn on a mountain peak
As varied as the desert's early bloom
A learning place.

No longer sequestered by distance or walls
This college must ride astride the
Volcanic changes of today
If we are to have a tomorrow.

And so we plan and build
An expression of hope and confidence
In many yet unborn
In ideas yet unthought
In undreamed dreams
In a tomorrow which begins today.

We build not isolated expanses
Which inspire by size and grandeur
But rather form a place
Whose miniature views and quiet spaces
Create a view of the wider world.
Like Spanish missions old
Whose walls turned back both heat and wind
And sheltered all who entered.

We build and plan
A place where time stands still
Where each student finds his way
To build a tomorrow which transcends
Today
To become more than he could be
Without this place
To discover
The richness of man's cumulative
Intelligence,
The excitement of
The application
Of that intelligence to life.

These open doors
For all
Who seek today
Tomorrow's dream,
Who take today
That first courageous step
To meet tomorrow's challenge
Yet these doors
Close out all that
Hinders, distracts, and flaws
The infinite process of passing ideas
From man to man
From mind to mind.

Doors for all
Who live today and
Dream of a tomorrow
With richer life and peace,
An open door we set
To knowledge and understanding,
A place so quiet one can hear the past
So busy one can know the present
And so full no one departs less than
He entered.

A Master Plan
That encapsulates
Man's pride in his past,
Man's passion for the present,
Man's faith in his future.

In all the Universe
Only man
Plans.

Awareness of where we have been, and the steps in our path of becoming, are important to the transformational leaders of the community college movement. We know that we are different today from what we were yesterday. We also know that we are different today from what we will be tomorrow. In attempting to address the unknown, the leaders in this study discussed concrete means of creating a shared vision for the future. Their reliance on others helped shape the pathway of their vision. The importance of involving both internal and external constituents in the process of shaping the future was identified as essential by these excellent leaders. It is through their vision that these leaders were able to effect change.

CHAPTER 7

LEADING: THE PROCESS OF EMPOWERMENT

❝ *Leaders are almost never as much in charge as they are pictured to be, and followers almost never are as submissive as one might imagine.* **❞**

JOHN GARDNER, *"Leaders and Followers"*

LEADERSHIP: Demonstrated Competencies

DELEGATING AND EMPOWERING

A BIAS FOR ACTION

STRENGTH THROUGH TASKING AND CONSIDERATION

SHARED DECISION-MAKING

THE INFLUENCE OF OTHERS

PROBLEM-SOLVING THROUGH COLLABORATION

BUILDING THE EFFECTIVE COMMUNICATIONS NETWORK

EMPOWERMENT THROUGH VISIBILITY

ENERGY FOR ACTION

LEADING: THE PROCESS OF EMPOWERMENT

INTRODUCTION

For the past 50 years researchers have vigorously attempted to increase our understanding of the concept of leadership. They have subjected leadership to microscopic examination and dissected each of its known components in their search to comprehend this critically important phenomenon. One idea we have come to value is that the gestalt of leadership is greater than the sum of its parts. Unfortunately, we have been guilty in the past of failing to examine the effects of the whole leadership continuum; we have been too preoccupied with examining the components only.

In spite of the plethora of efforts by researchers to analyze leadership, there has been no precise theoretical framework developed about either leaders or leadership (Burns, 1978). Rather, what has emerged is a paradigm or model of leadership. Jago (1982) has examined this paradigm by characterizing the component elements of leadership research, and we summarize those elements briefly.

Leadership has been described along two main dimensions: universal and contingent. Each of those two dimensions of leadership is affected by the styles and behaviors of the leader. For example, according to the universal concept, "great leaders are born;" they have genetically

determined traits that guide them. Jesus Christ and many of the
prophets, including Moses, Buddha, and Mohammed, are so regarded.
Other leaders are not and cannot be compared to these charismatic,
religious leaders; therefore, it is their styles and behaviors that we have
studied in order to classify the nature of the leader and leadership.
Through the scholarship of Weber and Simmel, we have been able to
examine leadership through the quintessential interaction between
leaders and followers. Moreover, we have learned that effective leadership depends on contingencies (or the interactions among situations,
leader behavior, and follower response). Leaders do not just solve
specific problems; they change people. Leaders make lasting impressions by successfully interacting with followers within the organizations
they lead.

Gardner (1987), in his article "Leaders and Followers," discusses
the suggestion of Georg Simmel, a pre-World War I contemporary of
Max Weber, that followers have about as much influence on their
leaders as leaders have on their followers. Simmel purported that
leaders cannot maintain authority unless followers are prepared to believe in that authority—a most appropriate observation, particularly
for those in leadership positions within such professional bureaucracies as community colleges.

Mintzberg (1979) would agree: he points out that the nature of public service bureaucracies is unique. In other words, they do not follow
the pattern of classical bureaucracies, which have a strong element of
control and are known for their chain of command. Rather, the "professional bureaucracy" focuses on the expertise of the professional. Because of the rigorous nature of their profession and the demands that
they make on themselves, professionals have a completely different
orientation regarding their roles in the organization and tend to balk
at traditional bureaucratic controls. In such professional bureaucracies the role of the follower becomes especially important—leaders must
acknowledge and support their followers because of the expertise and
knowledge they bring to their colleges.

Gardner (1987) addresses this unique situation in corporate and
governmental bureaucracies where employees are not always acknowledged for their "professional" status. Moreover, he emphasizes the importance of the leader and follower relationship when he writes:

*THEY are supposed to accept their superiors in the hierarchy as
their leaders, but quite often they do not. One of the reasons corporate and governmental bureaucracies stagnate is the assumption*

by line executives that, given their rank and authority, they lead without being leaders. They can be given subordinates, but they cannot be given a following. A following must be earned. They mistake the exercise of authority for leadership, and as long as they persist in that mistake, they will never learn the art of turning subordinates into followership (pp. 3–4).

In the past, the organizational structure of the bureaucracy was built on the premise that followers were bound to accept their superiors in the hierarchy as their leaders, regardless of whether the person in such a leadership position was, in fact, providing leadership. Leaders can be given subordinates, but that in no way guarantees that leaders will be effective or successful with a particular followership.

The assumption that many bureaucratic leaders have made over the years is that their position automatically provides them with the unchallenged right of followership. This narrow perspective of leadership has given most bureaucratic organizations little hope of achieving a high level of effectiveness. There has been and will continue to be an opportunity for individuals in leadership roles to use the power of their position in the accomplishment of organizational goals. However, in dynamic organizations, the style of leadership exhibited at the top promotes and models the importance of followership rather than assuming the unchallenged right of such followership.

In the community college movement we have seen, in part, an evolution in the style of leadership that has been exhibited over the past 25 years. The leadership style generic to the era of the 1960s reflected that of the authoritarian builders. The style of the 1970s focused on a systems approach to effective leadership and the introduction of the concept of "management by objectives." Leadership in the 1980s has cultivated and promoted the concept of "participatory management." Although the concept implies a more egalitarian approach to the leadership phenomenon and a closer relationship between the leader and the follower, it does not always follow that the leader "naturally" adopts this style of leadership.

When participatory management is effectively utilized, it fosters meaningful leadership/followership interaction. The misuse of the concept has resulted in great disillusionment among followers. When leaders profess to believe in participatory management but do not fully comprehend or integrate the process, the confusion and frustration that result create an adverse impact on leader and follower interactions.

Thus, those leaders who can successfully use the concept of participatory management become pioneers of new territories and can therefore use resources previously ignored or underutilized in the community college movement.

The leadership behaviors of those identified in our study demonstrated that they not only grasped the wholeness of the concept of participatory management but also understood the intricacies within it. Most of the CEOs we interviewed were concerned about the abuse and misuse of this concept. They emphasized the importance of utilizing "participatory leadership," not just participatory management. A common approach the CEOs shared with us was that of delegating and empowering individuals within the organization. Those who best understood an issue and who were most directly affected by its results were given an opportunity to respond directly and influence the outcome of the decision-making process. Involving those grass-root individuals most affected by a decision was an important component of participatory leadership.

In dealing with the challenging problems and issues facing community college leaders, these presidents exhibited a style of leadership that closely aligned leaders and followers in such a way that collaboration, in conjunction with delegation and empowerment, was accomplished primarily through following their intuition.

DELEGATING AND EMPOWERING

What has become increasingly apparent in analyzing the data of the current study is the relationship between the philosophical themes. As we examine the underpinnings that enable a leader to delegate and empower followers within the organization, it is obvious that delegation and empowerment cannot happen unless the leadership within the institution enables it to happen. The idea that the chief executive officer sets the tone for the organizational culture is solidly supported in the literature (Vough and Asbell, 1979; Peters and Waterman, 1982; Hoyle, 1985; Roueche and Baker, 1987). Transformational leaders are able to develop and communicate a new vision; they get others not only to see the vision but also to adopt that vision as their own. They not only lead and inspire others to move toward that vision but also provide individuals within the organization the opportunity to assume some degree of ownership in accomplishing the shared task.

Although each individual's leadership style varied somewhat, dependent upon the situation, the overwhelming theme of the leaders in this study was their commitment to the concept of delegation and empowerment. As President Ron Horvath, Jefferson Community College, Kentucky, stated:

I have great respect for the ability of those individuals who work in this institution. When people in our college come up with good ideas, I try to provide them with not only the responsibility but also the authority to carry them out. If possible, I also try to provide some resources for implementation. Thus, there is a good deal of delegation—both responsibility and authority. Part of the realization is really knowing when to stay out of the way so that when people have some good ideas they can go out and get those ideas put into practice. I think this is an important part of leadership—the ability to have the confidence in your followers so that you can let go and enable them to pursue their good ideas. This is certainly one aspect of my leadership style.

Effective leaders rely on others. The entire college is an extension of the president. President Ruth Shaw, Central Piedmont Community College, North Carolina, notes:

I am a strong delegator. I really expect people in the broad framework to determine the particular way in which they best contribute and then to get active. I would much prefer to orchestrate and coach. I tend to be very much a participative leader; my instinct, virtually any time there is a problem issue, is to call together a group of people, not necessarily in the chain of command, in order to consider that particular task. I tend to look at a much broader picture to bring together a particular group of people who have something to offer toward the problem and solution. Then I let them "have at it" and develop a good action plan. Later I sort out the responsibilities for the plan into the appropriate areas.

But it is not just the college presidents or CEOs who express their participative style. It is also their administrative teams who confirm that their presidents do indeed empower them. In a response from an administrator at Metropolitian Technical Community College, Nebraska, we learned:

WHEN the new president came to Metro in 1981, the staff and faculty operated within a rigid hierarchical structure with each employee in his or her proper place. What impressed me when I returned to the college after a hiatus in industry was that to-day's leadership team is made up of every employee at the college. While maintaining a traditional organizational chart to define the structure of the college, our president has managed through generous empowerment to provide opportunities to every-one to contribute in significant ways to the fabric of the institution.

A BIAS FOR ACTION

E ffective transformational leaders exhibit confidence in how they achieve their defined institutional and community related goals. President Ron Lingle, Coastal Carolina Community College, North Carolina, suggests:

HOW we accomplish a particular task is never the issue because we are going to do it the best way we can find. If the approach to be used comes from the ranks—great! If it comes down from above—great! If it comes from outside constituencies in the community—great! It doesn't matter where the plan of action is generated, as long as the emphasis is that we are going to get done the things that we have to do. But we cannot achieve them alone. The president cannot do them; the faculty cannot do them; the board cannot do them; the community cannot do them. However, all of us working together are pretty much an irresistible force.

John Keyser, Clackamas Community College, Oregon, is aware of the importance of the various representative groups of the college and their critical relationship to decision-making. He states:

OUR college has a different decision-making process from what many other colleges might have, and I think it exhibits my philosophy of providing the opportunity of involving all constituents in decision-making in a clearly defined way. We developed a booklet on the purpose and values related to the decision-making process. We give a copy of this booklet to everyone within the college. It describes our Presidents' Council, which consists of not just the deans and/or others associated with the management team, but also includes the president of the student association, the president of the faculty association, and the president of the classified association. All the various sub-council committees, such as the deans' council, the student development council, the instructional council, and the business services council, feed into the Presidents' Council. Thus, all major matters of college-wide importance are discussed within this particular council.

WE also have several review groups that function informally on campus. These groups include the exempt employees group (consisting of administrators, supervisors, and classified employees removed from the bargaining unit—confidentials), the classified association, the student government association, and our faculty association. All of these function as a feedback group, even though these groups are not part of the formal decision-making structure. However, they are very much a part of the total process, not just in an informal sense; they are specific entities that are officially designated to provide an important function. These groups have a chance to get their "teeth" into any kind of issue and report back to the Presidents' Council regarding their feelings on that issue. They may initiate concerns and/or review issues. Their role is very open-ended.

WE have found that this decision-making process works well. It involves representation from all the college constituent groups; and as a result, not only does it facilitate the decision-making process and save time, but it has greatly enhanced campus communication.

One of the major issues facing many of today's CEOs is that of collective bargaining. The degree to which the collective bargaining process has contributed to the polarization of the management team and the various unionized sub-groups within an institution varies from college district to district. It is difficult to suggest how one might initiate change to improve adversarial relationships. However, President Richard McDowell, Schoolcraft Community College, offers an outstanding example of what might and can be accomplished when all the primary college actors—administration and college union leaders—commit themselves to improving the collective bargaining process by changing the traditional governance power struggle. For Schoolcraft the traditional collective bargaining process fostered only continuing animosity among all constituent groups of the college. McDowell reasoned that if the gamesmanship associated with the collective bargaining process remained within the walls of the bargaining room, the process could become less detrimental:

I come from a state in which there is a lot of union activity, and nearly every group of public employees belongs to some kind of union. That is true of our employees at the college: the faculty, the support staff, the maintenance people, the food service, and even the middle-management administrators belong to some union. Somewhere along the line in the course of the history of our college, quite an adversarial relationship began to develop. It began to interfere with other kinds of agendas, especially those related to instruction, curriculum, and quality. All of our energy was being challenged on governance issues, and battling between faculty and administration about "who had the right to do what" became the norm. Three rather serious strikes took place. When I came to the college, the situation looked like it called for a change of players. A new president might bring a new opportunity to start over with new relationships.

ONE of the first things we did was to research a new form of relationship called mutual-gains-collective bargaining. We no longer worked with the adversarial power relationship, where information is hidden and where it seems more like a chess match than a building program for improving the quality of the institution.

Mutual-gains-collective bargaining becomes more a problem-solving situation. There are techniques and ground rules in which the players are trained. The concept has to do with identifying issues. An issue is given a very specific identification or a very specific set of criteria. If an issue involves only one person, then it is not an issue. Issues must have broad application across the college. After the issue is identified and both sides concur, there is a brainstorming process about possible solutions to the issue.

WHAT happened was, through the process, we developed a sense of trust that overrode the adversarial components of collective bargaining. For many critical issues we were able to say, "Well, why don't we go and have some people look into this? Whatever they decide, we'll do." And we did that! It was a matter of taking maybe a faculty member and an administrator and saying, "Here, go find a solution." They would come back and say, "We think this is a good answer." Usually we agreed. Our criterion was simply: 'Is this what's really best for the institution?" We gained a sense of really trying to find a solution as opposed to transactions in which we said, "I'll trade you this for one of those."

THERE has been, in six years, a dramatic turnaround in the attitudes of the people at the college because now they don't have to wait every two years to come up with their list of things they need fixed. They send them up through the chain of command and remark, "Here's the situation that we have, and we need it fixed now, rather than saving it for next time or wanting to 'bargain' for it." As a result, we have all demonstrated some leadership. The faculty and the administration are making a better working relationship that takes away the sting and the emotion from collective bargaining. It's still not perfect; but we've negotiated two contracts this way, with another one coming up next year.

This complex issue of collective bargaining was also cited from a follower's perspective. The following example was provided by a member of the leadership team at Monroe Community College, New York:

PRIOR to the appointment of our present president, union negotiations with the faculty and the professional staff were always marked with a degree of hostility and the constant threat of an impasse. As a result of this president's non-adversarial approach to negotiations, I have been allowed to hold some face-to-face informal meetings with the leadership of the union in an effort to explore ways to overcome difficulties, which had caused previous breakdowns in the negotiation process.

THE president agreed to an off-campus day-long meeting prior to negotiations with the leadership of the Faculty Association and the President's Executive Cabinet. Faculty from the Cornell Industrial Labor Relations School were invited to make presentations during this day-long meeting. The result of this effort, which was initiated by our CEO, was that for the first time the negotiation process did not become overly adversarial and resulted in a fair contract, completed in a timely manner. Through the excellent leadership provided in this important area, union relations were greatly improved. Morale of the faculty and professonal staff was dramatically improved, and educational goals of the institution were more easily achieved.

STRENGTH THROUGH TASKING AND CONSIDERATION

The results of more than four decades of objective research on leadership enable us to say that "followers do like being treated with consideration, do like having their say, do like being able to exercise their own initiative—and participation does increase acceptance of decisions" (Gardner, 1987, p.5). Chancellor Tom Van Groningen, Yosemite Community College District, California, explains:

NO matter how good an idea I've got, if I don't go through a process of enlisting the kind of identity and property interest in the concept with others, it's not going to go anyplace. If a concept has merit, it has to be institutionalized and be able to survive without my being involved and without my being here. If the idea cannot do that, then it may not be the time or place for such a thought. If it is dependent on the strength of one individual or more specifically the CEO, then the concept is in trouble. Thus, one of the tests that I apply periodically is to take that step back and remove myself from the process. I transfer responsibility for the idea to others, and often I find that the idea is not just being maintained but is also improving as a result of others picking it up and taking it beyond where I could take it.

The following is an example from a member of the leadership team of the Yosemite Community College District. It reinforces the importance of college involvement in dealing with complex problems:

SEVERAL years ago during very tight financial times, it was evident that the college needed to do better planning and budget development. Everyone needed to be involved, and people needed to understand the reality of the situation and have the opportunity to be involved in the decision-making process. There were few resources, and people were discouraged. Faculty members were skeptical about being involved in planning. Managers resented the additional work. Resistance was great. Our chancellor articulated a vision of what we could accomplish if we all participated. He supported the effort financially. He chaired the steering committee for the first five years. He used the process, made decisions, and allocated resources based on the input from the process. He was persistent and patient. The process worked! We now have an exemplary planning and budget development process in which every district employee is encouraged to participate. While we revise and refine the effort annually, it has become accepted and institutionalized. The process will continue with or without our chancellor remaining in his position.

SHARED DECISION-MAKING

The transformational leader is able to involve others in the decision-making process. It follows that if the CEO empowers others and delegates responsibilities, then subordinates share in decision-making. As Allison (1971) notes, the mix of personality, expertise, influence, and temperament that allows the group to clarify alternatives, even while it pulls and hauls for separate preferences, must be better understood and accommodated. Results of Allison's examination of the decision-making process further underscore the necessity of ensuring that all those affected by the decision-making process (leader and the led) be involved in the process. In his analysis of decision-making, he demonstrates that one model for decision-making is not thorough enough. Perspectives and policies from all actors in any transaction or interaction must be acknowledged and integrated for acceptable outcomes. David Ponitz, Sinclair Community College, Ohio, says:

NOBODY has got a lock on truth. We talk about ideas, and after agreeing upon the parameters appropriate to the situation, we set about to reach a hybrid solution to the tough problems. Once we find the hybrid solution that fits the particular parameters, the individuals responsible for implementation are empowered with getting the task done. Not only has this approach worked, but it has proven to be a good training ground for those aspiring to higher levels of leadership.

Multi-campus operations must become more integrated and better able to share their existing resources—both people and materials. A member of the leadership team at Eastern Iowa Community College, who later moved to St. Louis Community College with Michael Crawford, reinforces the value of shared decision-making from a follower's perspective. He says:

OUR CEO decided to attempt to resolve this concern through the use of telecommunications. He felt that the use of telecommunications had the potential not only to bring the group together on the use of telecommunications, but also to enable individual campuses to understand better the need to have *additional information and resources. By using discussion groups and meetings that involved people at all levels in each of the three institutions, by utilizing outside resource people, and by establishing an open communications environment in general, what could have been a negative and threatening situation was turned into a positive and meaningful activity.*

AS a result of team work, open communications, and extremely positive leadership, our CEO was able not only to demonstrate the positive use of telecommunications, but also to use this activity to open discussions in a variety of areas to bring a greater understanding of overall college direction and goals. This approach to leadership truly makes a difference.

However, President Al Lorenzo, Macomb Community College, Michigan, reflects upon the concept of leadership style:

I think your style of leadership changes somewhat as you settle into a presidential position and begin to prove yourself. I think the first period of time, which is measured in months rather than years, is difficult. However, after you have been there awhile and the organization has had some success, you tend to feel a little more secure yourself. I don't believe that you can give something that you don't have—I don't think you can give freedom if you don't have freedom; I don't think you can empower if you yourself haven't been vested with some power. The more that presidents can become secure, then I think the more they can let go and allow others to let go. I am not afraid any longer of someone who makes a mistake because he took a risk, since the reputation of the college and the reputation that I have been allowed to develop will hold us in "good stead" and enable us to get over the bump in the road. But that may not be the case in the first six months of a new presidency. Risk-taking is a by-product of tenure, and I'm not sure I'm going to do much letting go until my feet are solidly planted.

THE INFLUENCE OF OTHERS

One of the behaviors identified as critical to the CEOs sampled in this study was the significance of follower input. CEOs emphasized that the influence of others, primarily from within the institution, was extremely important to the overall functioning of their respective colleges. President Patsy Fulton, Brookhaven College, Texas, said:

I believe that administration, first of all, is a service function. If we approach our administrative role from a "service first" perspective rather than from a position of control and power, we are better apt to maximize the potential that exists within our professional bureaucracies. In fact, power in its positive sense is the capacity to translate educational needs into concrete plans and to carry these plans through to their successful completion for student learning and employee growth.

President Anne Mulder, Lake Michigan College, Michigan, tells a wonderful story that focuses on how others can influence decision-making:

WHEN I first came on board, there was a marketing committee meeting in progress. I went in and said to the faculty, "Can I help you do whatever it is that you want me to help you with?" Suddenly, there was a hand that came up from the back of the room; a fellow said, "Yes, Madam, we want to know what you're going to do about the ducks." (The ducks swam in the moat that surrounds the campus.) And I said, "The ducks? What seems to be the problem?" He replied, "To tell you the truth, we have been sliding through their droppings into this building for years!"

DOESN'T it get to be an incredible picture—sliding into the building? "There are students who are outraged because the ducks have been mating on the yard and then laying their eggs, and breaking them, and the cycle begins again."

THE picture got to be more than I could imagine, so I said, "Have you ever asked anyone if there might be a solution to this problem?" He said, "Yes, all you have to do is move the feeder!" Well, truly the feeder for the ducks was located right there on the edge of where the students and faculty entered the building. I said, "Move the feeder? Have you ever said this to anyone?" He looked at the stack of paper he held in his hand and waved it toward me: "Six years worth of memos!" I saw that he had a stack of memos about the size of a large telephone directory. I asked, "Is there anyone here in charge of the feeder?" After one of the staff responded that he was the responsible party, I said, "Move it!"

YOU see, those kinds of quick decisions can occur. Maybe this example illustrates how I can be influenced. I do not have a committee to decide on the ecological imbalance that would be created because of the move, because the college is made for people, not for ducks. I try to weigh decisions based upon the immediate need to be responsive to people, keeping in mind that it is the people who are the important products in our institutions. The outcome of that incident was that the feeder was moved, and I was declared a heroine. We have a college made up of people who now know that the college exists for people, and not for ducks.

Our transformational leaders emphasized the importance of providing people within the organization an opportunity to have input. An important component of participatory management is the ability to enable and allow decision-making to take place throughout the hierarchy of the institution. These leaders not only delegate and empower their followership, but they also expect followers to accept the responsibility that goes with the process.

PROBLEM-SOLVING THROUGH COLLABORATION

A collaborative effort among administrators, faculty, and staff may seem to be an insurmountable task for making decisions. But we know that good leadership is dependent on building a network of relationships so that decisions can be affected by the constituent groups involved. Richard Ernst, Northern Virginia Community College, Virginia, reflects that trait:

WHENEVER we undertake a major thrust, one of my responsibilities is to assure that we involve the entire institution as best we can. For any extensive planning process that we undertake, be it the development of annual goals, five-year goals, ten-year goals, and/or our master plan, we attempt to solicit broad-based participation from all our internal constituents—board members, faculty, classified staff, and students.

The importance of a leader's ability to implement this behavior is further reinforced in the following example, provided by a member of the administrative staff at Gulf Coast Community College:

CAMPUS enrollments of traditional and lifelong learners had far exceeded facilities and appropriate resources for quality service and growth. Yet we appeared to lack the appropriate financial resources to address the problem. The situation was further complicated by the fact that there were several "pockets" of "vested interests" attempting to deal with various aspects of the problem. Our CEO was extremely successful in helping us examine the focus of our mission, shape a vision of the future in terms of potential service, facilitate problem-solving, mobilize appropriate resources, and energize staff to action, commitment, and enthusiasm—for the construction of an 8.5 million dollar facility for student and community service.

OUR CEO created and maintained a collaborative, problem-solving environment that kept us clearly focused on our broad college mission of service to traditional and non-traditional students. This environment caused the campus "family" to feel that quality growth was possible, empowered the campus at large to help formulate a plan, and facilitated communications and interaction regarding the problem-solving process to develop a prioritized plan for growth. It also motivated the entire campus to participate, feel valued, and take pride in the process, while mobilizing local and state "political" resources to lobby for funding.

OUR president is truly a working example of the qualities identified in the Multifactor College Leadership Questionnaire. As we reflect upon his qualities, we are reminded: "A leader is best when people barely know that he exists, not so good when people obey and acclaim him, worst when they despise him. Fail to honor people, and they fail to honor you. But of a good leader, who talks little, when his work is done, his aim fulfilled, they will all say, 'We did this ourselves' " (Lao Tzu).

Another example that relates to one of the major issues facing today's CEOs is that of aging faculty. Non-growth enrollments coupled with shrinking financial resources no longer enable colleges to add any significant number of new full-time teaching positions. Those in present full-time positions face little opportunity for mobility. Thus, as senior faculty members retire and/or a limited number of new positions is achieved, it is important that a clearly defined rationale exist to make the most of each new hiring opportunity. Los Rios Community College District has begun to address this specific issue. In our interview with Dave Mertes, former Chancellor, he discussed this particular situation:

WE have not yet had many opportunities to replace faculty, but we are starting this year to get the first group of retirements and vacancies that will permit us to start hiring some new full-time people. To deal effectively with this situation, we formed what we called a "shared governance" committee consisting of representatives from the collective bargaining unit, representatives from the academic senate, and a representative from my office.

THE presidents of those two faculty groups and I met with a very small group (we each brought two people), and we discussed and developed a strategy for hiring someone to replace ourselves. We all felt the importance of developing such a strategy, knowing that what we agreed upon would have a significant impact on the future direction of the district. Together we sat down and restructured the hiring process for faculty. We built or frontloaded the hiring policy, so that before any unit could hire a faculty member, that particular unit had to do an assessment of where they were at the present time, where they wanted to go, and what kinds of human resources they needed to get there. The faculty, therefore, were required to do an in-house (departmental) self-evaluation. They then shared their assessment with the campus president. Once the campus president had the opportunity to interact with those involved and work through the merits of each individual case, departments were either authorized a position or not authorized a position dependent upon the needs of the total college.

The shared decision-making process adapted and communicated in this particular college district clearly indicated that there was not an automatic replacement of any position; but, in fact, faculty openings created opportunities to hire for the future, not to maintain the status quo. Through such a shared decision-making process, the needs of the community, in concert with the future goals of the college, are being addressed in a way that promotes openness and understanding of the need for possible change, rather than paranoia and determination to maintain the past.

This example proved to be significant enough to be cited also by a member of the administrative team at Los Rios Community College District. The information shared by the administrative team member paralleled that of former Chancellor Mertes and then went further:

THIS clearly shows a commitment on the part of the Chancellor and his administrative team to the concept of shared governance. The shared governance committee at Los Rios has become a model for shared governance in the state of California. The faculty, both union and senate, address statewide conferences on this subject and ask David Mertes to be a guest speaker. Examples of the actions of the committee include: 1) faculty representation on the district curriculum committee (previously, faculty input was only at the colleges; now the faculty participates in the district-wide coordination); and 2) review and revision of the hiring procedures for faculty and management. Also, future topics for shared governance will focus on the needs of the district in preparation for the changing demographics of this area. This shared governance approach is now an integral part of our problem-solving process, and we all appreciate the opportunity for involvement that it provides.

BUILDING THE EFFECTIVE COMMUNICATIONS NETWORK

A college CEO is the spokesperson and leader of the institution. What he says, how he says it, and how he models what is desired all have a tremendous impact on the perceptions of those who have an interest in the college. Keeping people in the organization informed and establishing and maintaining an effective two-way flow of information are essential, no matter what the size of the organization. Communication must be an open process and one that encourages participation from all its constituents. President Joseph Hankin, Westchester Community College, New York, said: "If you value keeping in touch with the various constituent groups within the institution, it takes a lot of hours a week to accomplish. However, I think it is worth it." Hal McAninch, College of DuPage, Illinois, says:

ON one hand, it is important that I try to be extremely open with faculty and available to them. I try to accomplish this through walking around and talking with them, seeing them at coffee, and attending various college events. At the same time I recognize that you have to be clear regarding faculty involvement in the decision-making process.

ON the other hand, you don't want to create a situation which inadvertently allows follower expectation levels to be something you can't live with down the road. To give people the impression that they are making the final decision is very wrong.

CERTAINLY in our institution the reality is that followers have a lot of input and that a decision will be made based on their input. I strongly believe in that philosophically, and I want to make sure that message is communicated so that all our employee constituents know that. However, having said that, I believe the CEO is still the individual who is ultimately accountable for all decisions and who therefore on occasion may need to challenge or overrule a comprehensive committee decision. This is not a good practice for many reasons, the least of which is that the committee members who have worked so hard to arrive at their decision end up questioning the purpose and value of the time expended.

President Al Lorenzo believes that "regardless of the constituency, most individuals given the same set of facts will probably make a similar decision. Thus, by promoting open communication and sharing information with all the constituents within the institution, people better understand what's going on and why decisions are being made the way they are."

However, to achieve effective communication we must recognize that one-half the communication process is listening. Many of our CEOs noted that a good communicator is a good listener. We all like to talk, but it is difficult to learn much when we do all the talking. If one is able to stimulate conversations and not only listen to but also understand and appreciate what followers are saying, then meaningful communication will result.

Effective and open communication is achieved in a variety of ways, but the approach utilized by many of the CEOs in the study is characterized by the following example provided by President Patsy Fulton:

IN helping people to feel a valued part of the team at Brookhaven, I have focused on communication and appreciation. I "walk and talk" constantly and encourage all administrators to do the same. It is and has been important to me as the leader of this institution to find out who the people at our college are, what their goals and aspirations are, and to let them know who I am. I attempt to accomplish this by engaging both faculty and

administration on a one-to-one basis. It takes a great deal of time,
but it certainly promotes effective communication.

A member of the administrative team at Rancho Santiago Community College, California, had this to say about the communication effort of their college CEO:

OUR president has worked hard in his four years at RSC to
bring the management team along and to encourage them to share
more information with faculty, thereby minimizing the spread
of rumors and "misfacts." This has required him to walk care-
fully so that he won't lose the support of managers as he changes
their management styles through effective communication.

EMPOWERMENT THROUGH VISIBILITY

Peters and Waterman (1982) made famous their concept of "management by walking around." They captured the idea that good leaders have contact with their team and their organization. They do not wait to hear secondhand what is going on, they are out there in the trenches where the action is, and they experience firsthand the day-to-day routine of the workplace and the lifestyles of the workers. Bass (1985b) reinforces the observations of Peters and Waterman (1982) in his identification of consideration for others. He states that consideration contributes to follower satisfaction with the leader and, in many cases, leads to follower satisfaction with productivity. Our CEOs also valued management by walking around. Although the application of this activity varied somewhat from CEO to CEO, the fundamental purpose was constant. David Ponitz, Sinclair Community College, said:

YOU need to spend time out of the confines of your office through
such practices as management by walking around. I think many
people defined Peters' concept incorrectly. They think that manage-
ment by walking around is just that! I walk around, say "hi,"
and engage in a little chit-chat. But management by walking
around is walking around and asking the right questions, and

listening, and being vulnerable, and having a real understanding of what that person's perception of the truth is, which may be different from yours, and being open enough to let them "zonk" you and let them really tell you where things are wrong. You may disagree with them, but you need to know how people are thinking.

People who manage by walking around do not do so aimlessly. They have a purpose, a mental agenda. Chancellor Michael Crawford, St. Louis Community College, expressed it this way:

I also believe that no matter what the size of the college, be it small or a large multi-campus organization, I have a responsibility to be highly visible with the faculty and staff. I do that. It takes time and a concerted effort, but I make a point of getting out and meeting with them regularly and informally, just sitting down and talking.

As we know, external constituents, at both the local and state levels, consume much more presidential time than in the past. However, in spite of the external demands, President James Hudgins, Midlands Technical College, South Carolina, notes that it is important to be visible and accessible in one's own institution:

I think it is important that a president pay attention to followers and not be perceived as working only with the external constituents of the college. To facilitate this leader-follower relationship, I created an internal structure that gave me more personal contact with my colleagues so as to enhance my interaction with them. My approach emphasizes the personal touch. I really try to be available and participate in activities that our faculty and students consider to be important. Rather than looking for a reason to be absent from an activity, I really look for reasons to be present. An important part of the process is being visible. Since I, and I'm sure other presidents, have a limited amount of time, I consciously minimize random walking around the campus— although I do some of that—and really seek out and plan in my schedule to be at key locations. This has led folks to be somewhat amazed at my ability to be in so many different places. That is not by accident, but rather it is a planned process of being close to the right people on a regular basis in an effort to keep in touch at the grass-roots level.

Brunetta Wolfman, former president of Roxbury Community College, Massachusetts, also maintains institutional fluency by walking around:

I walk around a lot, and I talk to people. I get acquainted. I find that if I walk around and bump into faculty, I can find out what is going on in their minds, what is bothering them, and what good things are happening to them. The feedback that I get justifies this casual approach of being around. I try to be in the cafeteria several times during the week and eat there with faculty, sometimes with students. Also, a number of students come into my office and talk to me because they know that I'm accessible. Another thing I can do by walking around is to see what the environment is like. I sort of "poke around" to see where people are and how they are using things, and I pick up a lot of information which I can then share with the deans of the faculties.

These examples demonstrate the CEOs' interest in their followership and their ways of showing that they value the followers' perspective and effort. Additionally, this behavior reinforces consideration for others and initiates in followers the expectation that there will be continued and future interest by the CEO for follower participation. This, in turn, establishes the responsibility in the follower to strive continuously to reach for higher levels of achievement.

ENERGY FOR ACTION

There was among the CEOs that we interviewed a vitality that is described best by integrating it with the ideas that Gleazer (1980) talked about in his work *The Community College: Values, Visions, and*

Vitality. Gleazer suggests that the "nature" of the community college is such that the expectations placed on it and its administration go beyond traditional educational practices. Community colleges are in the job of extending educational opportunity where none existed before.

In order to bind the foundations of the community college educational mission, its leaders must exhibit a special energy and a vitality that maintain the institutions in times of personnel, student, and financial needs. The CEOs studied have exhibited a vital strength that seemed to transcend both their job and their institution. They used words like "excited," "revitalized," "invigorated," when they talked to us. They seemed to be able to draw on the resources of their personal strength, both to lead the college and to support their followers. This high level of energy was critical to situational control and contingency situations in which the presidents took risks, changed long established routines, or handled controversial issues with unions, their community, or their boards.

Indeed, what we have identified is a kind of instinct that these CEOs exhibit in spite of the fact that the environment draws them in many directions. Our CEOs recognize the "burden" of their responsibilities and the commitment they make to their institutions. Chancellor Larry Tyree, Dallas County Community College District, Texas, and others called themselves "workaholics." President McCabe warned us that "the thing that might get you down is the commitments that go beyond the parameters of the job." But each president really said: "We have the energy for the situational need," "we have the strength to continue in the face of adversity," and "we can accomplish these things with a positive spirit!"

We found that the concept we used, "energy for action," affected all the attributes of our transformational leaders, including vision, leadership, follower reciprocity, motivation, or values. In spite of the fact that they noted that they could not be "all things to all people," the energy and enthusiasm they exuded was contagious.

CONCLUSION

Leadership, according to research, has become more than defining the attributes or characteristics of the leader: it involves understanding the leader-follower relationship. The CEOs of this study have aided in that understanding by sharing their perceptions and experiences with us. They have demonstrated that talented and excellent CEOs have trust and faith in their staff and faculty. They exhibit respect for and caring toward their subordinates and truly epitomize the leader-follower relationships in which a match or a bond is formed that allows participatory leadership to occur. Not only do leaders want others to "see" their vision, they also want to be influenced by their followers. They bring the values of their team to their own leadership style. The team's ideas become more important than the person or the personality. Critical decisions are made jointly through a shared process. And, finally, this process is usually accomplished with a great deal of energy and vitality. The next chapter examines those behaviors identified by the "blue chip" CEOs that make a difference.

CHAPTER 8

LEADER AND FOLLOWER COHESION

❝ *We are no longer constrained by the man on horseback theory of leadership (where the hero seemed linked only to his horse), by the old 'traits approach' to leadership, by the 'gee whiz' aspects of the theory of charisma. We recognize, I believe, that leadership is interpersonal, that leaders cannot be seen in isolation from followers, that the linkage between the two embraces the dynamics of wants and needs and other motivations, that leadership is largely a teaching process beginning with the parental nurturing of children, that creative leadership is closely related to conflict and crisis or at least to debate and dialogue, and that—above all— transforming leadership carries grave but not always recognized moral implications.* **❞**

JAMES MACGREGOR BURNS, *Preface to Leadership: Multidisciplinary Perspectives*

PEOPLE ORIENTATION: Demonstrated Competencies

UNDERSTANDING CAMPUS ETHOS

REWARDING OTHERS

RESPECTING THE INDIVIDUAL

STUDENT-CENTEREDNESS

SEEKING AND VALUING OTHERS

LEADER AND
FOLLOWER COHESION

INTRODUCTION

Tracing the historical development of leadership, we have come to
recognize and appreciate that many situational elements affect the
process of leadership, apart from the characteristics of the leaders
and the followers. Organizational culture is one such element. In the
past, much emphasis has been placed on administrative processes and
structures and perhaps too little on understanding the people within
the organizational structure. This complex intertwining of organizational structure, philosophy, and values has come to be known as organizational culture (Steers, 1979), an element in which leaders play
an important role in the formation and continuation of its various components (Peters and Waterman, 1982; Koprowski, 1983; Peters and Austin, 1985; Schein, 1985; and Roueche and Baker, 1987). However, the
processes by which leaders go about influencing culture and embedding cultural values and beliefs are not all that clear to those in leadership roles in most organizations.

Schein (1985) says that "the only thing of real importance that
leaders do is to create and manage culture" (p. 2). He defines culture as

A pattern of basic assumptions—invented, discovered, or developed by a given group as it learns to cope with its problems of external adaptation and internal integration—that has worked well enough to be considered valid and, therefore, to be taught to new members as the correct way to perceive, think, and feel in relationship to those problems (p. 9).

If we appreciate the value and importance of Schein's perspective, then certainly part of leadership effectiveness lies in understanding those embedding and managing processes that have the greatest impact on the campus ethos.

Culture is a learned phenomenon which evolves with new experiences; it can be changed if one understands the dynamics of the learning process. Since very few organizational leaders have the opportunity to develop the culture from the organization's beginnings, it becomes apparent that the impact of leadership, especially new leadership in an established organization, will be directly related to (1) how harmonious the existing culture is with the leader's vision and goals for the organization, and (2) how successful the leader is in developing a strategy for changing the culture within the parameters that this harmony creates.

We have defined leadership as the ability to influence, shape, and embed values, attitudes, beliefs, and behaviors of all the college members. The "knack" of how to move all members of the college community from where they are to where they need to be is indeed one of the formidable challenges facing today's transformational CEOs. As noted earlier, the history of the institution is an important element to consider—particularly when new ideas that will influence the status quo of an existing situation are generated. We all know that presidential turnover exists at a significantly higher rate than faculty turnover. The turnover rate, in and of itself, creates an interesting challenge to CEOs, particularly new CEOs, who might wish to redirect the existing focus of the college to meet changing institutional and community needs. Obviously, presidents who walk to their own beats without ensuring that others understand and are in tune with the game plan have little chance of achieving their objectives. Understanding the concept of *team* and being a team player is essential if CEOs wish to initiate change successfully. Institutions have little chance of achieving change if attention is not given to both the organizational and individual dynamics associated with all the steps involved in the change process (see Figure 2.1—Roueche-Baker-Rose Adaptation of the Tichy/Devanna Transformational Leader Model).

The importance of attending to both organizational and individual dynamics throughout the complete process cannot be over-emphasized. Change constantly runs into resistance when those in leadership positions neglect to ensure that the triggers for change incorporate the distinct phases found in our adaptation to the change model identified in Chapter Three. The three phases—recognizing the need for revitalization and new direction around the mission, creating a new vision, and institutionalizing change to accomplish the mission—are essential to initiation and implementation of change. Once again, our CEOs clearly indicated their understanding of the intricacies involved in being a transformational leader. They appreciated the importance of involving and supporting the appropriate actors to accomplish the process of transformation.

Accomplishing change requires patience. Often new presidents with the desire to effect institutional renewal fail to recognize the complexity of the process. Not only must the CEOs understand the historical culture of their institutions, but they must also realize the significance of follower entrenchment and the human tendency to resist change. The average tenure in the present positions of our CEOs is approximately eight years, higher than the national presidential average of five years, but considerably less than the average tenure for faculty—14 years, according to a recent study by Dr. M. C. Keim (1988). Acknowledging these variables and being committed to patience have enabled these transformational leaders to change their respective institutions significantly. This change has been accomplished over time and through their ability to create a climate in which a shared vision and values permeate the culture, thus dissipating the natural reluctance toward change.

UNDERSTANDING CAMPUS ETHOS

"Leaders can and do affect the success and 'social health' of a group, organization, or nation" (Hollander, 1978). The essence of this statement is played out in many successful community colleges across this nation. Cognizant that today's leadership style is an interactive process that involves the leader and followers, many of the CEOs studied here attempt to set a particular "tone" in their institutions. "If what I say is not reflected in what I do, then my leader-follower relationship is in serious jeopardy" (Chancellor Larry Tyree, Dallas County Community College District, Texas).

Setting the "tone" is a critical component in the style/behavior arsenal of the transformational leader. As Thomas J. Watson, Jr. (1963) noted, the most important action his father took in building IBM was to set the tone for the organization. Vough and Asbell (1979) commented that persons in positions of leadership are responsible for setting the tone in their workplaces. Hoyle (1985) stated that although school leaders by themselves cannot create a positive school climate, they can set the tone for their staffs to do so. Roueche and Baker (1987) reported that President McCabe set the tone at Miami-Dade Community College District with his unwavering commitment to high standards. Indeed, setting the tone is the process of channeling the organizational climate to create a culture supportive of productivity for successful student outcomes.

Transformational leaders set the "tone." They understand the relationship between leadership and followership—each dependent upon the other. Thus, transformational leaders promote an environment in which the followership plays an important and active role; that is, they empower the followers with leadership roles. From this perceptual foundation the leader recognizes the intrinsic motivation the followers receive from "doing" and encourages the followers to "run the show" whenever possible. By delegating and empowering those informed followers with shared goals, the transformational leader conveys a belief in followers by giving them the opportunity to succeed, supporting any endeavor by establishing parameters, providing information, and identifying resources.

This style of leadership requires cooperative followership from those in leadership roles at all levels within a hierarchy. Moreover, transformational leaders do not confuse leadership with authority; they understand where leadership and followership reside in any situation. Achieving balance in a situation is a necessity for successful outcomes and often requires a tolerance for considerable ambiguity. In essence, the understanding and acceptance of situational leadership and followership allow the development of a trust relationship that is open, sharing, candid, and even critical when the situation demands criticism.

Leaders create a working environment that promotes within followers a feeling of being valued, not only for their potential, but also for their actions. Successful transformational leaders change the outlook and behavior of their followers by openly communicating with them and actively engaging them in the process.

The leaders identified in this study were pleased to discuss their perspectives on how and why their colleges were successful in accomplishing change. They emphasized that by achieving a collective understanding of the issues facing the college and by sharing their dreams and aspirations of where the college was headed, they were able to engage the followership in the concept and the process. It was apparent that success was the result of the ability of the leadership team, under the guidance of the CEO, to articulate and collaborate with followers on the direction and goals of the institution in such a way that the followers were provided with a sense of ownership. This, in turn, affected followers' and others' perceptions of the leader, particularly their expectations about leader competence and motivation, which were positively influenced under such working conditions. This approach is consistent with that of Robert House (1971), who suggested that the leader-follower bond is not so dependent on an emotional appeal—such as that associated with a charismatic leader—as it is on the leader's gripping followers with a program of action: a goal and the path to achieve it.

The leaders in our study fully appreciated Robert House's perspective. They indicated that one of the significant components of their job was to be aware of and in tune with the particular community that they serve. Of the number of similarities among community colleges across the country, one in particular was that community colleges were trying to focus on the needs of their respective communities. To accomplish such a task, community colleges by design are constantly changing. This ebb and flow in relationships to community needs significantly affects these institutions.

The successful institutions that we studied clearly indicated that one of the ways that they dealt with this constant change was through follower involvement. For example, in order to facilitate this ongoing process, Chancellor Michael Crawford, St. Louis Community College, noted:

THE way I approach it is that I see myself as being in charge of the climate within our institution. I'm in charge of setting an atmosphere that is sufficiently open and direct, relaxed, flexible, with cards on the table. It is a risk-taking kind of atmosphere that will allow us to do what we have to do for the community. It is a climate control, constantly prodding the internal constituents in an appropriate kind of way.

This, in turn, is translated into a value for followers, and our CEOs work hard at showing their appreciation to those who work within the organization.

REWARDING OTHERS

Classical behavioral conditioning theory supports the idea that positive reinforcement is one of the strongest embedding mechanisms available to persons wanting to influence others. Unfortunately, very few organizations adequately structure their reward systems to motivate workers effectively and to reinforce behaviors consistent with organizational goals.

Roueche and Baker (1987) point out that a structure of rewards is necessary for a climate of excellence. In the educational setting, this refers to students as well as to members of the faculty, staff, and administration. Positive rewards specifically targeted at desired behaviors are fundamental to the full integration of behaviors consistent with institutional values.

Peters and Waterman (1982) and Peters and Austin (1985) cite positive reinforcement as key to motivating desired behaviors. Peters and Waterman (1982) suggest that positively reinforced behavior slowly comes to occupy a larger and larger share of the time and attention of employees. They say that management's most significant output is getting others to shift their attention in more desirable directions. Peters and Austin (1985) note that the success of Tupperware and Mary Kay Cosmetics is directly related to the festive nature of the celebrations around individual successes. Systems for recognition and reward have a direct impact on employee behavior and thus reinforce values. Conscious attention to the rewards in an organization represents a clear identification of the organization's values and culture.

Understanding one's internal institutional environment is obviously essential for any community college CEO, particularly as it relates to the intrinsic rewards offered to the followership. The value of caring for people was a consistent theme of the CEOs interviewed in this study. President Chuck Carlsen, Johnson County Community College, Kansas, reinforces the value of recognizing the worth of every individual:

EVERYONE in our college plays an important role. It is not enough to deal with just the faculty, although they certainly have a great deal to contribute. I also make a point of talking with all our employee groups—groups such as our maintenance crew, custodial staff, and secretarial staff. I also come back at night to meet with our night crew, adjunct staff, and part-time faculty.

Each individual within these work groups plays a critical role in achieving what we are. This is their institution. They are proud of it and take pride in their contribution in making the institution what it is. My role is to let them know—face to face, if possible—that I value their contribution and commitment.

Regardless of these individuals' positions, it is important they know that they are appreciated. This appreciation may be expressed in a number of different ways, but perhaps the most powerful way is the extent to which the leader involves followers in providing input into the problem-solving/decision-making process of the college. Excellent leaders are in touch with their internal constituents. They share information, and they listen. They build bridges that facilitate effective communication; through such efforts, followers feel involved.

Positive reinforcement takes many forms. Often it is difficult to predict the impact that a CEO's actions will have on an institution. Such is the case in the following example related by James Chasteen, President of John C. Calhoun State Community College, Alabama:

WE had a big snowstorm, and we had to close down Thursday and Friday. I decided to open and have class on Monday. Maybe it wasn't a good decision. A lot of the students came, but a lot of faculty and staff people weren't able to come. A staff person wanted me to "say something" to those who didn't show up. Instead, I got a list of all who did show up. I wrote personal notes thanking everyone who showed up for work on Monday, difficult as it was. At the ball game last week, a security guard said, "Hey, listen, I want to thank you for that note." I've gotten more positive response for that than anything we've done for a long time.

The value of this involvement is multifaceted. Employees throughout the institution have a greater sense of ownership as it relates to their working environment. Their sense of commitment and pride in what they do permeates the institution, and as a result the accomplishment of the mission is enhanced. This positive attitude is then reflected in working with students. Thus, when the culture of an institution promotes recognizing and rewarding individuals, this intangible feeling powerfully affects all constituents. Not only are the followers affected; so are the clients. Colleges that emphasize or promote a rewards orientation appear to be more student-centered. They focus directly on assisting students at all levels of development to be successful. Employees who enjoy their work, regardless of their institutional role, significantly affect the working environment. Leaders are appreciated, employees feel positive, and students reap the intangible rewards.

Although this concept is obvious to the participants in this study, many of the colleges across the country have failed either to understand or to communicate how much they value their employees. Transformational leaders, however, emphasized the importance of recognizing and rewarding others. They noted that without leader-follower reciprocity, change is exceedingly difficult. Their appreciation for the individual was clearly evident. President Raymond Stone, Sandhills Community College, North Carolina, succinctly captured this concept: "I think recognizing the value of the people within the institution is critical for anybody in a leadership position. Our institution is people, and surely we can value what we are all about."

RESPECTING THE INDIVIDUAL

As noted earlier, respect for the individual is one of the fundamental values shared by our transformational CEOs: "This is an institution made up of people." "This is a people place." "Our product is people." Therefore, it makes sense and is constant with our underlying mission that respect for the individuals who make up the organization is significant.

The value of the individual is certainly not unique or exclusive to community college institutions. As Thomas J. Watson, Jr., stated:

> IBM's philosophy is largely contained in three simple beliefs. I want to begin with what I think is the most important: our respect for the individual. This is a simple concept, but in IBM it occupies a major portion of management time (Peters and Waterman, 1982, pp. 14–15).

An underlying theme of our transformational leaders' thoughts mirrored Watson's sincere respect for his individual followers. Many of the CEOs noted the importance of recognizing and knowing every employee's name. Others mentioned how important it was to keep informed regarding the accomplishments of their followers and to indicate in writing and/or in other appropriate ways their best wishes regarding such accomplishments. Still others discussed the importance of creating an environment that provided maximum opportunity for individuals to take risks and "let their creative juices flow."

Chancellor Michael Crawford, St. Louis Community College, responded to the following questions: "How do you know when your team is fully functioning? When are you achieving what you really want to achieve? When is there an awareness of unity achieved by your administrative team?" His answer was direct and reflected the fine balance of individual recognition and team success: "When the people who are part of that whole team get as much satisfaction from others' successes as they do their own."

Building and developing cohesive teams throughout the institution is essential and is accomplished much more readily when the relationship between leader and follower is based on respect for the individual. President Raymond Stone, Sandhills Community College, illustrates this concept:

I appreciate my colleagues. Over the years I have developed a close personal friendship with many of them as well as a great professional respect for what they do.

Chancellor Donald Walker, Grossmont Community College District, California, also reinforces the importance of recognizing that each individual can and usually wants to make a contribution. He noted:

I believe the name of the game is "bubble-up," not "hammer-down." Academic communities are full of talented people—the trick is to conjure up superior performance since it cannot be commanded. I really think that it is possible to get everyone into the act and still get something done. All of us are smarter than any of us, and therefore the emphasis should be on problem-solving rather than on the question, "Who is responsible?" People must be at the heart of the organization and the values of the CEO must reflect this priority. There is not anyone who doesn't count. Successful leaders, particularly in the community college arena, have

learned to work with committees and coalitions—not as neces-
sary burdens but as instruments that have the potential to pro-
duce truly satisfactory and even spectacular results.

President Al Wisgoski, Illinois Valley Community College, captured
the essence of this presidential behavior: "With openness and respect
for individual differences of opinion have come mutual trust and
respect."

On the other hand, we must remain cognizant of the shortcomings surrounding the human-relations approach to management (in
which some of these examples could be classified). Peters and Waterman (1982) expressed the view that the human relations movement has
been an "overwhelming failure" (p. 95) as it directly affects high-
productivity organizations. They noted that many human-relations-style
managers lost their focus on production and focused instead on creating a work environment in which everyone felt happy and content.
Their point is well taken, although it may not be as applicable to community colleges as it is to the private sector. Nonetheless, educational
productivity is a valued commodity within the community college
movement.

Another explanation, cited by Hoyle (1985), was that the human-
relations style of management, although appearing to be kindly and
democratic, was often simply manipulative. The idea of manipulation
implies that, although the importance of people to productivity was
realized, people were viewed as resources to be used rather than as
equals to be encouraged. It has been our experience that the issue of
manipulation is indeed a sensitive issue within the educational arena
and one that deserves the attention of community college CEOs.

The CEOs who participated in this study were well aware of Hoyle's
concern and concretely addressed the issue—not by simply talking
about respecting the individual within their institutions, but by modeling behavior consistent with the theoretical concept of Blake and Mouton (1964). It was Blake and Mouton who made clear, through their
work with the Managerial Grid, that effective management requires both
a high level of concern for persons and a high level of concern for
productivity.

When the leader of the organization is able to communicate a
genuine respect for the people who exist within the working environment, management errors related to the human relations movement
are minimized. The error of simply trying to make employees feel content will be avoided because having respect for people involves an

understanding that people want to work hard for something they understand, share, and respect.

The recipient of respect within the community college environment is the student. The changing and diverse nature of the student population of today's community colleges requires an institutional responsiveness unlike any in the past.

As the Commission on the Future of Community Colleges wrote:

BECAUSE our doors are open to students regardless of age, race, or ethnic origin, the nation's community colleges can be leading architects in building new communities in America. As partners in a network of institutions stretching from coast to coast, they can help the least advantaged move into the mainstream of American life, serve students of all ages, and provide continuing education, civic empowerment, and social integration for a growing number of citizens. Such community building amidst diversity is vital to the future of the nation (p. 10).

This open-door policy, however, elicits great uncertainty. It is not easy for the individuals involved in the internal organization to be proactive in meeting this challenge. The need to be responsive and compassionate to such student populations is fraught with ambiguity and a balance that focuses on students and their needs.

STUDENT-CENTEREDNESS

I n *Access and Excellence* (1987), an in-depth study of Miami-Dade Community College, Roueche and Baker concluded:

STUDENT achievement will result from a composite, interwoven pattern, or "gestalt" of attitudes, policies, and behaviors, all consciously designed to shape a positive institutional environment. These patterns of policies and behaviors interact to create a college "feeling"; in fact, they point to specific climate factors that appear to have a significant productivity and satisfaction (p. 13).

This feeling or "gestalt" is an attribute of what is valued in the culture and the resulting synergy that may result from a student-oriented
environment. As Bob McCabe so aptly notes, "Our students are the cen-
terpiece of our table." The theme of student-centeredness is common
to many colleges and is important not only to the presidents, but also
to their staffs. A member of the leadership team at the College of
DuPage reflected:

> OCCASIONALLY, staff get so caught up in doing their jobs
> (teaching, filing, managing, etc.) that the real purpose of our work
> is obscured, namely valuing students and their needs. Our leader
> makes a point of reminding staff and the board through group
> meetings, individual sessions, and/or in writing that our reason
> for being is to serve the students, and in so doing to develop into
> an outstanding institution. The college is recognized as highly
> student-oriented. Students' needs are considered and valued first,
> before the needs of the staff or the institution.

Without question, the CEOs involved in the study strongly reinforced the importance of institutions being student-centered. They emphasized not only their need to model behaviors consistent with this
theme but also the importance of all the other employee work groups
to do so as well. This common theme appeared to be achieved in many
ways. President Henry Wagner, Chattanooga State Technical Community College, Tennessee, discussed the significance of student centeredness as follows:

> ALL programs belong to the institution, and ultimately those
> programs belong to the students. We try to involve students regu-
> larly and sincerely in all programming and committee structures.
> I meet and my key staff meets with a Student Cabinet, a represen-
> tative group from each of the program areas of the college, on
> a monthly basis. That meeting is wide open; students are allowed
> to take any direction they wish, in terms of questions, or sugges-
> tions, or comments. We write minutes of those meetings and carry
> them back to our executive staff meeting the following Monday,
> where each of those suggestions or comments is taken very

seriously. We decide if there is a need to change whatever program area is addressed in those comments.

Many of our CEOs addressed it by emphasizing the importance of the classroom activity and their dedication to the teaching/learning process, while others discussed the importance of meeting and interacting with students. For example, President Peter Spina, Monroe Community College, states:

I involve myself with students in a number of different ways, which I feel enables me to keep some contact with our primary clientele. I do things that are of a structured nature, such as meeting regularly with the student government, attending a variety of student events, and visiting student center areas. In the state of New York, we have an elected student trustee on our board, so I spend time orienting and educating that student each summer. I also participate in what we call the President's Forum. Once each semester the student government invites me to an open meeting, to which all students are invited. It is held in a large lecture hall, and students are invited to ask whatever they wish. I am on the "firing-line," so to speak, since I don't get an agenda prior to the forum. The tone of these forums has been very positive. Most of the questions are well thought-out, and I think the activity has helped maintain good communication and understanding between myself and the student body.

For CEOs to be effective in their role as transformational leaders, they must constantly focus and refine the institutional shared vision. It is important for CEOs to have a sense of student needs. This is best achieved through the development and implementation of systems designed to promote student success. Such systems must address the following concepts: student acquisition, student matriculation, curriculum integration, and student monitoring.

Over the past several years, community colleges have been making great strides in improving their student information systems in an attempt to become better apprised of student success. Some colleges have been more successful than others in addressing this challenge.

Miami-Dade is one of the acknowledged leaders in the implementation of a total student program designed to meet the four previously mentioned concepts (Roueche and Baker, 1987). While some colleges have made great strides in addressing the issue, still others are in the planning stages for such systems.

In addition to systems they have designed to focus on student success and centeredness, outstanding leaders use a variety of techniques to emphasize the importance of students. The commitment to student-centeredness is well-illustrated by Brookhaven College's organizational chart (Dallas County Community College District), which clearly demonstrates the importance of students within the organization.

SEEKING AND VALUING OTHERS

Peters and Austin (1985) quote former New Orleans Saints coach Bum Phillips who said, "The main thing is getting people to play. When you think it's your system that's winning, you're in for a damn big surprise. It's those players' efforts" (p. 326). Nothing motivates players, team members, or followers more than feeling that they are partners and contributors to the goal. Coaching is face-to-face leadership that pulls people together and encourages them to step up to responsibility and achievement. Leaders are aware of the value of teaming, and they select team players—those who will complement and strengthen the team.

The first step in creating a strong leadership team is understanding the needs of the institution and selecting the best individuals to address those needs. Variables that must be considered in the selection process relate to the shared vision of the institution, the demands of the position, and an awareness of perceived inadequacies that may exist in the leadership team. Leaders who are cognizant of not only their own particular strengths and weaknesses but also those of other members of the leadership team emphasize the need to select individuals who possess the strengths that will enhance team effectiveness.

This approach was clearly evidenced in our interview with President Ray Hawkins, Tyler Junior College, Texas. He was discussing his five-year campus development plan and noted:

FOR each of the proposed projects, I have chosen, by design, to use a "bottoms up" planning process. It is not highly formalized where the process strangles the product or the people; rather it

Figure 8.1 **Brookhaven College's Organizational Chart**

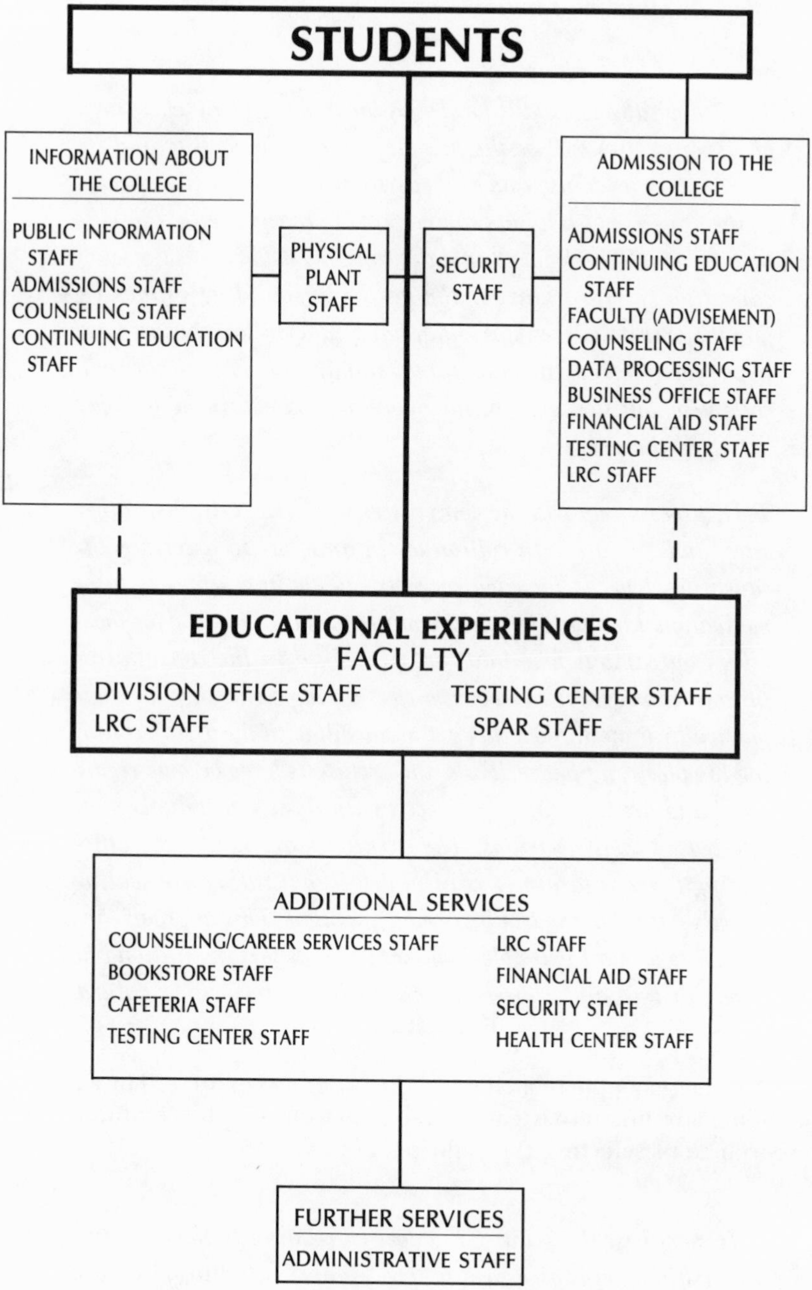

STUDENTS

| INFORMATION ABOUT THE COLLEGE | | | ADMISSION TO THE COLLEGE |

PUBLIC INFORMATION STAFF
ADMISSIONS STAFF
COUNSELING STAFF
CONTINUING EDUCATION STAFF

PHYSICAL PLANT STAFF

SECURITY STAFF

ADMISSIONS STAFF
CONTINUING EDUCATION STAFF
FACULTY (ADVISEMENT)
COUNSELING STAFF
DATA PROCESSING STAFF
BUSINESS OFFICE STAFF
FINANCIAL AID STAFF
TESTING CENTER STAFF
LRC STAFF

EDUCATIONAL EXPERIENCES
FACULTY

DIVISION OFFICE STAFF   TESTING CENTER STAFF
LRC STAFF   SPAR STAFF

ADDITIONAL SERVICES

COUNSELING/CAREER SERVICES STAFF   LRC STAFF
BOOKSTORE STAFF   FINANCIAL AID STAFF
CAFETERIA STAFF   SECURITY STAFF
TESTING CENTER STAFF   HEALTH CENTER STAFF

FURTHER SERVICES

ADMINISTRATIVE STAFF

*is an informal process to get input. In each case I have appointed
a facility planning advisory committee specific to the particular
project.*

———

*THE committee is usually headed by the vice-president whose area
of responsibility will be the primary user of the facility and includes several faculty and staff personnel most directly affected
by the project. The advisory committees are charged with a specific
task in which the final product is to hand the architect a set of
education specifications for the particular building so that before the architects ever start, they have, in writing, what we need
in the facility from an educational standpoint. This is not radi-
cally new, but it is critical in involving and obtaining follower
input in the process.*

———

*THE process requires the committees to read, study, visit other
sites, and consult with colleagues in an effort to ascertain the
educational needs for each project. The activity appears to be
motivational not only for the committee members but also for those
others on campus who have been involved in the consultative
process. It has resulted in committees taking ownership for their
particular project. Also, they get to consult with the architect during his planning phase. Thus, the architects have become reedu-
cated and are now talking directly with those individuals most
affected by their decisions. The architects are not in my office
talking to me regarding technical details but rather are dealing
directly with those individuals most involved. This approach has
proven to be most valuable. The employees at this institution like
to be involved and appreciate that their involvement is valued.*

———

Another example related to this behavior was expressed by a member of the administrative team at San Juan College, who reinforces the
importance of selecting the right people:

———

*THE very best thing our CEO does in relation to the executive
leadership team is hire good people—people with integrity, good*

ideas, energy, experience, and initiative. One important reason that the college works is that we as an administrative team work well together. Our strengths complement each other as we all work at achieving the best we can for the college. This team functions as a genuine team.

And a member of the leadership team at John C. Calhoun State Community College, Alabama, said:

OUR CEO typically has surrounded himself with capable, energetic, loyal people. Each is dedicated to the concept of the community college and appreciates the opportunity to serve the college.

As we discussed with our CEOs the relationship that existed between themselves and their followers, the importance and value assigned to employees within their institutions were obvious. Our CEOs emphasized that they worked hard at maintaining effective channels of communication and creating an environment based on mutual trust with their employees. Followers were encouraged to speak openly and honestly about issues. One example that highlighted this leadership behavior was provided by President Ruth Shaw, Central Piedmont Community College, North Carolina:

I have not been in this institution very long (20 months), so there are a number of transitional issues presently on the table. One of them has to do with some reorganization in various departments. I'm looking at combining some departments into larger divisions. Such decisions have traditionally been viewed as administrative prerogative. However, I expect greater participation in such decisions. Unfortunately, many of the faculty and staff are having difficulty getting accustomed to the idea that their input is valued. If they have something to say about these issues, it is important that they do so. My style of leadership is not something where a decision is just made and announced and where people are left to figure it out as best they can.

WHEN it came up that reorganization was being considered, some people leaped to the rampart, anticipating that the battle was on because they thought something was going to happen to them. In this particular case, one department expressed real concern. So I went over to that particular department when I heard they were concerned and sat down with all the faculty, and we talked about "Here is the context for this, here is why it is even on the table as a question of discussion, and here is the background." We talked about positive ways in which faculty could be involved in decisions that would, in fact, benefit students. We basically laid out the issues and dealt with them face to face. It was direct. It did not hide behind a structure. It invited people to participate in appropriate ways, and it was also clear where the ultimate accountability lay.

AT some point the president has to accept the ultimate accountability for management and leadership in the college, and I accept that challenge. It is my responsibility to get the input and then to decide how to use it. The outcome is yet to be determined, although I am presently awaiting a recommendation from my vice president.

LET me reemphasize the process. The input provided by the faculty outlining their concerns was thoughtful and valuable. Not only was the input valuable, but so was the process. The misconception that the reorganization represented an administrative ploy to cut costs was put squarely on the table. The issue was confronted directly and immediately and, I think, to the satisfaction of all concerned.

SUMMARY

There is no doubt that the president has primary responsibility for creating the climate or tone within the organization. As such, it is extremely important that CEOs understand the impact of their leadership style. *Knowledge of self* appears to be a critical element in effective leadership. Bennis and Nanus (1985) suggest that positive self-regard consists of three components: knowledge of one's strengths; the capacity to nurture and develop those strengths; and the ability to discern the fit between one's strengths and weaknesses and the organization's needs. This positive self-regard appears to induce other-regard in followers, creating a sense of confidence and high expectations, not unlike the Pygmalion effect. This positive self-regard is translated to followers in a variety of ways. Through dignity and understanding, transformational leaders exhibit the qualities of patience, respect, faith in others, and the ability to listen. These nurturing qualities represent some of the values that were reported by our CEOs.

The impact of this style of leadership behavior is a modeling for followers, creating an organization in which individuals are consistently functioning at higher levels of performance and personal satisfaction. An atmosphere is created that not only is productive, but also is humanly satisfying, contributing to a high degree of synergy. This synergy results in the group's collective efforts accomplishing more than each member could accomplish by working independently.

Peters and Waterman (1982) pointed out that a strong organizational culture creates a coherent framework within which motivated persons are able to work. They noted that, without exception, excellent companies were characterized by a strong organizational culture. Thus, transformational leaders are adept at attending to both the organizational and the individual dynamics of their respective institutions. The challenge is neither simple nor ever fully realized. However, the proactive transformational community college CEO is the catalyst for change in the evolving and ever-shifting community college mission.

CHAPTER 9

MOTIVATION FOR EMPOWERMENT

66 *People who occupy critical organizational positions and act as gatekeepers with the external world tend to amass power. Others inside the organization become dependent on the gatekeepers for a vision of the outside world. Active power seekers strive to develop a team they can draw on for needed support and goal accomplishment. Such people collaborate with others and explore the knowledge that exists inside and outside the organization.... But power flows two ways. To achieve and exercise power both leaders and followers must become interdependent with one another. Both must be influenced as well as influence. Reciprocity and balance are essential.* 99

HAMPTON, SUMMER, AND WEBBER
Organizational Behavior and the Practice of Management

MOTIVATIONAL ORIENTATION: Demonstrated Competencies

STAGES OF MOTIVATION
MOTIVATING TOWARD COMMITMENT AND ACTION
THE EXPECTATIONS PROCESS
A CONTEXT FOR CREATIVE SKILLS
DEVELOPING FOLLOWERS
PEAK PERFORMANCE

MOTIVATION FOR EMPOWERMENT

INTRODUCTION

n examining the complex concept of motivation, significant attention must be given to the phenomenon of leader/follower interdepen-
dency. The overwhelming emphasis in studies of leadership has been
on the traits, behaviors, and/or situations that separate the effective
leader from the ineffective leader. Seldom is leadership addressed in
relation to follower involvement and responsibility. Little attention has
been directed toward the gestalt of leadership. However, we know that
leadership is greater than the sum of its parts—that it is the catalyst
helping colleges forge ahead in the face of great adversity, challenge
the status quo, and inspire great performance from those who collectively seek to move students toward success.

STAGES OF MOTIVATION

nfortunately, most research has been unilateral in nature, focusing on leader behaviors or traits; only recently has there been
analysis of the interaction between the leader and the situation.
Typically, leadership studies have focused on the shortcomings that

interfere with effective leadership. Such leader behaviors as the abuse of power, injustice, and indecision are consistently identified in the literature to the exclusion of a more comprehensive examination of the interaction between both leaders and followers.

As exceptions, Argyris (1957) and Hersey and Blanchard (1977) have attempted to convey the importance of maturity in the follower as it relates to leadership. Carew and others (1985) demonstrate how motivation for empowerment can be developed over time in an organization. They report that all groups are unique, dynamic, complex, ever-changing, living systems that are different from and subsequently more than the sum of the individual members. Blanchard's research supports the fact that groups go through similar stages as they grow from a collection of individuals to a smoothly functioning team. Blanchard supports the idea that transformational leaders must do more than listen and talk. They must interact with and be an integral part of the group.

In the current study, one deficit came through loud and clear. The CEOs' leadership teams want more quality time with their leaders. They want and expect time individually and collectively, and they want this time to be motivational and inspiring.

Blanchard supports the idea that CEOs must differentiate the content (what the team is doing) from the process (how the group is handling its communication and team activities) in order to transform the group from a collection of individuals to a motivated and integrated team. Our data support the idea that the truly exceptional CEO understands what is happening among the members of the leadership team and knows how to translate this interaction into productive group effectiveness. When CEOs work directly with the leadership team as a group, as opposed to tasking individuals one-on-one, motivation and performance generally are enhanced.

Blanchard indicates that research on small group interaction supports one consistent conclusion: groups, such as the leadership teams researched in the current study, pass through predictable developmental stages—including changes in personnel—during a CEO's tenure.

Lacoursiere (1980) envisioned five stages of group development that we were able to identify in the current study. These five stages of group or team development include

1) orientation
2) dissatisfaction
3) resolution
4) production
5) termination

These stages suggest that the CEO's task in empowering the executive leadership team differs at each stage and is complicated further during each addition or deletion from the team.

Stage One of motivation through empowerment—orientation—is a low team development level. Members are eager to serve but are often not sure of the directions and expectations. Most are excited about being members of the team and yet are anxious concerning their ability to make a major contribution. In this orientation stage CEOs must invest considerable time with the team and must be consistently visionary and clear regarding directions and expectations.

In Stage Two—dissatisfaction—many team members begin to experience a discrepancy between their initial expectations and the reality of being followers within the context of the CEO's vision and expectations. Members often experience dissatisfaction with the ambiguity of the goals and of the collective tasks designed (or not designed) to accomplish them. Cohen and March (1986) described this context perfectly when they said:

THE American college or university is a prototypic organized anarchy. It does not know what it is doing. Its goals are either vague or in dispute. Its technology is familiar but not understood. Its major participants wander in and out of the organization. These factors do not make a university a bad organization or a disorganized one; but they do make it a problem to describe, understand, and lead (p. 2).

The dip in motivation during the dissatisfaction stage is attributed to the degree of discrepancy between the followers' initial expectations and the institution's ambiguity and lack of clear outcomes. In this stage, a CEO must lead the charge toward redefining goals and tasks; an integration must occur between various units of the followers and the important/achievable outcomes. Lacoursiere concluded that this stage can be brief if the CEOs and their teams are able to throw out the old ways of measuring progress toward goals and substitute new ways of achieving these goals. To add new tasks onto old tasks is to ensure that the group remains at the dissatisfaction stage.

In Stage Three—resolution—CEOs and their teams resolve differences, reduce ambiguity, focus on new relationships, and begin to move toward productivity. Team members become less dissatisfied as ways of working together become clear. They also resolve differences in personality and style between the CEO and the team members. As feelings of mutual respect, harmony, and trust develop, group cohesion follows. During this stage of motivation, CEOs increase emphasis on group problem-solving. The CEO's full involvement in group problem-solving is critical in moving the group to the next stage.

Stage Four—production—should be the sustained stage for CEOs and their teams. The length and quality of the productive stage of development depend on the skills of the CEO and on the development and stability of the team. The ease with which the CEO and the team resolve new problems, learn new skills, and increase quality is a predictor of the success of the productivity stage of group development. The team members at this stage

- sustain positive feelings regarding team membership;
- begin to feel confident of the outcome of their collective problem-solving and decision-making;
- work well and effectively together;
- begin to work with less attention and support from the CEO;
- challenge and/or support other team members;
- focus their energy on the resolution of group activities and begin to develop synergy of complementary functions and interpersonal support.

Stage Five—termination—almost always occurs with the retirement or promotion of the CEO and can occur with major reorganization of the team members. If the CEO has exited the scene, the new CEO must be able to analyze the team and their new needs and then move quickly to restore productivity. In this case the CEO must maintain or restore morale and assume that competence remains intact. If there is a major change in team membership, the CEO may find the group regressing to the resolution stage.

When we analyze the group data from the current study and the research reported in this discussion, it is interesting to note that the amount of work accomplished by the CEOs and their teams steadily increases from low to high from the orientation to the production stages—while morale or motivation to perform begins high in the orientation stage, then dips in the dissatisfaction stage, only to recover and track performance in the production stage. In the terminal stage both the quality and amount of work and the motivation of the team to perform are affected by the skill and behavior of the current CEO (in cases where the composition of the team has changed) or of the new CEO (in cases where the CEO is the major focus of new demands).

In spite of the valuable work of Hersey, Blanchard, and Lacoursiere, the role of the follower in relationship to the leader has yet to receive the emphasis of research necessary to draw firm conclusions regarding leader behavior and follower response. While the leader-follower relationship is not a clear-cut issue, it behooves us to look at the reciprocal relationship between the two in order to understand leadership as a holistic concept.

Every relationship is a form of partnership, and partnership, by definition, denotes shared responsibilities. A "given" in our definition of leadership is that the full involvement of the follower is critical to effectiveness in any context. The concept of shared vision denotes more than a group of individuals functioning in "group-think." Rather, shared vision implies the development of a common belief system in which the product of group involvement exists throughout the institution. The role of the leader in achieving shared vision is to initiate a cycle of carefully developed stages that motivate followers to recognize the need for change and provide the opportunity for the transformation to occur. This style of motivational leadership generates a snowball effect, actively engaging followers in the accomplishment of activities deemed important by the college community. It is in this type of institutional environment that creativity, innovation, risk-taking, and responsibility flourish at all levels.

While Deming (1988) argues that 90 percent of the problems of an organization are managerial, he does not lose sight of the fact that the resolution of these problems must be accomplished through follower energy. These concerns generate a number of questions: Do leaders make a difference? How are followers involved in significant problem-solving? How much emphasis should be placed on follower responsibility? How can leaders determine the proper level of follower involvement? Although these questions may generate interesting scenarios, our findings clearly support the conclusion that transformational leaders are better able to engage their followers in change and new direction than are their non-transformational counterparts.

John Gardner, former Secretary of Health, Education, and Welfare, suggests some of the complex components involved in the interaction of leading and following:

———

IF one is engaged in administering, it makes a great deal of difference whether the people one is seeking to influence are subordinate, superordinate, or co-equal. Leadership overrides such distinctions. It moves in any direction it can. The key reality is that in a tumultuous, swiftly changing environment, in a world of multiple, colliding systems, lateral leadership—boundary-crossing leadership—is absolutely essential. Those who can exercise leadership from whatever they happen to be in the rush of events are priceless (1987, p. 6).

Gardner's idea that leadership moves in many directions was supported by many outstanding community college CEOs. Chancellor Jeff Hockaday, Virginia Community College System, answers the question of how CEOs pay appropriate attention to instruction:

THEY do so by their actions. They speak of good teaching and mean it. They require the staff to become involved in the learning process. They do not talk about the importance of good faculty and then give the rewards to administrators. They provide opportunities for recognition for teaching achievement. They provide opportunities for faculty development and involvement, and they maintain consistency of support in good or bad times. Educational leaders create atmospheres where good teaching is expected—where anything else is abnormal. They create environments where teachers are respected and their needs are addressed.

The means by which our sample CEOs motivated their followers varied, but in spite of the variance, a common theme emerged. Their behaviors indicated that leader motivation focused on caring, respecting, rewarding, celebrating, and promoting a creative, risk-taking environment where the emphasis was on the challenge of the unknown rather than on skepticism or failure.

MOTIVATING TOWARD COMMITMENT AND ACTION

C hapter 8, "Leader and Follower Cohesion," explored the concept of culture and the importance of leader understanding of his or her particular working environment. Schein (1985) noted

that an organization's culture may be affected by the values and beliefs of the leader through behaviors that are aligned and consistent
with underlying institutional values and beliefs. This alignment leads
to the successful completion of the organization's tasks and solution
of its problems. The more successful the solutions (and the stronger
the followers' perceptions of that success), the greater the likelihood
that the values behind the behaviors will develop into beliefs through
a process of cognitive transformation. If the solutions continue to work
and the leader continues value-consistent behaviors, then the beliefs
gradually become assumptions and ultimately become integrated into
the deepest culture of the organization.

This concept has been acted upon by our selected community college transformational leaders. Through their conscientious and deliber-
ate attention to promoting a campus ethos that focuses on developing a "shared vision," and in conjunction with their understanding
of the issues that influenced their particular culture, the outstanding
leaders have achieved collegial awareness and acceptance of the institutional and individual values that are revered within their college
or system.

Individual needs of followers—defined here in terms of motivational needs—are companions to institutional goals in the organizational culture. Klemp (1977) suggested that motivation is a key factor
in the successful performance of any job and is defined as "a need
state—a prerequisite for behavior" (Roueche and Baker, 1987). Research
has shown that monetary rewards (Deci, 1971), good player awards
(Lepper, Greene, and Nisbett, 1973), threats of punishment (Deci and
Cascio, 1972), explicit competition (Deci et al., 1981), and external evaluation of performance (Smith, 1974) can all affect motivation. Intrinsic
motivation, on the other hand, will be bolstered if experiences lead
people to feel more self-determination and competence. Intrinsic motivation and the rewards that such motivation produces are perceived
as pleasurable psychological states. Hackman and Oldham (1980) note
that there are at least three such states: (1) experienced meaningful-
ness of the work ("feelings" of arousal from rich stimuli, of competence
in performance, of closure of a work episode, and of connectedness
with others); (2) experienced responsibility for work outcomes; and (3)
knowledge of results.

The intrinsic needs for competence and self-determination motivate an ongoing process of seeking and attempting to conquer optimal
challenges, suited to people's own competencies, that are neither too
easy nor too difficult (Deci and Ryan, 1985). President Joe Malik, Grays
Harbor College, Washington, illustrates:

WHEN I think of my role as a motivator, two things come to mind. First, I work hard at my job; and I believe that behavior not only is obvious to others but, in and of itself, has a positive effect on others. Second, and perhaps more importantly, I ask people to work. I am direct with people. After getting institutional commitment to something, I ask individuals for help. I try to match different individuals with appropriate tasks so that they have an interest in what they are asked to do. If people have an interest in the task, they are much more committed. I also tell them directly that I think they are the persons to do the job. It is not very sophisticated or profound, but it is honest and it appears to work well.

Such an approach borrows heavily from the Japanese style of management as outlined in Ouchi's Theory Z (1981). According to Ouchi, the key to increased productivity is a focus on people with the central issue revolving around trust. The greater the trust, the more leaders know of their followers as individuals, thus building more cohesive and openly communicating teams. Trusted and trusting followers are given greater autonomy, because they are often in the best position to make effective decisions. Also, when they are given greater autonomy, they will display more intrinsic motivation (Deci and Ryan, 1985). Theory Z overlaps considerably with Theory Y (McGregor, 1960) in that the organizing concept for Theory Y is based on autonomy (participation in decision-making) while the organizing concept for Theory Z is based on trust. Trust and autonomy are companions. The autonomy of Theory Y requires a trusting environment, and Theory Z needs participative decision-making as a fundamental aspect of a trusting relationship between leaders and followers. Thus, the Theory Z approach to leadership relies on creating and sustaining an organizational culture that genuinely involves people in developing and fulfilling individual and organizational goals and objectives. Commitment is the psychic knot that ties individual meaning and institutional mission (Kuhn and Geis, 1984).

A member of the leadership team at Midlands Technical College, South Carolina, observed:

AS the third president of one of the largest community colleges in South Carolina, President Hudgins faced the central issue of pulling together a diverse leadership team and motivating it to inspire an entire institution of three campuses which had lacked vision and vitality for some years. The dynamics of this team, a combination of new team members coupled with two already in place, were immediately forceful and potentially excellent for the college. Their energies were focused through a series of retreats, calm yet consistent motivation, and professional development.

PRESIDENT Hudgins also started a college-wide study of the values and vision of the institution, and he made certain that the leadership team was fully involved in the process as consensus builders. Three significant results developed:

(1) Midlands Technical College is clearly on the move again. A faculty that had not trusted earlier leadership now openly expresses their trust. Staff who felt left out and unrewarded now express renewed belief that the institution can be excellent.

(2) The entire college feels a part of the new planning process and, in particular, a part of the new "Vision for Excellence." College faculty and staff also feel that the entire leadership team is working together and not simply "dictating" objectives and directions.

(3) The leadership team around President Hudgins now functions exceptionally well—anticipating, coordinating, and solving issues with openness. Thanks to this process of building a leadership team through the planning steps, Midlands Technical College now is positioned for significant change and future development.

Focusing on students is another effective way of motivating followers within the institution to initiate change. Chancellor Jim Kellerman, Orange County Community College District, California, shares the following:

EDUCATIONAL leaders must foster an atmosphere in which rapidly changing student populations will be well served, and in which unique forms of educational programming may be developed. An effective way to establish this atmosphere is through motivation of staff and faculty to pursue excellence while maintaining a focus on students. This process is facilitated through open communications, teamwork and participation, and a solid working base of information. To accomplish this, we do not need new and complex systems, but open, straightforward policies and procedures which are people-centered rather than thing-centered. Educational institutions are essentially personnel systems whose working parts are primarily people and whose products are almost entirely people.

In the interview, we asked CEOs to discuss how they motivated others in the work environment. Their collective responses centered on a deep sense of commitment to the community college mission. Many of those we interviewed said that they believed so strongly in the role of the community college that they had difficulty containing their enthusiasm. Others said they truly believed that they had found their calling and that they were doing what they should be doing. This missionary-like zeal regarding their leadership role was exhibited in a variety of ways and in a multitude of situations. Chancellor Michael Crawford, St. Louis Community College, Missouri, made the following statement, and it characterizes the CEOs' responses:

I truly believe in the mission of the community college, and more importantly, I see its potential or opportunity to change a community and the students we are designed to serve. We really have a dynamic mission, and I hope my enthusiasm is exuded and shared by others and thus becomes somewhat synergistic as others capture that spirit.

Still others discussed a more formalized approach. Chancellor Tom Fryer, Foothill-De Anza Community College District, California, notes:

THE team I try to build focuses around the budget and policy development group. The leadership group of this college district is not a management group. My philosophy is that if institutions are really going to achieve their mission, everybody needs to be pulling together in more or less a line and in the same direction. I believe that an excessive reliance on a management team to get that done leaves a lot of people excluded from the process.

THUS, it comes down to thinking about how I motivate people (a very, very diverse group of people) and helping them establish some common vision of the future and move toward it. I accomplish that in the following ways: I encourage open and frank discussions in which I listen intently to what they are saying and try to respond; I try to interpret what one person is saying to another; and I try to be a common advocate for all points of view. As far as I am concerned, if you exist and have a point of view, your point of view is legitimate and valid and deserves to be accounted for in the mix of ideas.

Individual and group motivation is enhanced when followers understand how they fit into the organization. When individual roles are clearly delineated, followers comprehend their role in the tapestry of the shared vision.

THE EXPECTATIONS PROCESS

Establishing clearly defined expectations is not a simple process. Victor Vroom (1964) of Yale University argues that the psychological press on followers to perform is a function of their expectancies about the future and the personal attractiveness of specific future outcomes. It calls for a comprehensive understanding and "felt need" by the leader of what is necessary to motivate followers to perform their roles effectively and efficiently. It is a process in which the leader ensures that the followers understand both the big picture and how each follower component role fits into that picture. The degree to which leaders and their administrative team are able to present the college gestalt (mission through shared vision—the big picture) is the critical initial step toward assisting followers in their efforts to identify with and assume ownership for the direction in which the college is moving.

Once the shared vision is valued, the leader must understand, accept, and translate the need for each component part to exist within the college. A significant part of this translation, perhaps the most important, is the personalization of these component parts into follower roles. It is here that understanding blends with responsibility and individual expectations emerge.

This personalization is well illustrated by President David Buettner, North Iowa Area Community College:

IN the process of accomplishing our shared mission and communicating that to each and every one of our employees, I think it is important that employees know what they ought to be able to count on from the institution. Let me share with you a rather simple four-point list of principles that I have used and that I teach to achieve this goal:

1. *Provide a good job description—an accurate description of what it is that we expect of them.*

2. *Provide a good, honest evaluation of their performance—it may be subjective by its nature, but employees deserve to know how the institution feels about their performance.*

3. *Provide support for the discrepancies that arise between the expectations of the evaluator and the perceived outcome. Also, those who go beyond the job description and its expectations need to be recognized and rewarded.*

THE problem I see regarding performance shortcomings is that many times the efforts an institution makes or individuals make to remedy the shortcomings of people under their supervision are really anemic. In many cases, by the time you get around to really telling them in a bold, straightforward fashion that there is a problem, you almost have decided in your own mind that they are not going to work out. I've tried to prevent that in my own mind first and then in others, so that employees can count on an honest evaluation and an honest ethical effort to help them in alleviating any problems. The parallel to this, which we do not talk about enough, is that when employees really excel, they should be able to count on our help to raise that excellence to public view inside the institution and, at times, externally.

4. The role of the leader is to ensure that followers are provided with a job description, systematic evaluation, and the necessary support to maximize their role effectiveness.

IF, for example, an employee excels year after year, we should have in our mind that that employee should be rewarded and advanced, consistent with his or her wishes and abilities. We shouldn't expect them to stay there and deliver year after year without any recognition or reward. For example, our salary systems are not capped—a 20-year employee who does an excellent job can get the same raise as employees who have been here five years.

ON the negative side, let's consider an employee who has been made aware of certain problems and has been the recipient of our honest efforts to help alleviate the problems. If this fourth point is intact and working, we are doing an honest evaluation of what progress has been made, and we don't kid ourselves if the person has not, in fact, worked out. If the performance is not there, we look for a solution—either a reassignment, a smarter way of trying to help, or in some cases, actual termination.

This concept is further reinforced by President Bill Scaggs, Meridian Community College, Mississippi, who summarized his approach to motivating others:

I have confidence in others. When you let people know what you expect and give them the responsibility to take action, they respond well. I also make sure that I praise them when they succeed. I know this is not very original. But it works.

When those in positions of leadership understand these individual roles, the value of each and its part within the institution is further strengthened. Astute leadership lays the foundation for cooperation and teamwork by promoting this value within and throughout the entire organization. The clarification of individual roles within the institution also generates a value for followers regarding their specific relevance to the organization. The reward for the leader and administrative team in this process is the internalization of the value by each follower who, in turn, will create his or her individual intrinsic motivation.

Because intrinsic motivation has been associated with creativity, flexibility, and spontaneity, the presence of such characteristics has powerful implications for an institution. Problems discovered by employees themselves are more likely to be solved in a creative manner than are problems presented by superiors (Getzels, 1975). Thus, the leadership should be prepared to foster creativity and to capitalize on follower willingness to participate at higher levels of involvement.

A CONTEXT FOR CREATIVE SKILLS

In establishing a creative environment, those responsible for the organization must understand the context of creativity. Creativity requires an extensive background of knowledge related to the problem. Creativity, as opposed to more mundane thought processes, includes the willingness to accept an unstructured problem, give the problem form, and persist as long as necessary to solve the problem. This perseverance requires commitment and discipline, often in a non-linear fashion. This knowledge base is an important prerequisite of the creative thought process (Simon, 1983). These conditions—knowledge, tolerance of ambiguity, persistence—relate directly to an individual's or group's ability to resolve a problem creatively. The degree to which the leader is able to function with these variables defines the extent to which followers feel their own creativity is supported.

Transformational leaders, by definition, are change agents. They live in a world of shifting sands and take risks by stepping into the unknown. They model the type of behavior that promotes creativity and risk-taking, and they are not satisfied with the mundane.

President Al Wisgoski, Illinois Valley Community College, illustrates these characteristics:

I believe the first responsibility of enlightened educational leadership is to create that environment where people are encouraged to perform to the very best of their abilities, where there is a free and open exchange of ideas and opinions, where there is a striving for excellence—an environment where people are not afraid to dream the impossible dream. Such an environment is often facilitated through modeling. Effective leadership is founded, in part, on the principles of openness, shared information, and integrity. When such an environment is created, followers are more apt to take creative risks. Complacency with past achievements must be gently but firmly discouraged; striving for excellence must be continuously encouraged and rewarded. In fostering this desired creative environment, we must exhibit respect for the dignity of all persons, loyalty, integrity, and a sense of duty. These elements are critical but difficult to achieve unless trust is exhibited by those in leadership positions within the college. Having the confidence that the leader will act in the best interests of those who follow enables the follower to be the creative academic risk-taker who is necessary to bring about committed curricular change.

An organizational leader who recognizes the need for and provides the opportunity to develop creative ideas establishes a culture in which individual ideas are valued. Such a leader understands that the creative imagination of each individual within the organization can spark the creativity of others. The potential of this sort of spontaneity can have dramatic results throughout the institution, providing the yeast for innovative growth and change. The following example from a member of the leadership team at the College of DuPage, Illinois, illustrates this concept:

STAFF members were not examining operational efficiency as rigorously as desired. The president created a Risk Fund to promote efficient operation and accountability. Faculty and staff are encouraged to prepare proposals to borrow from the fund to accomplish an efficiency-related goal. The fund is paid back over several years from the savings which result from the accomplishment of the goal. Staff are encouraged to be accountable, to be concerned about efficiency, and to be creative in solving problems. Risk-taking is supported through the process.

This kind of activity reinforces the value of creative problem-solving and, at the same time, provides opportunities for institutional redirection. The understanding of various organizational components and how they must integrate for institutional effectiveness requires a knowledge base beyond the normal perspective that most people possess. This knowledge is enhanced by attending to the development of the individual in a variety of ways.

DEVELOPING FOLLOWERS

I n recent decades there has been increasing support for the view that the purposes of the group are best served through a relationship in which the leader helps his or her followers develop their own judgment and provides a nurturing environment that enables them to grow and become better contributors. The more that leaders are able to encourage followers to develop their own initiative, the more effective the leaders will be in promoting the followership to create something that can survive the departure of the leader (Gardner, 1987).

The ways in which followers are developed and the extent to which they are able to function independently within a team framework vary significantly from institution to institution. However, the importance of this underlying theme comes through loud and clear in our CEO interviews. Chancellor Larry Tyree, Dallas County Community College District, says:

I believe it begins with the CEO's philosophy and the way he or she values people. You need to like people, enjoy being with them, believe that all people have the potential to become better than they are, and believe that most people want to grow when given the opportunity. If that is your orientation, then I think you as the leader are committed to working hard with your faculty, staff, and administrative team in order to help them achieve their potential. As a result, and perhaps even more importantly, the payoff does not stop there. This prevailing attitude enables our people to work with students in such a way as to help them achieve their individual potential.

An important vehicle for helping followers achieve their potential is a development program that attends to the needs of faculty, staff, and administration in relation to the goals of the institution. Indeed, many colleges have components of staff development in place, but few encourage and provide the opportunity for the development of all. Staff development programs that promote individuals or small groups working in isolation minimize their own potential value. It is counterproductive to have one segment of the organization receiving professional development in isolation from the others. In attempting to incorporate the outcomes of a staff development opportunity, these individuals, or small groups, should not have to utilize time and energy to convince others, especially those they report to, of the value of an idea or concept. Rather the discussion should focus on the process of implementation.

Unfortunately, staff development programs rarely provide a "big picture" for participants. Individuals often come away with new knowledge and a high degree of motivation to implement it; however, if the individual's colleagues and/or superiors do not support the new knowledge, then both the knowledge and the motivation to implement it are lost. Moreover, a possible catalyst to stimulate others is lost, as well.

President Gunder Myran, Washtenaw Community College, Michigan, illustrates the importance of a staff development activity designed for institutional impact:

WE have initiated a management development approach, based on the concept of Executive Issues Management. This approach assists staff (along with the leader) in learning how to solve problems without blaming other persons or offices. It helps individuals learn how to understand others' needs, and their own, and then find ways to collaborate on solutions that are mutually beneficial. This approach creates a strategy that is very similar to the "win-win" and/or mutual gains approach to problem solving.

THIS approach suggests that people must be taught how to solve problems by attending to the needs of others, and there is a process to achieve this problem solving. First, you have to identify the problem in more detail than might occur normally. By determining the needs of the other person, you move toward strategies that focus on the situation and end up with solutions in which both parties feel that they have met their own needs and solved the problem.

Deci and Ryan (1985) note that quality performance is an indicator of the presence of intrinsic motivation. Transformational leaders, as we have indicated, motivate followers toward commitment and action in several ways:

1) by developing a process of expectation around individual roles;
2) by providing an environment for creative skills to originate and flourish;
3) by providing opportunities for increased knowledge through the development of followers.

The culmination of such directed motivation sets the stage for followers to maximize their potential and perform optimally.

PEAK PERFORMANCE

How is peak performance achieved in an organization? The transformational CEOs in our study recognize and place a value on the human resources within their institution, understanding that the institution can only be as effective as the quality, the vitality, and the commitment of the people within it. Leaders appreciate the differences in followers' characteristics and recognize that the leader's role is to move each follower as close to peak performance as possible.

Characteristically, one group of followers has an internal locus of control. To maximize the potential of these followers, outstanding leaders must provide an environment for optimum performance. Then the peak performers will intrinsically motivate themselves to be the best that they can be and to do the best that they can do. "The motivational bedrock will continue to be achievement and external mastery on the one hand, and self-development and internal mastery on the other" (Garfield, 1986, p. 300). These followers possess the ability to function at high levels, peak performance levels, whatever their tasks. And they give back to an institution work and loyalty in direct proportion to the latitude they are given and the value that is placed on their efforts.

Outstanding leaders must also lead a second, more challenging group of followers—a group with an external locus of control. Our transformational leaders motivate this group toward peak performance by demonstrating commitment and expectations and by providing a context for creative skills and development.

A common approach to inspiring followers, as noted by our leaders, is the creation of enthusiasm and excitement around important issues and tasks. Generating enthusiasm often results in follower participation and involvement. "People have a stake in an idea if they have participated in its creation and will work much harder, in a more dedicated way, to bring it to success" (Chancellor Bob Jensen, Rancho Santiago College, California).

When followers understand the expectations of the organization and have the desire and skills to perform, their ability to be effective participants is greatly enhanced. A member of the administrative team at Meridian Community College, Mississippi, noted:

THE president was effective in creating enthusiasm for cooperative action among all participants. He certainly utilized a creative approach to development of knowledge and awareness among individuals from four different institutions and agencies. This example is just one of many regular occurrences. He is a CEO who is not bound by tradition. He readily inspires his management team by example and stimulates us all to participate in the important mission of our community college.

While many of our CEOs expressed some apprehension about their own ability to motivate others, they were all cognizant of the effect that people external to the institution can have on the inspiration and motivation of followers. President Jim Hudgins, Midlands Technical College, South Carolina, addressed this issue:

OUR faculty and staff sometimes lose their appreciation of what it is they are accomplishing and contributing through their efforts. One of the things that I did to address this issue was to invite community leaders onto campus. I then shared with our faculty and staff the reports I received from these community

*leaders about how the college was valued in the community. This
helped us immensely in our planning for the future. At the same
time, the feedback from community leaders helped us toward
rebuilding our convictions about the value of this institution.
The result was that our people became believers in what we are
all about.*

Peak performance is not only difficult to achieve, but difficult to
sustain. What is most effective for the institution over an extended
period of time is not necessarily that large numbers of individuals perform at a peak level at the same time, but that there are some peak
performances occurring all the time. Enabling these peak performances
to happen requires knowledge and commitment on the part of the
leader. An illustration by President Jim Henderson, San Juan College,
New Mexico, follows:

---

*WE have attempted to study and identify elements that make
a great organization. What kinds of ingredients are essential?
We know that salaries are important, but we also believe that
there is more than that, that there has to be job satisfaction. The
results of our recent questionnaire dealing with situational analysis clearly indicated that employees were happy and they liked
their jobs here. That is exactly what we try to build into the environment. We all understand that we are here to serve students,
and so we want to make it fun, make it so that people want to
be here.*

---

*RECENTLY, we brought in someone from Disney World who
discussed with us what good organizations are doing to motivate their people and make them feel good. We attempt to incorporate those ingredients. It is important for people (all of us within
the organization) to model appropriate behavior. This modeling
starts with telephone behavior. We are very sensitive to how we
answer the telephone and how we react to people. I have high
expectations for our people and for our administrative team. They
have to be top performers and top people, but they also need to*

be stroked. We have built-in faculty awards, staff awards, and a number of different ways that we try to recognize excellence. I appreciate the efforts of our people, and I want to ensure they receive the recognition they so rightfully deserve.

CONCLUSION

Effective CEOs recognize that they must accomplish the mission of their colleges through empowering others. They instinctively recognize that their personal leadership behavior plays a major role in the development of leadership teams and, hence, the college. They resolve the crisis of availability by being physically present and personally emphasizing both tasks and morale-building behavior. Effective CEOs constantly sharpen their skills in observing and diagnosing team and college behavior. They demonstrate a wide range of tasking and consideration skills and use them appropriately. They see their teams and their colleges as living systems that are constantly in need of influence and attention. Our data lead us to conclude that community colleges that are characterized by faculty and staff participation, cohesive leadership teams, and total college collaboration, are led by CEOs who demonstrate the maximum empowerment of followers through motivation.

Motivation only *appears* to be a simple process of getting an individual to do what you want him or her to do, yet the process is amorphous and complex. Transformational leaders understand both the simplicity and the intricacies involved in successful motivation. Our CEOs understand this concept instinctively; thus, they work at inspiring and involving their followership.

Sharing is basic to the concept of shared vision. Shared vision is achieved, in part, by a leader's motivating his or her followership to accept this shared vision. It is the followers' acceptance that is the first manifestation of institutional transformation—a change that is accomplished through the leader's ability to transform people. The transformational leaders interviewed in this study understand the psychic knots that tie individual interests and institutional mission.

LEADERS AND THEIR VALUES

66 *Do not confuse leadership with status.... Do not confuse leadership with authority.... Do not confuse leadership with power.... Leadership is the process of persuasion or example by which an individual or leadership team induces a group to pursue an objective held by the leader or shared by the leader and followers.* *99*

JOHN W. GARDNER, *"Leaders and Followers"*

VALUES ORIENTATION: Demonstrated Competencies

A COMMITMENT TO LEARNING
A COMMITMENT TO QUALITY EDUCATION
A COMMITMENT TO ETHICAL BEHAVIOR
OPENNESS AND TRUST
CONSISTENT JUDGMENT
HUMOR AS INFLUENCE
LEADERSHIP THROUGH EXAMPLE

LEADERS AND
THEIR VALUES

INTRODUCTION

The fifth theme identified by the transformational CEOs was values—effectiveness blended with the moral aspect of leadership. In addressing this theme, we asked our presidents to discuss their personal values and share how these values affect their position. The transformational leaders reinforced the findings of Peters and Waterman in *In Search of Excellence* (1982): the chief executive officer is the most important individual influencing the excellence of a corporation. They noted that one of the CEO's most important roles is that of value leadership.

Value leadership is leadership by which the CEOs exemplify, through their behavior, the values upon which an organization is founded. Value leadership does not seek to command, but to influence. Value leadership does not seek to coerce, but to inspire. "Values are the leverage point for the whole internal impulse to excel, because they encompass not only *what* and *how* but *why*" (Garfield, p. 266). By exercising value leadership, the CEO sets the tone for an environment in which human and material resources can be used to their fullest potential to achieve the mission and goals of the organization and/or institution.

213

Ford Motor Company developed an excellent and succinct statement regarding its mission, *values*, and guiding principles. Ford's "mission is to improve continually our products and services to meet our
customers' needs." Ford indicates that *how* they *accomplish* their *mission*
is as *important* as the mission itself.

Fundamental to success for the Ford Motor Company are the following basic values:

---

*People—Our people are the source of our strength. They pro-
vide our corporate intelligence and determine our reputation and
vitality. Involvement and teamwork are our core human values.*

---

*Products—Our products are the end result of our efforts, and
they should be the best in serving customers worldwide. As our
products are viewed, so are we viewed.*

---

*Profits—Profits are the ultimate measure of how efficiently we
provide customers with the best products for their needs. Profits
are required to survive and grow.*

The guiding principles Ford has adopted to meet these values are:

---

*Quality comes first—To achieve customer satisfaction, the quality
of our products and services must be our number-one priority.*

---

*Customers are the focus of everything we do—Our work must
be done with our customers in mind, providing better products
and services than our competition.*

---

*Continuous improvement is essential to our success—We must
strive for excellence in everything we do: in our products, in their
safety and value—and in our services, our human relations, our
competitiveness, and our profitability.*

---

*Employee involvement is our way of life—We are a team. We
must treat each other with trust and respect.*

Dealers and suppliers are our partners*—The company must maintain mutually beneficial relationships with dealers, suppliers, and our other business associates.*

Integrity is never compromised*—The conduct of our company world-wide must be pursued in a manner that is socially responsible and commands respect for its integrity and for its positive contributions to society. Our doors are open to men and women alike without discrimination and without regard to ethnic origin or personal beliefs.*

In spite of some of the obvious differences that exist between the Ford Motor Company and a community college, Ford's mission, values, and guiding principles are both applicable and appropriate to today's community college.

Selznick (1957) stated that in both creating and maintaining an institution, leaders require techniques for infusing day-to-day behavior with long-run meaning and purpose. He noted that one of the most important of these techniques was the elaboration of socially integrating myths. Peters and Waterman (1982) reinforced this idea indicating that the excellent presidents they studied were collectors and tellers of stories, legends, and myths to support their basic beliefs. These stories, legends, and myths are a primary medium for transmitting the value system of the organizational culture. The focus of these activities is often on reported behaviors of the CEO or on instances in which a company performed well under pressure. Whatever the nature of the example, the significance of the stories was to reinforce qualities that were highly valued in the organizational culture. Peters and Waterman (1982) further suggest that when the CEO is directly involved in sharing myths during face-to-face interactions, the CEO is fulfilling an important aspect of his or her role as a value leader for the organization.

This face-to-face contact initiated by the CEO with followers within the organization also creates the opportunity to discover what people are doing and provides an opportunity to reward those who are doing their jobs well. This activity enables the CEO to be visible and engage in rich, informal communication. It also allows the CEO and follower to become involved in face-to-face interactions in the follower's own work space—an environment less formal and intimidating than that of the CEO's office—where the CEO can listen, share myths, and recognize follower competence and commitment.

As in the private sector, the CEOs of the community college play the primary role in setting the tone for excellence within their institution. The overriding theme, generated from both the interviewing process and from the participants' written educational philosophies, emphasized the importance of a comprehensive set of clearly defined institutional values. However, it is important to note these institutional values reflect the values of both the CEO and the institutional followers. Schoolcraft College, Michigan, is one example of an institution that has successfully meshed the personal values of the leader and followers with a common set of institutional values. As President Richard McDowell related:

*SEVERAL years ago we undertook not only to examine our own personal values, but also to try to translate those values into some organizational values that other people would buy into. We successfully achieved this objective through conducting a session in which we invited over forty campus leaders to discuss what it was about our college that they thought made us better than other colleges. The process generated about eighty separate values that were reflected by the following three values that we adopted. The first value was **quality** in everything we do. The second value was **caring**—caring for students, for staff and faculty, and for the people in the community. And the third value was **creativity**—developing the new and improving the old.*

The importance of value clarification and commitment to a set of values forms the base upon which excellence is built. Let us now examine the values that have been shared by some outstanding community college leaders.

A COMMITMENT TO LEARNING

I n *Higher Learning* Derek Bok examines the university environment and asks, "Is it still possible for academic leaders to bring about significant change?" He notes that "many observers seem to doubt it," but offers a more helpful reply of his own. Even though faculties properly represent the locus of educational policy-making, "it may be

too soon to write off the luckless administrators [who] possess attributes and powers that put them in a unique position to foster educational reform" (as cited in O'Neil, 1987, p. 40). This cautious but op-
timistic view surrounding the university president's educational role,
as reflected by Bok, is not shared by our outstanding community college CEOs. Those in the community college arena see a mandate to
anticipate and lead their respective institutions, to be responsive to the
educational reform needed to better serve their communities. The members of our transformational institutions, from the CEO to the rank
and file, relish the challenge to be responsive to community needs.
These institutions whose constituents understand and share the vision
of who they are and where they are going work in a creative, risk-taking
environment, confronting and achieving the changes necessary to serve
their communities better. "I believe so strongly in the mission of the
community college that it is obvious to all those I come in contact with
what our role is" (Chancellor Larry Tyree, Dallas County Community
College District).

At times, the message of the CEOs was filled with strong emotion
and deep inner commitment about the concept of mission and community. Chancellor Michael Crawford articulated what appeared to be
in the hearts of many of the outstanding CEOs we interviewed:

---

*OUR mission is achieved by constantly applying ourselves to what
we are really all about, and values have a great deal to do with
that. It is hard to nail down what is constant about the community college. However, I think now we are coming around to a
better understanding of what it is that we are all about. Those
people who are successful in this business, at whatever level, but
especially faculty members, are those who really have that deep,
gut-level, burning understanding that they are in this business
to serve people and to help people accomplish whatever their individual goals might be.*

---

*WE need to make sure that we keep the mission broad so that
we are dealing with the current crisis of literacy, as well as dealing with the more traditional transfer situation. We are moving
out in all those directions in an effort to serve our communities
better. I know we cannot be all things to all people, but both as
a chancellor and as an educator I am going to attempt to achieve*

*that goal. I think we ought to keep trying to be as many things
as we possibly can. I argue with those that think we ought to
narrow our mission. I disagree because I think we can deliver
the highest quality and still be a lot of things to a lot of people.
I believe very strongly in a broad, flexible mission.*

This idea seems to be the constant in all those who are committed
to the community college movement. Regardless of their educational
background, their experience, their age, where they came from, and
their specific role, they all have that burning desire to confront and
conquer the educational challenges facing the community college.

Another excellent example that reflects a president's commitment
to providing learning opportunities designed to meet the needs of the
community is that illustrated by President John Cavan, Southside Virginia Community College:

*OUR mission at Southside Virginia Community College is not
unlike that of our sister colleges throughout the nation. We provide educational opportunities to a wide range of constituencies
within our college's service area. In many ways, Southside Virginia epitomizes this educational philosophy. We are an extremely
comprehensive community college. On one end of the spectrum,
we have the largest sex equity program in the Commonwealth
of Virginia and the largest educational program for mothers
receiving funds for Aid to Dependent Children. We have the
largest inmate education program in the state as well. One of
the correction centers we serve is a maximum security prison that
houses Virginia's most dangerous inmates. (As an example of
our college's success in inmate education, 24.3 percent of the inmates housed in that maximum security prison are registered
college students. Enrollees in our inmate education program are
doing extremely well academically and providing some interesting challenges to our faculty.)*

ON the other end of the spectrum, we developed the first comprehensive honors program of its type at a community college in the Commonwealth of Virginia. This program has been highly successful and has acted as a catalyst for the formation of honors programs at other community colleges within the Virginia Community College System. Although not a large program, it certainly reflects on the college's thrust for excellence.

There has been a strong emphasis here on the importance of valuing others and providing the opportunity for followers to "share" in the development and implementation of change. The following statement by a member of the administrative team at Meridian Community College, Mississippi, illustrates this attitude:

ONE recent event brought out vividly how quickly and effectively our president acts to set values and demonstrate commitment. Recently, in order to develop knowledge and commitment to the 2 + 2 concept, he invited university representatives, community college staff, and a foundation representative to accompany him to community colleges in South Carolina and Pennsylvania. The 2 + 2 concept has not been understood and accepted by university representatives in our community. In order to develop programs, university representatives must be "educated" about 2 + 2 and how it has been effective in other locations of the country. The CEO did not try to convince them personally; he let success speak for itself. He took members of his management team with him to visit 2 + 2 sites, but he did not bias them in advance by telling them what to expect. He let them see and learn for themselves. He thus allowed his management team to share in his vision.

To meet today's challenges successfully, many leaders have strongly committed themselves to promoting and providing opportunities that facilitate the development of their followers. In order to respond and to create educational services for new constituencies, colleges must constantly find ways to expose faculty and staff to new methods of teaching and more efficient ways of administering our institutions.

A COMMITMENT TO QUALITY EDUCATION

O ver the past several years there has been increased concern nation-wide regarding the exit skills of our high school and college graduates:

OUR once unchallenged preeminence in commerce, industry, science, and technological innovation is being overtaken by competitors throughout the world. We report to the American people that while we can take justifiable pride in what our schools and colleges have historically accomplished and contributed to the United States and the well-being of its people, the educational foundations of our society are presently being eroded by a rising tide of mediocrity that threatens our very future as a Nation and a people. What was unimaginable a generation ago has begun to occur—others are matching and surpassing our educational attainments (National Commission on Excellence in Education, 1983, p. 5).

Yet we stand steadfast in our fundamental belief that

all, regardless of race or class or economic status, are entitled to a fair chance and to the tools for developing their individual powers of mind and spirit to the utmost. This promise means that all children by virtue of their own efforts, competently guided, can hope to attain the mature and informed judgment needed to secure gainful employment, and to manage their own lives, thereby serving not only their own interests but also the progress of society itself (National Commission on Excellence in Education, 1983, p. 5).

W. Edwards Deming is known as the father of the quest for quality in American and Japanese industrial circles. Through his life's work he has developed a process of organizational transformation through revitalized leadership. Deming (1988) suggested that quality is improved in three ways: through innovation in design of a service, through innovation in processes, and through improvement of existing processes. Hard work will not ensure quality, best efforts will not ensure quality, neither will gadgets, computers, or investment in machinery. A necessary ingredient for improvement of quality is the application of profound knowledge. There is no substitute for knowledge. Knowledge we have in abundance. We must learn to use it.

The transformational CEOs articulated the importance of quality education in a variety of ways; although their language differed, the message they shared was extremely consistent. "Our community colleges serve students. Students' needs and expectations must inform our work. Colleges best serve students by ensuring that the education provided is of the highest quality. Thus, the institutional values which we believe to be important are those which enable us to better serve students" (President Jess Parrish, Midland College, Texas).

Quality education, community college style, is not bound by only traditional classrooms. A member of the leadership team at Meridian Community College observed:

MERIDIAN Community College is situated in Meridian, Mississippi. Its district entails Lauderdale County with a combined city/county population of approximately 76,000, most of whom are blue-collar workers.

ALTHOUGH the city boasts an active community theatre group and a symphony, its residents were not exposed to other types of cultural arts on a regular basis. Two facts made it appear unlikely that any group would sponsor such a program: the community-at-large would not respond to expensive tickets for such programs, and an appreciative audience would have to be cultivated through an elaborate and creative promotional campaign.

VIEWING the lack of such a program as a detriment to the college students and faculty as well as community residents, MCC President William F. Scaggs mapped out a plan for the college to sponsor such a program. He committed the necessary funding and supported the presentation of a varied and adventuresome program. Since initiating that program in 1979, he has continued to support and expand the MCC Arts/Letters Series.

STUDENTS, faculty, and community people representing a veritable cross-section of Lauderdale County are now broadening their cultural horizons via the MCC Arts/Letters Series. Dancers, musicians, lecturers, authors, poets, storytellers, and theater troupes of state, regional, and national acclaim have brought exciting and stimulating programs to the college stage. Many of these programs have been taken to a variety of locations around the community to expose specific groups to a discipline, and there are periodic class dismissals for MCC students to see programs during the day rather than just in the evening. Students and faculty are admitted free of charge. The cost of the tickets has remained nominal in order to encourage community participation. The Series has won acceptance by the community and is now even showcased as an asset of this community for prospective industrial and business developers. The MCC Arts/Letters Series is indeed a prime example of Dr. Scaggs' commitment to "access and excellence" in the community college mission.

Commitment to quality has been translated into educational terms by all the presidents who participated in the study. Their commitment to the value of quality education was evidenced by their verbal and written comments. Dallas County Community College District notes that although high expectations may sometimes exceed what is immediately possible in a complex organization, providing excellent education is more likely to result when expectations are clear. Therefore, the district leadership holds to the following commitments:

WE serve students. Their needs and expectations must inform our work. We serve them best by ensuring that the education we provide is of the highest quality. Thus, the organizational values that we believe to be important are those which enable us to better serve students.

WE must insist upon **excellent performance** *from each employee through*

> *clear expectations and evaluation,*
> *continued professional growth,*
> *reward and recognition for outstanding achievement.*

WE must provide a **quality work environment** *for each employee through*

> *work that is meaningful, that is productive, and that encourages individual initiative and offers enjoyment;*
> *salary, benefits, programs, facilities;*
> *mutual support for each other and our work groups.*

BELIEVING these two tenets to be primary, we therefore assert the following behaviors to be crucial to the achievement of quality in our work:

> **Mutual Trust:** *We value each other as persons—sharing perspectives, accommodating differences, assuming motives are trustworthy. This quality undergirds the others.*
>
> **Honesty:** *We speak and act truthfully, without hidden agendas, admitting when we make mistakes or do not know, keeping commitments, avoiding silence when it may be misleading.*
>
> **Fairness:** *We treat each other justly, applying rules with equity, providing opportunity based on qualifications, giving each other the benefit of the doubt.*
>
> **Considerate, Open Communications:** *We share information, ideas, and feelings, listening carefully, speaking forthrightly, respecting opinions of colleagues.*
>
> **Cooperation:** *We work together to achieve common goals, looking beyond self-interest, remaining helpful in difficult situations, encouraging compromise and positive change.*
>
> **Creativity:** *We value originality and vision, freeing professionals to try something new, expecting follow-through, using ideas that work.*

Responsible Risk-taking: We respond well to challenges, considering carefully, acting although uncertainties remain, moving forward in spite of possible criticism.

BECAUSE these commitments and behaviors are of great significance, we hold them as essential to our task as educators, and we hold ourselves accountable to achieve them.

The outstanding leaders that we talked with emphasized the importance of and a value for commitment to quality education. However, the CEOs emphasized that education in a vacuum is not enough. They went on to say that this education must be interwoven with the ethics of a solid value system to ensure that quality education is achieved.

A COMMITMENT TO ETHICAL BEHAVIOR

With shared vision comes shared norms, expectations, and purposes. The moral fiber that encompasses institutional sharing is the ethical behavior modeled by the leader. John Gardner (1986) notes:

VALUES always decay over time. Societies that keep their values alive do so not by escaping the process of decay but by powerful processes of regeneration. There must be a perpetual rebuilding. Each generation must rediscover the living elements in its own tradition and adapt them to present realities. To assist in that rediscovery is one of the tasks of leadership (p. 23).

As we attempt to understand the nature of behavior in human organizations, particularly the community college, we need to be cognizant of the nebulous role of institutional conscience. By institutional conscience we mean a system of values which is embodied in the conscious or unconscious levels of an institution's personality against which attitudes, actions, and judgments are examined apart from any outside control (Brown, 1973). We also suggest that this institutional conscience is significantly affected by leader behavior.

Conscience also deals in values and is composed of many parts of human experience: background, thoughts, and feelings that are unique to each individual. Because of the interactions and associations of the individual, it is impossible to sort out and measure individual values in definite, objective terms. Likewise, a measurable group value cannot be obtained from collectively combining individual values. Thus, the conscience of an organization must be reflected in the leaders. This concept, in turn, reinforces our definition of transformational leadership: *the ability to influence, shape, and embed values, attitudes, beliefs, and behaviors consistent with increased staff and faculty commitment to the unique mission of the community college.*

THE most valuable guide available to the leader in his efforts to understand human nature is as complete an understanding of himself as he can possibly attain. The understanding of self, which comes with introspection, provides the responsible leader with one of the most fundamental attributes of effective leadership—integrity. In the meaning here intended, integrity implies that a person has developed, over time, a consistent ordering of his system of values, attitudes, and goals. In common terms, he has come to know his own mind, conscious and unconscious, and for what he stands and for what he will fight. In the effective leader, this kind of integrity is not alone a moral or intellectual qualification for appointment. It is an attribute functionally prerequisite to continuing effectiveness in directing day-to-day operations in human organization. The image of the leader is not his superficial self, but rather the personification of a system of values which he has demonstrated over time. When this manifestation is clear and consistent and reflects a quality of personal integrity, it is a powerful instrument (Brown, 1973, p. 22).

Fundamental factors of fairness, foresight, wisdom, and responsibility are valued elements in leader behavior, for these elements provide a clear-cut understanding of the leader that followers can comprehend.

However, Brown (1973) also notes that integrity is not a quality derived from logic alone. He suggests that the ability to draw intuitively upon one's total experience, of which logical reasoning is only a part, is a precious attribute of leadership, particularly to those in senior decision-making positions, and that the attribute of intuitive integrity is an important ingredient in leadership.

In interviews, our leaders reinforced this concept. They emphasized the importance of ethical behavior and talked about it from several perspectives. The following statement by President Bob Riley, Howard County Junior College District, Texas, is one such perspective:

I have always believed that outstanding administration can only occur in an environment that communicates the worth and dignity of all persons. I deal honestly and fairly with all persons with whom I come into contact, and I expect my administrative team to do the same. I have always found that when faced with tough decisions, it is easier when you have created and work in an environment of honesty and straightforwardness. Trying to find an easy way out of a difficult situation just doesn't work for me. I will not tolerate anything less than honest and sincere answers to inquiries about the college operation. When high standards of integrity are communicated to the college constituency, the opportunity for complete confidence in the organization exists. I feel that everyone associated with the college should expect and receive treatment with the highest standards of integrity.

Riley's comments reinforce the idea that for a leader to permeate an organization's conscience, the leader must strongly communicate what it is that he or she values. The ways in which the influence of conscience moves down through an organization parallel those other behaviors of leadership. Leaders model behavior; they set the tone; through their ability to let their followers know who they are and what they represent, leaders demonstrate their commitment to ethical behavior.

This point was clearly illustrated by a member of the administrative team from Maricopa County Community College District:

ABOUT ten years ago, the Maricopa District was having a great deal of difficulty with the Governing Board. Individual members were contacting employees directly for information and

*involving themselves inappropriately in the day-to-day operations
of the District. Activities of the Board were having direct and
very counterproductive effects on the organization. There was
a great deal of polarization and unethical behavior on all sides.*

*AT a particularly crucial point, Dr. Elsner tendered his resig-
nation during a Governing Board meeting, stating, in effect, that
he could not and would not be party to unethical behavior. His
personal and professional ethics would not allow him to continue
as chancellor unless the situation changed.*

*THE Governing Board agreed to adopt a Code of Ethics, and
their actions had a great impact on the management of the District. By his actions, Dr. Elsner established the level of ethical
behavior he expected for Maricopa—from the Governing Board
to the individual employee!*

This ethical behavior is further strengthened by the conditions that
enable the risks of transformation in an institution to take place—
openness and trust.

OPENNESS AND TRUST

Of all the values shared by CEOs interviewed in this study, openness and trust, in conjunction with integrity, were identified
by all. They collectively felt that how they were perceived in
relation to these values permeated both their internal and external environments. These values enabled them to set a tone, a climate, within
their respective institutions. The CEOs' ability to achieve whatever institutional success they were realizing had little to do with elaborate
facilities or high levels of financial support, but rather with the openness and trust that exist within the institution.

The importance of such values was clearly identified by Peters and
Waterman (1982). They expected that excellent companies would be
distinguished simply by a unique set of cultural attributes. However,
what emerged from their study of the successful corporations was that
almost every excellent company had a strong leader. The chief executives of the management for excellence were persons who served as

value leaders for their organizations, managing the organizational culture to create and sustain a climate supportive of excellence.
The importance of the CEO as value leader was stressed repeat-
edly throughout *In Search of Excellence*. In the opening pages of their
book, Peters and Waterman (1982) referred to Chester Barnard's as-
sertion that "the leader's role is to harness the social factors in the organization, to shape and guide values" (p. 6). *In Search of Excellence*
devoted an entire chapter to an explication of the principle "Hands
On, Value Driven," which focuses on the importance of the CEO's role
as value leader for the organizational culture. The chapter concluded
with the statement that a CEO's most important role is to serve as an
organization's value leader, "clarifying the value system and breathing
life into it" (p. 291). Clearly, management for excellence theory holds
that managing the values of the organizational culture is one of the
most important contributions that a leader makes.

Another significant component associated with openness and trust
was highlighted by Stewart McLaurin, President of Kilgore Junior College, Texas:

---

*IT is my belief that effective leaders can ingest a large volume
of information from a wide audience and take that information
so that it sifts through the screen to the benefit of all. I rely heavily
for input on both formal channels such as administrative and
advisory councils and informal sources such as my monthly
luncheons with groups of randomly selected college employees.
It is important that people don't work out of deference to you.
A challenge of leadership is to get that rapport, that relationship with people, so that input will be realistic, critical, and
analytical. It takes time to develop that type of collegial
environment.*

Bennis and Nanus (1985) suggest that openness and trust imply
accountability, predictability, and reliability. We seem to know when
these elements are present; we also know when they are absent. When
attributes of predictable and consistent behavior are present, followers
within the organization have an increased sense of security.

CONSISTENT JUDGMENT

The unstable, external environment surrounding the community college has a significant impact on the internal workings of the organization. Declining enrollments, diminished resources, and increased student diversity compounded by underprepared learners are some of the problems faced not only by CEOs, but by all those involved in the community college. These problems often create a sense of uncertainty and, to some extent, insecurity within the minds of followers in the institution.

Predictable behavior exhibited by those in leadership roles throughout the institution in dealing with such uncertainties minimizes concern and insecurity. Consistent judgment has a stabilizing effect on followers by lending itself to a culture that provides an attitude of efficacy; that is, problem solving occurs in a predictable and consistent manner, minimizing crisis management and resulting in the collective belief that we as an institution can effectively handle critical challenges. This is accomplished, in part, through the establishment of a systems process that provides for the development of shared goals, allowing for routine, problem-solving, and innovative objectives.

An example of consistent judgment has been provided in the following example by a member of the administrative team at Danville Area Community College, Illinois:

THE situation that Dr. Lingle is handling in an impressive way is the process of reducing our personnel budget line item by $200,000 within the next two years. A number of factors have contributed to this situation including enrollment concerns, declining EAV, failure on the part of the state to pass a tax increase, and others. Dr. Lingle has taken the lead in addressing this situation in a very thorough and understanding way. He has done many of the things that a successful CEO does in these situations. He confides in his staff with a great deal of candor, he has addressed all campus constituents, and he has held a Board retreat to convey thoroughly his plan of action. His position has been to take a proactive approach. These are only a few of the many actions he has taken to strategically accomplish what needs to be done. I would be remiss not to say that he has his weaknesses, as we all do, but there is no other person I would rather

have at the top of our organization as we go through these
challenging times.

———————

This approach, in concert with wise decision-making and consistent judgment, not only facilitates the day-to-day operations but results in found time, enabling the leader and followers to direct their energies toward the shared vision and the planning necessary to accomplish that vision.

Another aspect of confidence gained from sound judgment is the ability to meet the unexpected. When an institution is not functioning in a state of crisis management at all times, the unexpected crisis can be handled with greater efficiency and effectiveness. An example of crisis in isolation was shared by a member of the leadership team from Sinclair Community College, Ohio:

———————

DURING a period of one week, two floods resulting from a city
water main break destroyed library facilities, the cafeteria, chemis-
try labs, and common facilities. The estimated cost of this damage
was $3 million. This was a circumstance unfamilar to college
administrators, but it was handled superbly. The Board was
immediately informed and kept current on a daily basis; faculty
and staff were invited to meet at 7:00 a.m. each morning to receive
updated information and assignments; the leadership team met
every evening to plan the following day's activities; the president
met with the media daily in an effort to keep the public informed;
and the president and vice-president for instruction were involved
in radio and TV call-in shows to inform the community as to
what to expect when coming to the campus. Students lost only
one week of classes, and what appeared to be a major disaster
for the college and its constituents resulted in some positive
outcomes. The community rallied to provide various types of
support to the institution, including donations, moving of books
at no charge, the freeze-drying of valuable books, and food provided
and delivered at no charge. And perhaps most important, public
attitude and respect were enhanced for the college and our CEO.

———————

President Byron McClenney, Community College of Denver, rein-forces the need for consistent judgment:

WITH all the talk about leadership these days we sometimes forget that group movement toward defined ends is the only way to demonstrate that leadership has really been exerted. What I am trying to say is that skillful college leaders must be able to use sound judgment in conducting college operations in order for the institution to achieve the purposes for which it was created. No longer is the primary emphasis on process and resources, but rather on an increased concentration of results and learning outcomes.

There are no guarantees that consistent judgment will eliminate all problems; however, it provides a framework that enables an organi-zation to deal more effectively with uncertainties. The context of relia-ble and consistent judgment is often perceived to be rigid, with little room for levity. Some of our outstanding CEOs indicated that humor can play an important role in problem-solving and wise decision-making.

HUMOR AS INFLUENCE

The literature on leadership supports the fact that humor is a power-ful tool that can be used to influence followers. However, humor did not prove to be a significant factor in the interviews conducted with the CEOs in our study. Although followers rated their CEOs highly on the Multifactor College Leadership Questionnaire, the item related to humor was not seen as a significant influence on follower behavior. The conclusion that we draw from this phenomenon is that humor is typically used in a more casual context than writing, responding to in-terviews, or completing questionnaires. Therefore, while this behavior remains in our model, the methods that we used to elicit it did not pro-duce meaningful, significant findings.

LEADERSHIP THROUGH EXAMPLE

Socrates once said, "The way to gain a good reputation is to endeavor to be what you desire to appear." Indeed, the CEOs studied here truly believe that the behavior they model has a significant impact on their respective organizations. This statement is consistent with the literature surrounding the concept of culture. "There is no doubt that actions speak louder than words. I think modeling is extremely important" (Chancellor Tom Van Gronigen, Yosemite Community College District, California). If a leader possesses an understanding of self, while at the same time understands that everything he or she does in the organization communicates something to the followers, then it is possible to begin consciously to embed values, attitudes, and beliefs. This, in turn, establishes a culture and climate which allow a greater likelihood for organizational success. A leader can speak long and hard about excellence and quality, values and beliefs, but the message will be delivered only if the leader pays attention to those areas of the organization that are the same as those he or she says are believed in and valued.

This point is well made by President Robert Miller, Quinebaug Valley Community College, Connecticut:

I believe that setting an example is very important. I feel a strong obligation to set an example in terms of my own personal conduct and in terms of the way in which I interpret my philosophical beliefs and values. I try to live these values in my day-to-day life. I apply them in the way in which I interact with my family, both privately and in public, and through positions I take on issues that are important to me. I am also very cognizant of the example that I hope the college sets for those in the community. I think that is why the work in the community college sector has been so important to me. It provides the opportunity to work with people in all walks of life, from all backgrounds, and to try to inspire them to raise their sights, to live out the kinds of values that are important in our American society.

If acted out in an institution, the adage, "Do as I say, and not as I do!" creates an environment of distrust in which the leader lacks credibility. It is important that the leader pay attention to and exhibit behaviors consistent with his or her values and beliefs.

A collage of the comments from Presidents Al Philips, Gunder Myran, Jim Hudgins, and Chancellor Larry Tyree exemplifies the importance of credible behavior:

IT is not an overtly conscious act, but I try to motivate faculty, staff, and students through my strong commitment to my job, my commitment to the institution, and my desire for this college to be the best community college. My enthusiasm for the college is contagious. It is important to show people, and I don't mean to just put on a show; they must be shown a genuine enthusiasm, a genuine sense that what we are doing is important, valuable, and wholesome and is worthy of a life commitment. I am willing to work hard, and I demonstrate that I am willing to do the kind of things that I ask others to do. I prefer to motivate people by example.

The message of this chapter is that modeling appropriate behavior is important. Our CEOs recognize that the behavior that they exhibit truly has an impact on their institution in relation to organizational effectiveness. But this modeling has an intangible and even greater impact on the lives of the students, for whom the institution was created. As a gardener attends to the growth and development of a plant through care, sunlight, and water, so our CEOs nurture and cultivate the growth and development of those within the institution. By modeling values that transform the organization, the CEO influences the behaviors of others who, in turn, influence attitudes toward learning in the classroom.

CONCLUSION

The values that a leader brings to the position of president have a significant impact on the institution. As value leaders, the CEOs studied both consciously and intuitively blend follower values and institutional values in concert with their own. This totality is the undergirding for the community college, and from it flows vision, influence, cohesion, and motivation.

Jefferson Community College's excellent institutional values statement provides an inspiring conclusion to this chapter:

*OUR primary goal is to be a quality institution, operated by dedi-
cated people providing educational services and opportunities
which meet the needs of our students and community. We aspire
to be recognized in our community as a caring institution, dedicated to high academic standards in our credit and non-credit
programs. As a publicly supported community college, we make
every effort to provide opportunities for the educational development of our students and a fulfulling work environment for our
faculty and staff. When students enroll in the college and when
employees are hired, we expect them to commit themselves to these
institutional values.*

CHAPTER 11

WOMEN IN LEADERSHIP ROLES *

❝ *GLAUCON: There will be ruling men who are morally good and noble.*
SOCRATES: And ruling women, too.
GLAUCON: Don't suppose that what I have said about leadership applies more to men than to women. **❞**

PLATO, 4th Century B.C.

TRANSFORMATIONAL LEADERSHIP: Gender Differences

VISION

INFLUENCE ORIENTATION

PEOPLE ORIENTATION

VALUES

MULTIFACTOR COLLEGE LEADERSHIP QUESTIONNAIRE

---

*Rosemary Gillett-Karam developed Chapter 11 from her dissertation which examined transformational leadership and gender differences of community college presidents identified in Phase I of this study.

WOMEN IN
LEADERSHIP ROLES

INTRODUCTION

The literature and research on college presidents have failed to analyze a new dynamic of leadership in America today: the emergence of a growing number of women as college and university CEOs. Although the number of women who are executives of colleges and universities remains small, trends indicate that more and more women will assume leadership positions throughout our society, whether in academia, politics, or business. Changing social and cultural norms have been responsible for this emergence of women in positions of leadership. Over the past 25 years we have seen an erosion of the social and cultural barriers that had previously prevented women from attaining executive positions. Male-centered biases and patriarchal thinking have been critically challenged by many in the literature (Woolf, 1938; de Beauvoir, 1949; Rich, 1977) and in research (Horner, 1971; Miller, 1976; Kanter, 1977; Bernard, 1981; Gilligan, 1982; Shakeshaft, 1987). Common among all these thinkers is their rejection of the treatment of women as deficit or discrimination models, and the need for and understanding of women's voice in scholarship.

Gilligan (1982), writing from the tradition of the philosophies of Locke, Mill, and Hume, challenged the human development philosophy

237

of Kohlberg (1972) and others when she reported that women's development is equal to but separate from that of men. Kohlberg's (1972) theory suggested that mankind has six stages of development; people advance along these stages by moving from deferring to authority, to
satisfying their own needs, to seeking others' approval, to valuing the
social order, to associating morality with the rights and standards endorsed by society, to thinking in terms of self-choices, based on universal
principles of justice (ethic of justice-rights). Gilligan's challenge to Kohlberg's theory, which he claimed was universally applicable, is based on
her objection to his single-track conception of human and moral development. She claims that difficulties arise when the same criteria for
moral maturation are applied to both women and men. Moreover, she
rejects the idea that there is only one correct way to pursue truth and
justice or self-autonomy based on moral development. In her empirical studies of women, she observed that women also are characterized
by levels and stages of progress of moral maturation, including the following six stages of development: personal survival, recognition of the
selfishness of caring only for self, taking responsibility for personal actions, conformity with and self-sacrifice for others (goodness), concern
for truth (dissipation of tension between self and others), and finally
interdependence of care for self and others. These stages focus on the
ethic of care, rather than on Kohlberg's ultimate stage, the ethic of
justice-rights. In Gilligan's research the moral problem (arising from
liberalism and social contract theory) comes from conflicting responsibilities rather than from competing rights. She claims that research
cannot continue to diminish the voice of women and that the process
of human and social development can be viewed from the voices of
both women and men. She writes:

---

*TO understand how the tension between responsibilities and
rights sustains the dialectic of human development is to see the
integrity of two disparate modes of experience that are in the end
connected. While an ethic of justice proceeds from the premise
of equality—that everyone should be treated the same—an ethic
of care rests on the premise of nonviolence, that no one should
be hurt. In the representation of maturity, both perspectives con-
verge in the realization that just as inequality adversely affects
both parties in an unequal relationship, so too violence is de-
structive for everyone involved. This dialogue between fairness*

*and care can not only provide a better understanding of rela-
tions between the sexes but also gives rise to a more comprehensive portrayal of adult work and family relationships (Gilligan,
1982, p. 174).*

Gilligan (1982) has influenced the writing of a new generation of
researchers who portray and examine the voices of women in various
disciplines (Lyons, 1983; Noddings, 1984; Belenky, et al., 1986; Kittay
and Meyers, 1987).

In the discipline of education, too, research has focused on the
emerging and developing status of women. Solomon (1985), Rosenberg
(1982), Simeone (1987), Komarovsky (1985), and Shakeshaft (1987) have
written about women in higher education and educational administration. In a few cases, studies have examined women as college presidents (Berry, 1979; Taylor, 1981; Evans, 1985). Moreover, in the last
five years more and more dissertation studies have focused on women
in leadership positions in colleges and universities. Only a few studies
have compared women and men college presidents (Miller, 1987; Gillett-
Karam, 1988); in each of those studies, differences between women and
men were reported in leadership behaviors.

Twenty-one women college presidents from throughout the nation
were named in Phase I as outstanding community college presidents;
all of those women were interviewed. They represent about one-third
of the total number of women nationwide who are community college
CEOs. The women of the study are listed in Appendix 11. Twenty-one
male college presidents, all of whom were "blue chippers," were also
interviewed. Comparisons were made on the basis of the three instruments that were used for the norm group and the "blue chippers" of
this study: the Presidential Information Questionnaire (Appendix 5),
the interview process (Appendix 7), and the Multifactor College Leadership Questionnaire (Appendices 8 and 9). Although we were primarily
interested in the question of how differences by sex or gender affected
leadership, we nevertheless assumed that effective leadership is not dependent on the question of gender. Our presidents were all transformational leaders; therefore, we sought to discover the strengths of their
behaviors as effective and exemplary presidents. It is critical to state at
the onset of this female-male comparison that our findings focused on
the behavioral strengths of the transformational presidents and that the
extent to which those strengths were exhibited sometimes had a feminine predominance and sometimes had a masculine predominance.

The differences we observed are not based on deficit behaviors; rather, they indicate areas of unusual strength.

The women of the study exhibited strong characteristics in all the dimensions of leadership, and in general their interview "scores" matched those of the men studied. When we compared exemplary female and male college presidents, we found areas of leadership behaviors in which women demonstrated stronger patterns of behaviors than did the men and other areas in which men demonstrated stronger behavioral patterns than did the women. We also found that women and men differed according to their biographical, experiential, and time utilization data. The two instruments which measured leadership behavior, the interview process based on the transformational leadership behaviors and the Multifactor College Leadership Questionnaire, did not demonstrate gender differences when evaluated overall on the basis of the cluster dimensions of vision, influence orientation, people orientation, motivation orientation, or values orientation. We did find differences, however, in the item analysis in the interview process—six of the 34 items listed below were found to have "feminine" or "masculine" characteristics of leadership behaviors.

Table 11.1

LEADERSHIP BEHAVIORS

FEMININE CHARACTERISTICS	MASCULINE CHARACTERISTICS
VISION Takes appropriate risks to bring about change.	
INFLUENCE Is able to cause followers to solve problems to work together.	Is characterized by a bias for action.
PEOPLE Demonstrates respect and caring for individual differences.	Rewards others contingent on their effort and performance.
VALUES Builds openness and trust through personal and professional behavior.	

Motivation as a cluster dimension was not found to have greater strengths for either women or men. We begin our examination of the feminine and masculine characteristics of leadership with the dimension variable **vision**.

VISION

T he literature supports the notion that vision is an essential quality of each of the attributes of the transformational leadership behaviors. Tichy and Devanna (1986) say:

VISION has two fundamental elements. One is to provide a conceptual framework or paradigm for understanding the organization's purpose—the vision includes a roadmap. The second important element is the emotional appeal: the part of the vision that has a motivational pull with which people can identify (p. 130).

To Bennis and Nanus (1985) "a vision is a target that beckons;" one of the critical factors which distinguishes a leader from a manager for these authors is "attention on vision: the leader operates on the emotional and spiritual resources of the organization, on its values, commitment and aspirations" (pp. 88–89). Walters (1987) said it most simply and succinctly: "Leadership means *vision* first and above everything else" (p. 19).

A member of the leadership team at Central Piedmont Community College said this about President Ruth Shaw:

THE college had a dispirited administration without a clear mission or unity of purpose. About a dozen vice-presidents ran uncoordinated programs on a decentralized basis. Our CEO reduced the number of vice-presidents, formed an executive cabinet, and held retreats to focus on a statement of purpose and mission. Then she empowered appropriately and instigated new designs of management. Slowly, the collective vision took place. Her correctives were handled with firmness, grace and consideration for the individuals involved. As a result, I expect us to remain a "top five" community college.

President Lois Callahan of the College of San Mateo spoke of vision and the connection between the vision of the leader and that of the college staff and faculty:

ONE of the things I do for the future of this institution is to clearly state the priorities for the college. Then as time progresses, we measure and critique those priorities. I think I establish a vision of what the college might be like and then articulate that generally among the faculty and with the administration to determine if there is consensus around my vision. If there isn't consensus, I continue to work on the idea, recognizing that the rest of the institution is not quite ready to see the vision in the same way I do. I think people are proud of what we have done; they can see movement in the institution. I wouldn't want to leave the impression that the president is the only one who has vision, but I do think the president is in the position of supporting and tying together the separate pieces that come from the members of the college and the community so that they come together for a whole vision for the institution.

President Flora Mancuso Edwards, Middlesex County College, New Jersey, expressed the concept of vision most eloquently: "The hardest thing to pull off is to convince people to dream and not be afraid. Then the next hardest thing is not letting them pull out of it."

By examining the **vision** theme with its seven attributes, we compared the female and male participants in the study for single-item comparisons. Figure 11.1 demonstrates the results of that comparison.

The question of leadership behavior and gender difference was demonstrated statistically in the behavior **"taking risks."** Unlike findings from early literature (Horney, 1967), which saw women deferring to male authority figures (i.e., unwilling to take risks to speak out), the female presidents of this study were willing to take risks to a greater extent than were our male presidents. For many of the college presidents' risk-taking had become almost second nature because they came to the presidency in a college surfeit with problems, such as those with curriculum, with boards, with budgets, with faculty, with the community, and with other administrators.

Figure 11.1   **VISION: Comparing Females and Males**

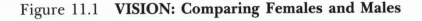

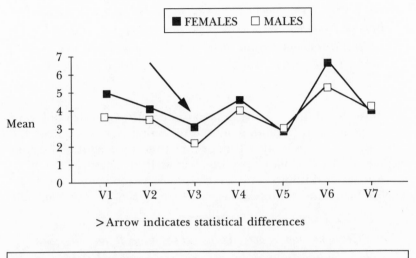

>Arrow indicates statistical differences

V1	Future orientation	V5	Articulating mission
V2	Shaping of future	V6	Sharing vision
V3	Taking risks	V7	Accessing students
V4	Taking action		

President Brunetta Wolfman, Roxbury Community College, Massachusetts, was the college's seventh president in nine years. Moreover, Roxbury had been moving from one temporary location to another and was in its third location when she was hired. She noted:

RISK-TAKING was something that was a given when I came to the college. It was important to redefine what the community wanted. They needed a new campus, they needed some stability, and they needed an academic program that would allow student success. What I did was to pull all this together and begin to write and talk about the future of the college. Faculty and others said to me, "You're the president—you make the decisions!" I had to risk their taking a new educational route to their own understanding. I replied to them, "I have to figure out with you the why and the what." Many were skeptical at the beginning, but later they came to recognize the benefits of what we could do together. We got a new campus! It was just the kind we needed, where students and faculty and staff all work together and learn from one another. We used a democratic process and created a multi-cultural egalitarian community in doing so. For me, the risk of breaking with tradition was well worth it.

President Marjorie Blaha, Solano Community College, California, talked about the uncertainties of funding both in her own college and in the state. Obviously, after Proposition 13 was passed in California, placing a rollback on local taxes which funded education, all the state's educational institutions suffered. Dr. Blaha had to contend with the state problems and her own college's budget quagmire. She remarked:

PRIOR to my coming here, the budget situation at the college was so bad. Feelings were so intense that the board had stepped in and taken over budget development. The board literally took it away from my predecessor: it descended on the administration and the institution directly—the college was experiencing a major crisis. I had to have a plan that would do more than pacify the board, and therefore I had to risk the kind of decision that the institution had never heard of—establishing a budget development committee that integrates budget planning with institutional planning.

THE committee is made up of representation from faculty, classified, management, and students; it keeps the board informed but not involved. What had to happen here was the board and the college family had to form some consensus on the values and attitudes we wanted to have at this college. We needed a participatory framework; we didn't have that. We wanted the proper assignment of roles for the board; we did not have that. Now the board members are quite relieved not to have that responsibility. I don't want to sound like a Pollyanna; there are still plenty of people who don't like the results, but they cannot say that they do not have an opportunity to participate.

A member of the leadership team at Lake Michigan College, Michigan, talked about the personal risk that President Anne Mulder took when she applied for state funding:

THE college was not in a situation of financial exigency—we had sufficient funding to continue what we were doing. Dr. Mulder felt it was "now or never" and laid out her concerns about future funding campaigns. She organized a campus effort and hired consultants (after she got board approval, a task in itself). We won with a two-to-one victory! Subsequent events have proven the president correct. Even six months later would have been too late. Most of the administrators had a significant involvement in the campaign. But mostly, the idea to go for it was the president's. It was an example of a president being able to take a risk and having others see that the risk was necessary in order to move the institution forward.

A member of the leadership team at Bristol Community College, Massachusetts, had this to say about President Eileen Farley:

WE had always talked about affirmative action, but we had made no real active effort to recruit minorities to our campus. It was easy to point to our books and say, "See, there it is: we do have a policy on affirmative action!" But that was just lip service. Dr. Farley was willing to risk the ennui and, in some cases, the opposition against active recruitment for minorities in our community and college. She authorized a strong recruitment effort, began advertising, went on recruitment searches, used personal contacts in minority communities to encourage applications, and provided incentives for successful efforts. In the 1987–1988 school year, three new minority faculty and two minority administrators were hired. Others were hired in technical and support services. I'll give Dr. Farley credit; she took risks that no one else was ever committed to take. Now we're all proud of her efforts.

INFLUENCE ORIENTATION

Kotter (1988) writes in *The Leadership Factor*: "Good leadership moves people in a direction that is genuinely in their real long-term best interests. It does not march people off a cliff. It does not waste their scarce resources. It does not build up the dark side of their human nature" (p. 17). Gardner (1986) put it this way:

WE need leaders in our organizations and in the nation who can bring alive the whole, down-the-line network of individuals with that kind of capacity to share the leadership task. Such a network will enliven and strengthen our society at every level. Sharing of leadership tasks will result in a more responsive and responsible system: this requires leaders who can delegate responsibility, who consult and listen, who have respect for human possibilities, who help us to help ourselves, and who help us grow. We must have leaders who are enablers, who help us remove obstacles to our effective functioning, who help us see and pursue shared purposes. Lyman Bryson said, "A democratic way of doing anything is a way that best keeps and develops the intrinsic powers of men and women" (p. 18).

President Patsy Fulton, Brookhaven College, Texas, articulates the role of leadership in the following statement and assumptions:

I believe Bennis when he talks about the fact that the leader must be able to articulate the mission and the vision. When I came to Brookhaven, I did a lot of listening. I still listen, and then I take what I hear and match it to my audience.

COLLABORATION is the critical element of my presidency. Why must we think as a group? It is because of the students: we care about the students and what students need; our job is to support what they need. My leadership style is collaboration, participation, listening and thinking and acting on what is ahead.

---

*AS far as I am concerned, if I can't see that picture of what is
ahead, then I don't need to be where I am. Our Directions Task
Force is marvelous because we really do some good thinking. We
started it with a reading list and excellent data. People don't
want to break at these meetings. They don't want to leave! I came
to Brookhaven believing I had better be straight with my audience.
I value honesty and fairness and the ability to disagree on issues.*

Both the feminine and the masculine characteristics of leadership
behaviors ("is able to cause followers to solve problems to work together" and "is characterized by a bias for action," respectively) are
represented in the following figure:

Figure 11.2   INFLUENCE: Comparing Females and Males

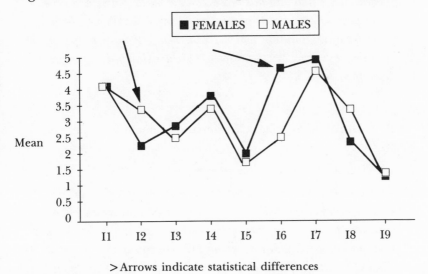

> Arrows indicate statistical differences

I1	Delegating authority	I6	Acting collaboratively
I2	Acting positively	I7	Listening and networking
I3	Tasking and consideration	I8	Being highly visible
I4	Sharing decision-making	I9	Being highly energetic
I5	Allowing others influence		

President Barbara Guthrie-Morse, West Virginia Northern Community College, West Virginia, talked about her leadership style in the following way:

I am a leader who uses a collaborative style. I like to hire the best and the smartest people I can get. There are so many things in which I don't have depth that I can balance out by hiring the most qualified people available for the job. Then I turn them loose as professionals to do their jobs.

I work collaboratively by having an open door and a computer. After I've written a draft copy, I turn to my "experts" and let them have a go at it. And vice-versa. In working on a budget problem, for example, I like to get several views from several sources. We individually bring pieces that we fit together collaboratively. I find that this process allows me to understand most of the pluses and minuses of most problems; it makes me a better defender of the solution which I can then articulate to groups outside the college. My solutions are always stamped "collaborative effort."

President Marilyn Schlack, Kalamazoo Community College, Michigan, said:

I am a consensus leader. I gather together many points of view and let every single person know that he or she has an important role to play. My style of leadership may change based on a situation: sometimes I'm caring and sometimes I'm directive. I tend to be inward and evaluate and assess what is going well and what needs to be changed in terms of greater effectiveness. I hope I'm a growing leader.

President Phyllis Peterson, Diablo Valley College, California, defined her leadership as consultative:

I'M very consultative in my style of leadership. For example, in our long range planning for coordination, we have developed a decision-making diagram which is based on participation, consultation, and consensus orientation. Input is dependent on the various constituent groups of the college, including the faculty senate and the cabinet. Although I have final decision-making authority, the decisions I make are not authoritarian. They are developed out of participation by key groups and actors from throughout the college and sometimes from throughout the community.

The male college presidents also were outstanding in the behavior **acting positively** (or "is characterized by a bias for action"). President John Kotula, Delaware Technical and Community College, spoke frankly about problems of racial divisiveness that had affected his college campuses:

STUDENTS had begun to make decisions about where to go to college not on the basis of programs offered but on the basis of the location of the school. The faculty were divided as well. That's no way to run a college. We had white and black racists. I think I treated everyone fairly, but I'm not soft. I saw a problem that was driving a wedge in our education delivery; it needed to be eliminated. Moreover, I believed we could establish a model campus. And if you go there now, you'll see that it is true. We don't have racial problems there. What I did was to merge the two campuses administratively. The move worked!

PEOPLE ORIENTATION

Both the women and the men of the study exhibited strengths in their people orientations that could be highlighted as feminine characteristics and masculine characteristics of behavior. The women mentioned "demonstrates respect and caring for individual differences" as a primary consideration in their relationships with people; their caring and respect for others was a theme which dominated their people skills. For the men of the study, the theme which dominated others in terms of people skills was their emphasis on rewards: the men of the study demonstrated a high regard for rewarding others on the basis of performance and effort. The figure that follows notes these differences:

Figure 11.3   **PEOPLE: Comparing Females and Males**

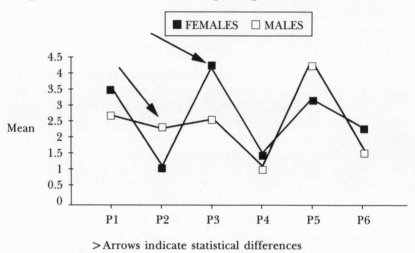

>Arrows indicate statistical differences

P1	Recognizing culture	P4	Meeting needs
P2	Rewarding others	P5	Valuing students
P3	Caring/respecting others	P6	Valuing others

It is not surprising that the concept of caring and respect for others was significantly correlated with gender. When one reviews the literature in women's studies, both Gilligan (1982) and Noddings (1984) use the concept as the basis of their studies of women in the fields of both moral development and education. For Gilligan, the caring or connection mode is that attribute that she posits against Kohlberg's (1972) justice rights mode which he, at one time, claimed was the ultimate stage of moral development. It is Gilligan's contention that "the different voice" that women contribute to the theory of moral development is that of **caring**. Noddings (1984), too, builds on an ethic of caring and of love. She argues that the mother's experience of caring and every-one's remembrance of being cared for constitute the basis of ethics. In her view, the ethic of caring gives joy to human existence: it is the recognition of and longing for relatedness that form the foundation of the ethic of care. Further, it is interesting to note the *cluster* of these three variables of connectedness and caring, collaboration, and trust. The three seem to be related empirically, but only the variable pair **"caring"** and **"openness"** has any statistical relevance; i.e., the quali-ties and behaviors involved with the variable caring are related to the qualities dealing with openness and trust; much of the variance of car-ing can be accounted for by openness and trust, and vice versa.

President Shirley Gordon, Highline Community College, Washing-ton, talked about how she valued her staff. She cited a campus crisis:

SINCE the early 1980s we have had to contend with financial reductions caused by the declines in our FTEs and state resources. We had to refocus the direction the college was taking, and at the same time we had to decrease our staff. We tried to accom-plish our changes without RIFing faculty and staff. We used every resignation and retirement as an opportunity to look at reassign-ments and retraining. I felt that a solution to the financial hard times could not be made at the expense of a fine faculty and staff. I know everyone. I've been here a long time. I try to keep in touch regarding things that are important in the lives of faculty and staff. I like to know when someone is hurting and when someone is happy. I care. I really like to have our people feel they are the college, not just employees.

Brunetta Wolfman came to the presidency at Roxbury Commu-nity College in Boston, Massachusetts, from a background in the YWCA and Campfire Girls leadership. She said:

I think there is a sensitivity that women have about gender and race. As women we need to recognize that sensitivity and the strength it gives us to act. Women are so much more fortunate to have been raised to be concerned about others, to be concerned

*about the environment, to be committed to helping others real-
ize their potential. That is something that ought to be valued
and not lost.*

President Virginia Holton, Lassen College, California, spoke of the
quality of care:

*I know I possess certain qualities that women may have to a
greater degree than men. I feel empathy and caring—qualities
that evoke the concept of nurturing. I like to emphasize the positive and make people feel good about themselves, but to do this
requires that we foster the essential qualities of creativity, dreaming, and vision!*

Rewarding others contingent on their effort and performance is
a behavior discussed by Heider in *The Tao of Leadership*:

*THE wise leader is not collecting a string of successes. The leader is
helping others to find their own success. There is plenty to go around.
Sharing success with others is very successful. The single principle behind all creation teaches us that true benefit blesses everyone
and diminishes no one. The wise leader knows that the reward for
doing the work arises naturally out of the work (1986, p. 42).*

President Robert Parilla, Montgomery College, Maryland, was
specific about the rewards of excellent work. He states:

*I strongly believe in and actively support staff development, es-
pecially faculty development and scholarship. That our faculty
pursue the role of scholar is something I always mean to reward.
Our programs for faculty don't just focus on "burn-out"; they
are set up to support scholarly activities. We buy the idea that
attention should be directed toward individual and professional
activities—programs that allow sabbatical leaves, released time*

for scholarly instructional projects, and institutional grants for instructional projects. We are committed to the students, and what better way to celebrate excellence for our faculty than to reward excellent teachers?

――――――

VALUES

The values dimension of leadership behaviors also demonstrated a statistically significant gender difference: the variable "builds openness and trust through personal and professional behavior" proved to be a stronger characteristic of the women CEOs of the study.

Figure 11.4 VALUES: Comparing Females and Males

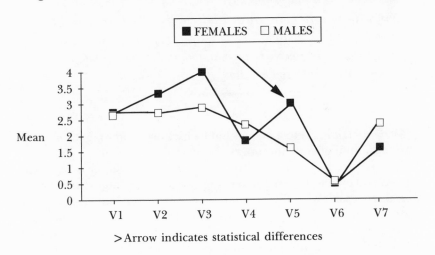

> Arrow indicates statistical differences

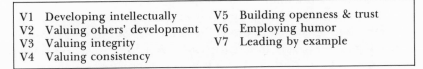

V1 Developing intellectually   V5 Building openness & trust
V2 Valuing others' development   V6 Employing humor
V3 Valuing integrity   V7 Leading by example
V4 Valuing consistency

President Karen Bowyer, Dyersburg State Community College, Tennessee, responded to the idea of trust and openness in the following manner:

I think the way you value people and respect people comes across in your day-to-day dealing with people. I try to treat people the way I value being treated. I'm forthright with people and as honest and fair as I can possibly be. If a problem comes up, I deal with it honestly and openly. I try always to be direct and open and available and honest in my dealings with others.

President Yvonne Kennedy, S. D. Bishop State Junior College, Alabama, said this:

I'VE never been able to separate my own values as a person from my values as a college president. Those values are ones that begin with integrity and trust; I believe that these are essential qualities for all individuals, but especially for a college president who must always be accountable to her faculty, staff, administration, and community.

The remaining research question focuses on examining the general cluster components of the interview process to determine if gender differences are critical to effective leadership. The answer is *no*. **When women and men were separated using gender as an independent variable to compare with the attributes of transformational leadership, there were no statistically significant differences.** Even when other testing procedures (cross tabulations, with corrected chi square) were used to ask the question, no significance was observed. Therefore, it would seem that gender does not make a difference in effective leadership. Figure 11.5 compares all leadership attributes to gender: **what is critically important about the figure is the similarity of the mean scores on each item.** The average difference between any two scores compared on the basis of gender differences is practically zero, suggesting a high degree of agreement between female and male college presidents. The women and men of the study are shown to have very similar behavioral characteristics and attributes when compared to overall cluster variables of transformational leadership. In the following figure, leadership attributes are compared by gender.

Figure 11.5 Leadership Attributes Compared By Gender

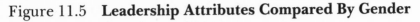

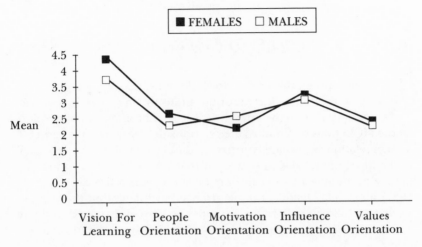

President Lois Callahan, College of San Mateo, California, captured and described a common concern shared by a number of the women presidents:

THE gender question is a tough one. I've always been a female. I am a product of being female, and my experiences in life reflect that. But I can't say that there have been any pluses or minuses based on gender—I think that this notion has played a critical role in my life. I don't approach things in a stereotypical masculine way either. I came to the presidency in a series of very traditional steps: I've been a teacher; I've been a department head; I've been a dean. This seems to be the normal progression of my male cohorts, as well. My approach to my job is as a human being, and I think it is important to care for people as human beings.

Effective leadership, therefore, is a concept relating attributes of presidents of community colleges without reference to their sex. The strengths of both the women and the men of the study are parallel strengths and contribute to their identity as transformational leaders. We turn now to an examination of the relationship of leadership qualities as perceived by the presidents and as acknowledged by the various members of their administrative units.

MULTIFACTOR COLLEGE LEADERSHIP QUESTIONNAIRE

As noted earlier, the Multifactor College Leadership Questionnaire (MCLQ) contains thirty-four questions which match those attributes described in the interview process. The intention of developing the MCLQ was to measure the relationship between leader and follower, a relationship which is critical to the concept of transformational leadership. Simmel (1950) suggested that followers have as much influence on their leaders as leaders have on their followers. Gardner (1987) states that "leaders can be given subordinates, but they cannot be given a following. A following must be earned. Leadership is not the exercise of authority, but the art of turning subordinates into followers" (p. 4).

The art of turning subordinates into followers is one that has been perfected for eighteen years by President Al Philips, Tulsa Junior College, Oklahoma. He said:

MY trouble is that I can't keep my good people; since I've been at TJC, eleven members of my administrative team have become presidents of other colleges!

The presidents associated with this component of the study were noted as having the tendency to respond, more often than not, to questions in the MCLQ with the response "fairly often," indicating they had room to improve in their presidency. In terms of general behaviors, the presidents tended to be most critical about their leadership styles or influence motivation; they gave themselves their lowest scores in that area. For one of those items, "my values are influenced by my leadership team," almost 50 percent of the presidents responded with "sometimes" or "once in a while." This rating was also demonstrated by the followers' ratings of their presidents. Although the presidents also questioned their behaviors concerning their abilities which "commit them to the quality development of others," and "to the development of their own intellectual self-development," these reactions seemed less critical to their subordinates. Finally, a majority of the presidents expressed the need to reward their administrative team more often.

In the figure that follows, we compare the responses of the female and male presidents as they responded to the MCLQ. What is most notable about this figure and the various analyses that produced it is that **no differences are found on the basis of gender either by cluster or by item analysis.** In the MCLQ, as in the structured interviews, we found no substantial differences that could be accounted for on the basis of gender. In fact, what is remarkable is the similarity between the female and male college presidents we studied in reference to the questions as a whole and the item-by-item analysis of the separate questions of the MCLQ. In the figures that follow (11.6, 11.7, and 11.8), the mean is given as a score between 3.5 and 5. Although scores could have ranged from 1 to 5 (by translating A, B, C, D, E, from the MCLQ), the range of answers from the presidents was from 3.60 to 4.95.

Figure 11.6   MCLQ: Comparing Females and Males

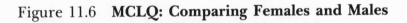

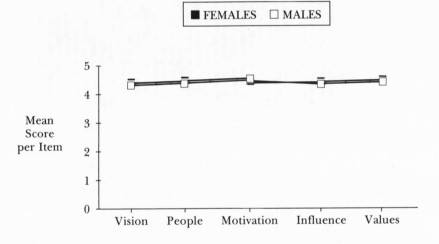

Finally, we come to that part of the analyses that determined follower response to leader, or the degree to which the follower was able to support what the president said about herself or himself. To paraphrase Burns (Kellerman, 1984), this is the test that takes the "gee whiz" out of the mystical theories of leadership. We have learned, moreover, that leadership is interpersonal and that leaders cannot be seen in isolation from followers. Although we found a relationship of 0.84 and 0.85, respectively, for the male and female presidents of the study when compared to their administrative teams, we were primarily interested in the percentage of agreement among all the followers and their leaders. The figure that follows demonstrates the similarities of responses by leaders and followers. Only in the variable "seeks and values the opinion of others" was there a statistically significant differ-ence; however, the argument here was not that one party reported ex-cellent behavior and the other reported poor behavior, but rather that each challenged the other on this variable for its highest rating.

Figure 11.7   **MCLQ: Comparing Presidents and Followers**

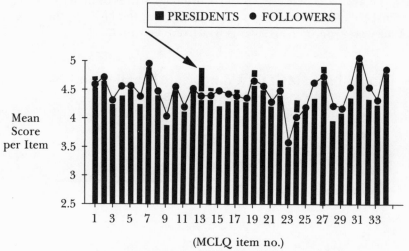

(MCLQ item no.)

>Arrow indicates statistical differences

What is most significant about the response by the followers is that they agree at the rate of almost 85 percent with their presidents. They see their presidents in much the same way the president sees herself or himself. An administrator at South Florida Community College made these comments about President Catherine Cornelius:

A local hotel, in considerable disrepair, caught Dr. Cornelius' attention. She wanted to see it renovated and used for college programs. This met with massive resistance from key members of the leadership team as well as from many of the district's board of trustees. Dr. Cornelius got the staff excited, from the ground floor up, about the potential for programs and benefits of the acquisition, by meeting with the leadership team, all the staff, and the local community. She made all the added work seem like a terrific opportunity for expansion and a chance to impact the community by saving an important landmark. She sold the idea to the board members individually—her vision was shared by all! I have no doubt now that, even in the face of adversity, SFCC will acquire the hotel soon—the leadership team and the board members will not let the opportunities fade away. They, too, have the vision inspired by the best CEO in the country.

A member of the administrative team at Lakewood Community College, Minnesota, related enthusiasm and support for President Jerry Owens:

DR. Owens is committed to providing postsecondary opportunities to reach underserved populations. So when community leaders from St. Paul approached her to initiate classes at a hospital site that was closing, she agreed. Many faculty members and administrators were less than enthusiastic. Dr. Owens' challenge was to seize the opportunity and open an off-campus site and to persuade reluctant faculty and administrators that the project was worthwhile.

SHE attacked the problem with determination and fervor. She delegated: one dean wrote a formal proposal, and another submitted a Title III grant to partially fund the project. She marshalled support both on campus and off campus, taking the proposal to the mayor, the city planners, the state legislators from our district, the media, the local community action councils, the high schools, and other postsecondary institutions in the vicinity. She brought the strongest proponents of the project on campus to promote the concept and dilute the financial obligations. She communicated, clearly and often, her own commitment and excitement about the project and her expectation that all administrators would assist with implementation.

LAKEWOOD'S Eastside Education Center opened in January, 1988, and currently enrolls over 500 students. An additional site was opened in April 1988, in a predominantly black neighborhood in St. Paul. The college has noticeably shifted directions, achieving a much greater emphasis and commitment of resources to programs and services to disadvantaged and underserved populations. Dr. Owens' enthusiasm was contagious, and many skeptical staff members are now eager supporters of the Center.

Figure 11.8 illustrates the relationship between the presidents as leaders and the subordinates as followers for the dimension "people orientation." The data are also represented in Figure 11.7 as a single

Figure 11.8   MCLQ: Comparing Presidents and Followers

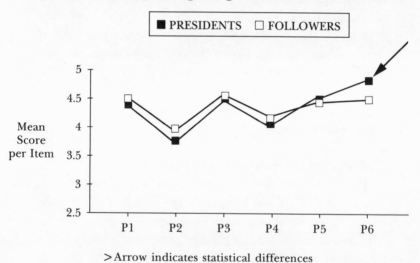

| ■ PRESIDENTS | □ FOLLOWERS |

>Arrow indicates statistical differences

P1	Understands organizational ethos
P2	Rewards appropriately
P3	Demonstrates respect toward others
P4	Considers individual needs
P5	Is student-oriented
P6	Values others

variable in the list of thirty-four variables representing the factors of the MCLQ. Again a caveat regarding this variable should be noted; it was not that the leaders and followers disagreed on this variable, but that they challenged each other on the strength of this variable as perceived by followers and leaders.

CONCLUSION

President Judith Eaton, Community College of Philadelphia, Pennsylvania, has written about women as community college presidents. She raises the question of empowerment of women as educational leaders of community colleges:

COMMUNITY *college education is being reshaped by the forces of limited financing, economic change, shifts in life-style and life expectations, and the demographics of our population. At the same time, a call is emerging for new leaders with new ideas to adapt our institutions to changing external forces. Where are the new leaders to come from? What is the present status of untapped resources—women and minorities—in leadership positions in community colleges? A focus on women may provide answers and insights for emerging leadership. Enriching community college leadership by increasing the diversity of participation could increase the variety of perceptions and insights into the decision-making process and influence community colleges to improve their services to specific constituencies (in Alfred, et al., 1984, pp. 93-94).*

Eaton specifically draws attention to the emergence of and need for women as college and university CEOs. She uses the word "empowerment" of women to suggest that leadership is the process of empowering others to lead. We noted in our study of transformational presidents that the women of the study did have the behaviors and attributes essential to effective leadership and that gender was not significant to leadership. Women as college presidents exhibited transforming behaviors which profited their colleges and their communities.

President Geraldine Evans, Rochester Community College, Minnesota, captured the essential nature of the transforming ability of presidents; she spoke of the difference between the junior college as it was when she came and the community college that emerged under her guidance:

I inherited a college which had been doing things the same way for almost thirty years. I inherited a junior college which valued an "egg-handling approach" to students. The students rolled in, they were sorted out, and they were sent out in a carton with a diploma. We have gone through a total revolution in the last five years, changing from a junior college whose attitude was "there would always be students—our job was to grade and sort them," to a college with a 25 percent drop in student enrollment. We had become a different college, with a different thrust based on our changing demographics. My job became one of redirecting the college and staff with more outreach programs; becoming involved in economic development; running classes early in the morning, late at night, and on weekends. Every facet of the institution has gone through revolutionary changes!

According to an American Council on Education survey of over 2000 colleges and universities (Mooney, 1988), women presidents of higher education institutions number only about ten percent. The council states that the number of women presidents has declined since 1984. That is of concern to all of us who are interested in providing opportunities for qualified rising administrators. Women as presidents have demonstrated exemplary practices and the ability to provide transformational models. They demonstrate vision about the future. Their style of leadership is collaborative and built on the premise of valuing the people in their institutions and their community. They are able to motivate their followers to "see" their vision and accept it as their own.

In the words of the gestalt psychologists, we are also suggesting that the whole has primacy over the parts. An analogy may be drawn from the ambiguous figures of gestalt psychology. At first the figure is seen as an image of either a vase or of two faces: the perceiver initially sees it in only one way, based on the pattern arrangement and the perceiver's past experiences. It is only when we call attention to the other pattern that the perceiver realizes the ambiguity of the pattern.

A similar phenomenon may organize thinking about gender. Although people may be aware of both genders in leadership roles, just as they are aware of both perceptions of the figure, they tend to adopt one or the other as their primary perception. But the concept and practice of leadership is holistic, a function of human behavior, not separate female or separate male behavior. Although some of the separate dimensions of human behavior may have a female quality or a male quality, that fact does not require that we abandon the need for understanding the conceptual whole. A holistic leader is needed to provide effective transformational leadership for the continued growth of the community college and the mission of egalitarian education in America.

CHAPTER 12

CONCLUSION

" *All men dream; but not equally.*
Those who dream by night in the
dusty recesses of their minds
Awake to find that it was vanity;
But the dreamers of day are
dangerous men,
That they act their dreams with
open eyes to make it possible. **"**

T.E. LAWRENCE

SHARED VISION
LEADERSHIP CONCERNS: MINORITIES AND WOMEN
IMPLICATIONS
VISIONS FOR THE FUTURE

CONCLUSION

INTRODUCTION

One of the greatest needs facing community colleges today is revitalized leadership—*transformational leadership to meet changing times.* The challenges that face those in community college CEO positions are formidable. President Dick Brownell, Rowan-Cabarrus Community College, North Carolina, suggests:

SUCH challenges demand today's leadership to be more aggressive if it is to compete successfully in the political arena, more dynamic if it is to keep abreast of rapidly changing times, and more effective in ensuring that teaching and learning are enhanced through participatory governance resulting from delegation and empowerment of others. The catalytic role of presidents in revitalizing leadership is paramount. The president must raise the level of awareness about change and create an organizational climate where change is accepted as natural and necessary.

SHARED VISION

T he success achieved in the face of these challenges results, in part, from the ability of the leader to create a working environment based on a "shared vision." Implicit in what "shared vision" meant to the CEOs we studied was the value they placed on *follower involvement*. This involvement, in turn, translated into building internal and external communities. This theme was significantly developed by Ernest Boyer in *College* (1987), a report of the findings of the Carnegie Foundation for the Advancement of Teaching. Dr. Boyer suggests that

> *what we need today are groups of well-informed, caring individuals who band together in the spirit of community to learn from one another, as citizens, in the democratic process. We need concerned people who are participants in inquiry, who know how to ask the right questions, who understand the process by which public policy is shaped, and who are prepared to make informed, discriminating judgments on questions that affect the future (p. 280).*

The recent report of the Commission on the Future of Community Colleges (1988), *Building Communities: A Vision For A New Century,* reinforces the significance of vision as it influences the community college. In their deliberations the members of the Commission defined the term *community* "not only as a region to be served, but also as a climate to be created" (p. 7) and commented on the process of building communities:

> *BUILDING communities is, we believe, an especially appropriate objective for the community college because it embraces the institution's comprehensive mission. But the goal is not just outreach. Perhaps more than any other institution, the community college also can inspire partnerships based upon shared values and common goals. The building of community, in its broadest and best sense, encompasses a concern for the whole, for integration and collaboration, for openness and integrity, for inclusiveness and self-renewal (p. 7).*

The Report included the following from John Gardner's 1987 Harry S. Truman Lecture to the American Association of Community and Junior Colleges:

THE community college can perform a convening function at which representatives of various fragments and interests come together in unofficial but serious discussion of community problems. [The college can] be an effective convener, a valuable forum, a meeting ground where the common good is discussed. (p. 7).

The Report continues, "In such a spirit, community colleges can, we believe, become sources of educational, civic, and cultural renewal" (p. 7). Renewal implies change, and change is best accomplished through shared vision and commitment. The transformational leaders identified in this study understand both the need for renewal, as articulated by the Futures Commission, and the ways in which such change can be accomplished within their own institutions.

The president is the key to establishing such a community. It is "the president who must be able to create a climate of teamwork so that resources will not be wasted by competing vested interests. By focusing leadership on change, the president can create dynamic structures and procedures which promote freedom and flexibility in matching resources to needs and which also unleash creativity to help the college cope with challenges" (Dick Brownell, Rowan-Cabarrus Community College).

Transformational leaders are change agents. They exhibit leadership behaviors that reflect vision, demonstrate the ability to influence others, acknowledge the importance of attending to and motivating people, and act on the importance of modeling values conducive to institutional excellence.

The CEOs in this study (1) demonstrated an understanding of the internal and external needs of their respective communities, (2) exhibited leadership attributes that reflected the themes of transformational leadership, and (3) collectively articulated these themes as the essence of effective leadership.

However, the five themes associated with transformational behavior are not of equal value. In fact, the theme of vision is of greatest value, is pivotal, is critical. The CEO must be able to comprehend the future needs of the community and to create an effective strategy that facilitates internal and external involvement. Vision is the umbrella under which all other transformational themes flourish.

VISION: a leader-conceptualized view of the future. When shared with others, the vision is the primary responsibility of the trans-formational leader.

Too many colleges stumble into the future because their leaders do not have the forward-looking perspective necessary to soften the shock of change. They are concerned primarily with the past and the present—with the now—so they spend most of their time administering and managing, rather than changing. This is not to imply that administration and management are not important functions, but these functions differ dramatically from the function of leadership. Transformational leadership demands foresight—looking into the future to provide a vision that can serve as a catalyst for action in the present. The function of leadership is to anticipate the future and determine in advance how best to deal with it.

We analyzed not only the five themes, but also the attributes within each theme. When we examined the seven attributes contained within the theme of vision, the primary component associated with transformational community college leadership was **shared vision**. The degree to which the CEO is able to achieve a "shared vision" is in a direct proportional relationship to the second and third most important attributes of vision: **commitment to change** and **future orientation**. All these attributes determine the CEO's ability to be an effective transformational leader.

INFLUENCE ORIENTATION: the process of shared attention to problems and understanding of roles to be played in resolution. Generally, it results in increased delegation and empowerment, promoting self-actualization of both leaders and followers.

The journey to transformational leadership includes lived and learned experiences which enable individuals to become what they can become. Along the way they acquire a true sense of self, leading to genuine self-confidence. Recognition and acceptance of one's own individuality translates into the ability for self-empowerment. This is the essential underpinning for the empowerment of others. Not to be confused with delegation in the workplace, empowerment promotes an increased awareness and the arousal of higher-level needs in others. Those so empowered have the ability to transcend self-interests; the result is frequently an extraordinary effort for the betterment of the institution.

Leaders committed to transforming their institutions also possess the ability to integrate the attributes associated with influencing others.

The most important influence attribute identified by the CEOs is **open communication**, which enables the involvement of others in the quest for "shared vision." Essential to this open communication is a second influencing attribute: the **delegation of authority**. When a CEO is able to delegate and empower others within the institution, the opportunity to initiate and sustain change is dramatically enhanced. The effectiveness of any transformational leader revolves around the ability to blend the attributes previously associated with vision and those critical attributes associated with influencing others.

> *PEOPLE ORIENTATION: the process of leader and follower interaction in which the team is considered a living system, focused on student success, and where the strengths of each team member are maximized. At the same time, there exists a strong focus on the individual.*

Transformational leaders are acutely aware of the importance of leader/follower interaction. The fundamental component to effective transformation is developing an institutional tone based on *sharedness* and a *value for others*, resulting in a living system of leading and following. The report of the Commission on the Future of Community Colleges (1988) cited an AACJC publication entitled "New Staff for New Students," which put the issue squarely:

> *THE staff of a college is its single greatest resource. In economic terms, the staff is the college's most significant and largest capital investment. In these terms alone, we affirm that it is only good sense that the investment should be helped to appreciate in value and not be allowed to wear itself out or slide into obsolescence by inattention or neglect (Commission on the Future of Community Colleges, p. 12).*

An examination of the six attributes associated with the theme of people orientation revealed the significance of **student-centeredness**. This attribute might appear to be obvious, but the passion and zeal our CEOs demonstrated for meeting student needs in their respective institutions was quite unexpected. The shared vision of *each* community college revolves around the mission of *all* community colleges: commitment to student access and success.

MOTIVATIONAL ORIENTATION: the process whereby the mass of the organization accepts a new vision and mission. Followers are motivated to achieve and are excited through performance and results.

Motivation is the glue that binds leaders and followers. "Work motivation is a set of energetic forces that originate within as well as beyond an individual's being, to initiate work-related behavior, and to determine its form, direction, intensity, and duration" (Pinder, 1984, p. 8). Motivated people draw from an inner source of motivation to meet new challenges and perform at ever higher levels.

Our CEOs associated the **development of followers** with motivation. Transformational leaders understand that change through shared vision demands not only commitment to the vision, but also commitment to the development of the followers as a means to reaching that vision. This development maximizes human potential by enabling creativity and innovation to flourish.

VALUES ORIENTATION: constitutes the moral fiber of the leader to include commitment, quality, integrity, trust, and respect through modeling. It is viewed as an ethical orientation, morally accepting to and uplifting for followers.

Fundamental to all of the CEOs interviewed in the study was the importance of modeling behavior associated with a value system based upon integrity, trust, and respect. We determined that the values of the living system of the institution were collectively derived from the leader and followers functioning in harmony.

Within this transformational theme, the aforementioned attributes were similarly important, the intangible links to the shared vision of educational opportunity for all who value and choose to acquire further knowledge. Transformational leaders emphasize the importance of providing these opportunities. Educational quality is a direct result of the transformational leader's success in assisting followers to accept and internalize institutional values for high standards, integrity, openness, and trust.

Earlier we suggested that the totality of the community college effort nationwide has established the institution as an essential component of the health and well-being of America. The community college is not alone in addressing the parameters of leadership, and the need for outstanding leaders is not restricted to the community college. But outstanding leaders are critical to meeting ever-increasing challenges and effecting successful change; they are sought in both public and private enterprises.

We offer these transformational themes as the essence of the behaviors exhibited by some outstanding community college CEOs who have the ability to transform the future educational direction of their institutions and ultimately the future direction of this country. We have attempted to isolate and illuminate the critical transformational behaviors identified by 50 outstanding community college CEOs to broaden our understanding of the unique leadership demands of the community college.

LEADERSHIP CONCERNS: MINORITIES AND WOMEN

A report by the The Commission on the Future of Community Colleges (1988) identified a critical deficit in leadership in American community colleges:

> . . . *there is a clear and pressing need to increase diversity among community college leadership. Currently, 10 percent of community college chief executive officers are women (121 of 1222), as are 35 percent of all administrators. There are 37 black, 32 Hispanic, and 8 Asian chief executive officers in the nation's community colleges. Blacks and Hispanics are underrepresented among all administrative and faculty groups. If the community college is to enlarge leadership from among underrepresented groups, intensive recruitment of women and members of minorities, as well as careful mentoring of the new recruits, must become long-term strategies.*

> *LOOKING to the year 2000, we recommend that community colleges collaborate with universities to develop creative programs aimed at preparing a new generation of community college presidents. A special effort should be made to recruit leaders from among minority and female populations (p. 42).*

Members of ethnic minorities and women are represented in this study; they are included in the original list of 256 community college

CEOs and in the "blue-chippers" in direct proportion to their representation in the general population of community college CEOs. However, we found, as did the American Council on Education, that less than 10 percent of the CEOs of American colleges and universities are minorities or women. Our sample reflects this data. It is important to note at this juncture, however, that our purpose was not to look at representative constituent groups but rather at the nature of transformational leadership in the American community college today. It was from that framework that we studied and discussed gender differences, noting the relationships between women and men as effective college presidents. We found, for example, a profound age gap existed between women and men entering administrative and executive positions—a gap of six and seven years; women obtained their executive positions later than did men. We suspected that gap to be similar for minorities as well, considering that one-fifth of the women studied also represented minority populations. Indeed, in our interviews with representative minority and female populations, we found the following:

• The age for entry level positions of upper administration was also deferred; where the average age of "first administrative position" for the norm group and the "blue chippers" was 28 years, the average age for the minority group members (including both men and women) was 31.25 years. Although the gap was not as large as that between women and men, it was nonetheless significant.

• In a comparison of the ages at which the different groups became presidents or CEOs, the following discrepancies appeared: men in the norm group were 36.1 years at the time of their first presidency; in the minority group we studied, males achieved this position at age 40.4 and the females at age 39.

• There were significant statistical differences between the minority group and the norm group in average number of years in present position. The norm group and the "blue chippers" reported an average tenure of almost 12 years, whereas the minority group reported an average tenure of 5.6 years for males and 3.8 years for females.

• None of this group began an administrative career as a college president, but that was also true of both the "blue chippers" and the female/male groups in our study; only in the norm group did about five percent of their number begin their college careers as president.

• All of the minority groups had prior teaching experiences either in public schools or in colleges and/or universities.

• Fully one-third of the CEOs in this study held the position of president prior to their present position; among the male members in the minority group, over one-half had previously been CEOs; among the female members, one-fourth had previously been college presidents.

A perfunctory glance, then, at the comparative picture of minority group members does not indicate wide disparities (e.g., the study of women as CEOs in Chapter 11); and if the comparison is extended, we can infer that these leaders can and do exhibit leadership capabilities and skills that will conform to our transformational leadership model.

However, in light of the concerns and recommendations of the Futures Commission and our own vision of improving the effectiveness of community college CEOs, we decided to explore the reasons for the underrepresentation of minorities and women in community college leadership. Furthermore, we would analyze the research data and recommend a process by which minority and female leaders would achieve full and productive representation.

To accomplish these tasks, we again drew from our list of exemplary CEOs—which included members of minority groups and women—plus critical members of the national leadership of Hispanic and black community college educational groups. Each of these CEOs was willing to share his/her own views of the status and future of minorities and women in American community colleges by answering the following questions:

1. What are your views on the issue that minorities and women are underrepresented in the leadership of American community colleges? Why does it occur? What factors contribute to this situation?

2. What recommendations do you have or would you make to change the current situation?

3. What would you like to see written about minorities and women in our book on leadership in American community colleges today?

Underrepresentation

The minority and women CEOs we interviewed shared their experiences candidly; consequently, they revealed many of the obstacles and barriers that contribute to the underrepresentation of minorities in positions of leadership. The statements we heard most often were not unexpected; they referred to a time in the 1960s in which the "vision" of a great dreamer and another transformational leader, Dr. Martin Luther King, raised the consciousness of Americans. He spoke of a United States of America where all people would share equally in the bounty of the nation and where political, social, educational, and economic rights would destroy the barriers of discrimination and inequality.

There was no doubt that our respondents felt they were the beneficiaries of this dream; this feeling was a common thread in their interviews. But even as they held to that belief and hope for the future of mankind, the contradictory nature of that promise manifested itself. A case in point is the issue of affirmative action, which was part of the civil rights legislation of the 1960s. Affirmative action was and is a policy advocating that people responsible for the allocation of services such as jobs, college admissions, or promotions, give some form of special consideration to members of groups who have been traditionally disadvantaged. Special consideration may be interpreted from its weakest form, in which jobs are widely advertised so that many applicants from different groups hear about them, to its strongest form, in which quotas are established requiring that a certain percentage of jobs or school admissions be set aside for previously underrepresented groups. But by 1973, the conflict over affirmative action found a critical battleground in the Bakke case. When Allan Bakke challenged the use of the quota system for college admissions, he initiated "reverse discrimination" court cases and confirmed the principle that advantages enjoyed by dominant groups for 200 years do not disappear with the pronouncement that discrimination is at an end.

There seems to be a paradox in the efforts of minority groups to achieve integration of political, social, economic and educational institutions: the move toward equality for one group may inhibit that right for other groups. All the leaders we interviewed observed this paradox. Don Phelps, Chancellor of the Los Angeles Community College District, commented:

———

WHERE minorities and affirmative action are concerned, I believe that you must work at the program constantly—you must look at affirmative action as purposeful; you must work on it every day or it can easily fall out of favor and be eliminated from the consciousness of employers. We must continue to nurture the idea of providing opportunity, because we must continue to nurture new people to move into the places that the minority initiates into positions of leadership have held. We are in danger every day of not having new members of minorities ready to take the places of those few slots which minorities now hold. We must remember that gradual losses are insidious losses. We can't give up what progress we have made. And if we do, we are giving up on our own leadership. I believe, furthermore, that good leadership must provide a model for underrepresented groups. Today, we lack moral leadership from the highest office in our nation; we continue to be victimized by benign neglect, and institutional racism remains as real today as it was thirty years ago.

Jerry Sue Owens, President of Lakewood Community College in Minnesota, spoke of underrepresentation and the deleterious effect of screening processes that demand "sameness":

WE are often underrepresented in general in community college leadership but also in teaching and classified staff—because of geographical location (suburban areas tend to be homogeneous and nonethnic), often because of low turnover. Those who were first in the door tend to stay there, so we tend to enter positions of leadership at an older age. Sometimes it's the "good ol' boy" network that stifles opportunity for women and members of ethnic minorities; but another part of this has to do with the nature of the early community college movement which drew faculty and administrators from high school ranks—those ranks were typically white, and the administrators were all men. Finally, I don't want to play down the role of racism; we are discussing this fact in forums among the Black Presidents' Round Table in Minnesota. People aren't moving up, and presidents aren't finding new opportunities to use their networks to promote new leadership. One factor in this lack of opportunity has to do with screening committees. Those committees are not representative of the diverse populations of community colleges. They apply a subtle racism by demanding that the best person for the job is the most published, the person with a Ph.D. in a particular discipline, and the person who has proven, by past successful experiences, to have qualifications that are highly competitive against any standard of performance. This is the "selection of sameness" concept in which a conscious decision is made to screen out women and members of minorities.

Earl Bowman, President of Minneapolis Community College, also referred to the screening process as a barrier for representation. His example describes a typical scenario for the minority applicant to leadership positions:

UNDERREPRESENTATION occurs because opportunities are not provided for minorities to enter into positions at an early point in their careers. Search committees (and presidents and chancellors) need to be educated to look for potential and promise in those people who are desirous of moving up. At the present time, we find minority candidates only by accident and certainly not by purpose. For example, a system that has a good minority administrator at upper administrative levels may be asked by a search committee if they know of someone who is a member of a minority whose attributes for a particular post are known and recommended. As those resumes come in, an "element of position perfection" enters the position race. Minority candidates are routinely screened out in the first phase of the screening because they cannot compare with some imaginary perfect candidate with a long list of successful experiences in his repertoire.

Eduardo Padron, Provost, New World Wolfson Center Community College in Florida, and Past President, National Community College Hispanic Council, referred to academia's perceptions of minority or female applicants for positions of leadership in the community college setting:

I feel we are underestimating the tremendous resources that the members of ethnic minorities and women can provide to leadership. Our student body for the year 2000 needs such role models because students continue to represent diversity and differences.

WHEN boards review the application of a minority or a female candidate for a leadership position, they must remember to include in their search a place for the underutilized talents and resources of members of minority groups or women. These applicants are not, as some believe, only one-dimensional in their thinking and their creativity, that is, only able to represent one particular group. They are, like their Anglo, male counterparts, "men and women of all seasons"—individuals who can lead and inspire all groups. They can deal well in a multi-dimensional society. But boards, selection committees and organizational associations (and their publications) need to become sensitive to these resources that are, at present, neglected and misunderstood.

These views concerning the underrepresentation of minorities and women in leadership positions follow the historical pattern of societal and legalistic changes occurring since the 1960s. The individuals expressing them are aware of the ebb-and-flow pattern of these changes; although they see factors which reflect the traditional barriers of gender and ethnic minorities, they have experienced what can happen once members of those groups attain positions of leadership.

William Segura, President of Chemeketa Community College in Oregon, painted an enlightening picture of the issue of underrepresentation and potential for growth by American society:

THE benefits to leadership that women and minorities can bring are too subtle for most mainstream individuals. These individuals do not appreciate subtle differences in people, such as the benefits of bilingualism or the attributes of growing up female. I think it's a shame because there is so much potential which is lost. For example, the potential of leadership that emanates from the concept of motherhood goes directly to the heart of the ideas of team-building and collaboration, concepts that we are learning are attributes of strong, ethical leaders. In the past, we have relied on women to do the soothing of our society—to solve problems and smooth things over for us, but we haven't seen the value in this for positions of leadership.

WHAT our contemporary society expects from us is that we will integrate into the established order without bringing our cultural and traditional character into that order. We are expected to know this process, but others do not have an appreciation of the things women and members of minorities can bring to positions of leadership. We must begin to enumerate and break down those essential qualities of the ethnic quality or the woman's quality of leadership. We must express what these groups mean to organizations by looking at the minority experience in America and then translate and elaborate on that meaning by pulling into common, everyday usage the characteristics of these groups that aid and contribute to leadership. We need to stop, take pause, and develop an appreciation for the power we are wasting by not taking full advantage of members of minority groups and women, by not bringing them along or asking for their perspectives. Change has to take place at all levels by building fires and creating the desire for something different to occur. More than likely it will take the equivalent of the "good ol' boy" network to get women and members of minorities to be seen and modeled by others. I think affirmative action is a trap of continuing racism; by hiring a quota of a certain ethnic group, the dignity of the accomplishments of this group is diminished as antipathy turns into disdain for the group as a whole.

Recommendations

President Segura knows that the litmus test for ensuring a greater role for women and members of minorities in positions of leadership in America is appreciating who those groups are and the talents and accomplishments they bring. This belief recurs as a major theme in our respondents' recommendations for change.

Flora Mancuso Edwards, President of Middlesex County College in New Jersey, and President of the National Community College Hispanic Council, takes a historic view of underrepresentation of minorities and women in positions of leadership:

―――――

IF we look at the history of the professional pool and the requirements and dynamics involved in deciding who can enter that pool, we note that the level of opportunity for the ethnic minorities and women is inadequate. One just has to look at the numbers of people in the traditional pipelines to discover that fewer department heads, fewer division deans and fewer vice-presidents in the community colleges are members of minority groups and women. Therefore, fewer provosts, presidents and chancellors are members of the underrepresented groups. This is a dynamic that goes on in terms of behavior we are comfortable with; it is basically modeled on white male behavior.

―――――

WHAT we as members of minorities find is that it is more difficult to learn and internalize the unwritten rules of the game. It requires some degree of schizophrenia to breech that gap to participate. Our society tends to distrust and dislike deviant behavior (and reject minorities, as such); therefore, when we make inroads, we must do so with creative schizophrenia. We must make a long-term investment in the future getting people into the pipeline—members of ethnic minorities need to be department heads and division deans and vice-presidents, and they need to be better prepared to do so. Minority leadership today must recommend more students for doctoral programs in leading colleges and universities. Doctoral recipients in key areas must be increased. The higher education community must strengthen the fabric of higher education departments in universities around the nation. Federal programs must be geared in this direction. Mentoring must occur at all levels—we at our own levels must assume responsibility to bring others along.

―――――

FOR the long view, when a black or Hispanic physics instructor is a common sight, then too will a black or Hispanic dean, and a black or Hispanic president be a common sight.

Tom Gonzales, President of Linn-Benton Community College in Oregon, responded to the lack of commitment and awareness of present leaders and leadership to instill in their own organizations the need to develop minorities and women for positions of leadership. He feels that the community college provides the "land of opportunity" for changes to occur. His recommendations involved two major groups:

THE AACJC Board should take the initiative in developing and setting the policy statement to impact leadership growth. This should be a very specific initiative and should draw on this known fact: there is a vast underrepresentation of minorities and women in community colleges today. It is almost an imperative that higher education leadership view these groups as new leaders for the future and pay attention to the changing demographics which affect the workplace, technology, the professions, and the colleges . . . we must have new role models. It just makes good sense to follow this logic. It's time—past time—to do so.

ALSO legislatures should be encouraged to promote leadership for groups who have been underrepresented in the past, especially minorities and women. The time is coming for this possibility. For example, this summer I addressed the National Conference of State Legislatures on this very topic. All 50 states were represented as I spoke of the underrepresentation of members of minorities in positions of leadership in our communities. I would suggest that the report of the Commission of Minority Participation and Education in American Life, One-third of a Nation, *be distributed to state and national representatives so that their awareness is heightened, and more importantly, so that they can get about the business of doing something to make things happen. Many potential leaders with all the necessary skills for leadership are around; all they need is the opportunity to work.*

Nolen Ellison, President of Cuyahoga Community College District in Ohio, made these recommendations:

OBVIOUSLY, the pool of minorities that might create a more representative group has not grown as fast as it should. There are deficits in this pool. There is a lack of aggressiveness in seeking minorities for leadership; and if institutions are not making a concerted effort to move minorities into positions of leadership, it will not happen. It seems that there has been a backward slide in the past couple of years in the commitment to the development of minority leadership. During the past five to ten years, minorities in large urban areas have been highly visible and as a result, highly stressed. These people are leaving the leadership roles; and because the pool is small, blacks are not replacing blacks.

I recommend that graduate programs, foundations and other leadership throughout the nation (including leadership development programs and college and university presidents) work in concert to develop the means to stimulate change. We need a collaborative effort rather than an individual one. Doctoral programs must be more aggressive in reaching out to minorities and nurturing them. Foundations and other leadership development programs must recruit minorities for leadership training. Local leaders must be more sensitive to the pressures and difficulties faced by minorities in large, urban areas. Their action, however, cannot be delayed; action must occur now!

Jerry Sue Owens pointed to some specific recommendations for change:

• A strong and powerful philosophy which specifically supports minorities' and women's growth in positions of leadership in community colleges must be espoused and acted upon by the AACJC.

• Boards of Trustees must be oriented toward diversity in hiring. They should, themselves, be appointed or elected to reflect the population and the service areas of the institution.

• Emphasis should be placed on cultural diversity throughout institutions, and this is a position that should be integrated into
the CEO's strategic planning.

• More minorities and women must be recruited for jobs and positions of leadership.

• A conscious effort must be made to mentor members of minority
groups and women for positions of leadership. A sincere mentoring program must assess, appraise, and interpret the modern
system as social reality and provide, through honest dialogue and
perhaps training, clues and tips and experiences on how these
groups can realistically make it in the contemporary world.

Carolyn Williams, President, National Council on Black American
Affairs, Highland Park Community College in Michigan, points to twin
deficits—good role models and adequate preparation for leadership
for minorities and women:

*WE need inspirational role models to prepare us to take and make
leadership positions in this society. Our self-concept needs bol-
stering; we can begin by demonstrating, in our research and in
the literature, the really outstanding examples of minorities and
women who have made it and who are doing exemplary jobs. Then
we can say, "Here are our successes—other groups can and should
do this, too!"*

*THE whole notion of the mentor is critical as well. We must
not only acquire mentors, but they must acquire us and encourage
us and support us so that we can begin to take their places without fear of failure or ignorance of what is expected of us.*

Charles Green, President of Rio Salado Community College in Arizona, spoke to readiness and mentoring:

*IF we find a situation where minorities and women are ready
but cannot get to the top, then we have a national problem which
must be treated. The AACJC and the ACCT must be the action*

arm to make this happen. They have a powerful ability to in-fluence the outcomes of what goes on in the community college movement in America.

READINESS is also a critical issue. Boards of Trustees must give serious consideration to getting ready to select a minority or a woman—they cannot say, "We are not ready." One should not command the company unless he or she has commanded the platoon. One has to be in the line movement to the top. There are politics involved in upward mobility and politics involve the use of power. To use power as a deterrent to a particular group or groups of society is not a wise use of power because the good leader eventually learns that he or she cannot practice leadership without followership.

Each of the leaders had recommendations for building and developing leadership for members of minority groups and for women. They sent loud and clear messages about the underrepresentation of these groups in the modern community college.

Messages

Jerry Sue Owens' message was eloquent: the changes that must occur are of benefit to all of society. She provides a critical global perspective:

THE value of cultural diversity and the tremendous contribution that can be made by different perspectives are the major themes that should be stressed throughout the community college movement; it isn't "sameness" that defines us but cultural diversity. We all need exposure whether we are faculty, students, or administrators. We need exposure to different perspectives to create healthy environments and to accept the value of differences as natural and normal to us. The more we value these differences, and the more we understand diversity, the greater our cohesiveness and strength as a college, a community and a nation.

Yvonne Kennedy, President of S. D. Bishop State Junior College in Alabama, also emphasized personal growth and development by encouraging the role of interdependence of people and our interaction with communities:

WE should not be discouraged or find despair in the situations that cause or contribute to the concept of underrepresentation for members of minorities or women in obtaining positions of leadership commensurate with their numbers in our population. We can cause change by having a joint direction for the good of education and mankind and by establishing a better network of communication and understanding.

Tom Gonzales offered some practical advice to members of minority groups and to women:

CONSIDER flexibility in your career; be ready to seek new opportunities outside your own district or state. Go after the opportunities; establish and connect with networks and mentors who build your confidence and in whom you can trust. There is a great deal in common between you and others who are members of underrepresented groups in society; join with them and work together. We need viability, new energy and new vision for the future. We as college presidents should commit ourselves to energize people to move in new directions for leadership by emphasizing varied backgrounds and varied experiences as well as academic training and knowledge.

Don Phelps and Earl Bowman both spoke of the rights of members of minorities and women to fail, to make mistakes and to grow from those failures and mistakes. Don Phelps commented:

THE majority group must remember that blacks have the right to fail just as whites fail. Right now that right is abrogated. We don't seem to give minorities the right to fail; we don't want to take risks when it comes to the failures of minorities. We only want to judge by positive experiences that withstand the test of time. Standards are different for whites and members of minority groups. Sometimes these groups are not considered to be qualified applicants for jobs because they do not conform to those standards developed and sanctioned by the majority society. If we are a plural, democratic society, then we should allow minorities all their rights—including the right to make a mistake and to fail. There is a real and covert danger in the judgment that says, "See, I told you they wouldn't work out. Now we just won't hire any more of them." Minorities and women can and should make mistakes and should be allowed to fail—they, too, will learn and grow from those mistakes and failures.

Summary

What are the implications of these findings? We think they are contained in the words of the men and women who have spoken. They have analyzed and interpreted a phenomenon which points up a known reality in our society—ethnic minorities and women are underrepresented in positions of leadership in our society and in the community colleges. They have honestly and candidly made recommendations to effect the changes that must occur in the community college movement. Their messages are clear and concise. They have identified the shortcomings of our system and recommended needed reforms.

We must look to these leaders to change our unintended neglect of members of minorities and women in positions of leadership for American community colleges. From these leaders we can expect great things; we can expect the manifestations of the attributes of transformational leaders—vision, people orientation, influence orientation, motivation orientation and values.

IMPLICATIONS

We suggest that the knowledge gained from this study has relevant implications for the identification, selection, and training of future leaders in the community college. Moreover, the opportunities for self-assessment and personal development for those presently involved in leadership roles should be enhanced.

One of the key roles of leadership is the responsibility to identify and provide for the development of future leaders. Due to the multifaceted demands upon CEOs, often this responsibility is not viewed as a priority. Thus, the absence of such modeling behavior thwarts this process throughout the institution. We offer the attributes discussed in this book as descriptors that can be utilized in the process of observation and identification of potential leaders with the intent to develop these individuals for leadership roles. Historically, people have been selected for administrative positions in community college leadership based upon their intellectual and cognitive prowess—typically beginning with an individual's first administrative appointment from a faculty position to department chairperson or another position on the administrative ladder. This promotional ladder leaves the concept of leadership readiness and training to a process of appointment. However, leadership is so important that leaders need to be fully educated to meet the challenges of their roles and to develop the skills of a transformational leader.

It is clear from our study and others of transformational leaders that the ability to have an impact on the behavior of followers is the critical variable in successful leadership. This knowledge may call for a rethinking of the admission criteria for graduate programs. The focus of most graduate schools in business and education has been on management. But while we do not disparage management skills, we must note that the ability to lead others is a combination of art and science that goes well beyond cognitive development.

What has become apparent through our previous experience and has been reinforced by this study is the lack of adequate preparation and leadership training for many involved in community college leadership at all levels. We understand that leadership is situational and training cannot prepare leaders for all of the unique demands encountered in the community college. However, the broad generic skills of effective leadership have been defined and described and can be taught and learned. Current situations and those to be met in the future demand that we make the most of the potential of those who aspire to and those who currently serve in leadership positions. We should focus on promoting their energy and understanding, so necessary to achieve excellent leadership. Without directed and individualized leadership training, we question how community college leaders can influence, shape, and embed values, attitudes, beliefs, and behaviors in their followers.

This study revealed the wide variance that exists among outstanding CEOs in relation to the five transformational themes and the 34 attributes found within those themes. This information indicates that among even the most outstanding community college leaders in the nation, there is always a need for continued professional development. We suggest that professional development in the community college has focused primarily on faculty and staff without attending to the needs of those in leadership roles. With this in mind, we offer these transformational themes and accompanying attributes as a guideline for self-assessment. Self-assessment, coupled with an effective professional development program, has the potential to make the difference between good and excellent leadership. However, it must be remembered that it is the combination of leaders at all levels in the institution that provides for successful outcomes. It is necessary that the professional development of these leaders be coordinated for maximum effectiveness.

VISIONS FOR THE FUTURE

Those who dream, those who have vision, have the ability to change their dreams and visions into reality. Columbus had a dream of a new world; he dared to act on that dream and sailed across a "flat" ocean to discover a new continent. Lincoln had a vision of saving and reuniting a nation torn by civil strife, and that dream cemented the power of the United States of America. Kennedy had a vision of a technology that would allow mankind to reach the stars; thus, our space program received the funding for the historic trip to the moon. Dreaming is an essential quality of individuals—we must dream so that change will benefit mankind. Transformational leaders possess imagination and creativity that, when combined with their ability to interrelate with their organizations or institutions, provide a climate conducive to new beginnings.

Visions are only the seedlings of reality. We must value and cherish our dreams and visions, nurturing them into fulfillment. Most of all, we must remember that few of our visions can be accomplished alone. The key to the achievements that we strive for is the ability to share our visions and thus earn the acceptance and assistance necessary for turning them into reality. What is truly important, what is lasting, is accomplished together. Be bold, be creative, be dynamic, and be willing to take risks to ensure the best possible education through the uniqueness of the community college. But do it together, leaders and followers, followers and leaders.

REFERENCES

AACJC Board. 1987. *AACJC Membership Directory 1987*. Washington, DC: American Association of Community and Junior Colleges.

Alfred, R., P. Elsner, R. LeCroy, and N. Armes (eds.). 1984. *Emerging roles for community college leaders*. New Directions for Community Colleges, No. 46. San Francisco: Jossey-Bass.

Allison, G. T. 1971. *Essence of decision*. Boston: Little, Brown and Company.

Argyris, C. 1957. *Personality and organization*. New York: Harper & Brothers.

Baker, G. A. 1984. Community college leadership: The crucial issue of quality control. In *Community college leadership for the '80s*, eds. John E. Roueche and George A. Baker III, 63–71. Washington, DC: American Association of Community and Junior Colleges.

Baker, G. A., J. E. Roueche, and R. Rose. (June/July 1988). Transformational leaders in the community college: The best of the best. *Community, technical, and junior college journal*.

Bass, B. M. 1985a. *Leadership and performance beyond expectations*. New York: The Free Press.

_____. 1985b. Leadership: Good, better, best. *Organizational dynamics* 13(3): 26–40.

Bass, B. M., D. A. Waldman, B. J. Avolio, and M. Bebb. 1987. Transformational leadership and the falling dominoes effect. *Group & organization Studies* 12 (March): 73–87.

Belenky, M., B. M. Clinchy, N. R. Goldberger, and J. M. Tarule. 1986. *Women's ways of knowing: The development of self, voice, and mind*. New York: Basic Books.

Benezet, L., J. Katz, and F. Magnusson. 1981. *Style and substance: Leadership and the college presidency*. Washington, DC: American Council on Education.

Bennis, W., and B. Nanus. 1985. *Leaders*. New York: Harper & Row.

Bernard, J. 1981. *The female world*. New York: The Free Press.

Berry, M. 1979. *Women in higher education administration: A book of readings*. Washington, DC: National Association for Women Deans, Administrators and Counselors.

Blake, R. R., and J. S. Mouton. 1964. *The managerial grid*. Houston: Gulf.

Boyer, E. L. 1987. *College: The undergraduate experience in America*. New York: Harper & Row.

Brown, J. D. 1973. *The human nature of organizations.* New York: Amacom.

Burns, J. M. 1978. *Leadership.* New York: Harper & Row.

Carbone, R. 1981. *Presidential passages: Former college presidents reflect on the splendor and agony of their careers.* Washington, DC: American Council on Education.

Carew, D. K., E. Parisi-Carew, and K. H. Blanchard. 1985. *Group development and situational leadership.* Escondido, CA: Blanchard Training and Development, Inc.

Cohen, M., and J. March. 1974, 1986. *Leadership and ambiguity: The American college president.* New York: McGraw-Hill.

The Commission on the Future of Community Colleges. 1988. *Building communities: A vision for a new century.* Washington, DC: American Association of Community and Junior Colleges.

Cornford, F. M. 1972. *Microcosmographia academica: Being a guide for the young academic politician.* Chicago: University of Chicago Press.

Cribbin, J. J. 1981. *Leadership: Strategies for organizational effectiveness.* New York: Amacom.

de Beauvoir, S. 1949. *The second sex.* New York: Knopf.

Deci, E. L. 1971. Effect of externally mediated rewards on intrinsic motivation. *Journal of personality and social psychology* 18: 105–115.

Deci, E. L., and W. F. Cascio. 1972. Changes in intrinsic motivation as a function of negative feedback and threats. Paper presented at the meeting of the Eastern Psychological Association, Boston, April.

Deci, E. L., G. Betley, J. Kahle, L. Abrams, and J. Porac. 1981. When trying to win: Competition and intrinsic motivation. *Personality and Social Psychology Bulletin* 7: 79–83.

Deci, E. L., and R. M. Ryan. 1985. *Intrinsic motivation and self-determination in human behavior.* New York: Plenum Press.

Deming, W. E. 1988. The need for change. *Journal for quality and participation* 11: 48–9.

Evans, N. 1985. *Facilitating the development of women.* San Francisco: Jossey-Bass.

Fiedler, F. E. 1967. *A theory of leadership effectiveness.* New York: McGraw-Hill.

Fisher, J. 1984. *Power of the presidency.* New York: American Council on Education.

Flanagan, J. C. (1954). The critical incident technique. *Psychological bulletin 51* (4), 327–358.

Follett, M. P. 1941. *Dynamic administration.* New York: Harper.

Garfield, C. 1986. *Peak performers: The new heroes of American business.* New York: Avon.

Gardner, J. W. 1986. *Leadership and power.* Leadership Studies Program, Washington, DC: Independent Sector.

———. 1987. Leaders and followers. *Liberal education* 73 (March/April): 4–8.

Getzels, J. 1975. Problem-finding and the inventiveness of solutions. *Journal of creative behavior* 9: 12–18.

Gillett-Karam, R. 1988. "Transformational leadership and the community college president: Are there gender differences?" Ph.D. diss., University of Texas.

Gilligan, C. 1982. *In a different voice: Psychological theory and women's development.* Cambridge, MA: Harvard University Press.

Gleazer, E. J. 1980. *The community college: Values, vision, and vitality.* Washington, DC: American Association of Community and Junior Colleges.

Hackman, J. R., and G. R. Oldham. 1980. *Work redesign.* Reading, MA: Addison-Wesley.

Hampton, D. R., C. E. Summer, and R. A. Webber. 1987. *Organizational behavior and the practice of management.* Glenview, IL: Scott, Foresman.

Heider, J. 1986. *The tao of leadership: Leadership strategies for a new age.* New York: Bantam Books.

Hersey, P., and K. H. Blanchard. 1969. *Management of organizational behavior: Utilizing human resources.* Englewood Cliffs, NJ: Prentice-Hall.

———. 1977. *Management of organizational behavior: Utilizing human resources.* Englewood Cliffs, NJ: Prentice-Hall.

Hickman, C. R., and M. A. Silva. 1984. *Creating excellence.* New York: New American Library.

Hollander, E. P. 1978. *Leadership dynamics.* New York: The Free Press.

Horner, M. 1971. Toward an understanding of achievement-related conflicts in women. *Journal of social issues* 28: 157–176.

Horney, K. 1967. *Feminine psychology.* New York: W. W. Norton.

House, R. J. 1971. A path-goal theory of leader effectiveness. *Administrative science quarterly* 16: 321–338.

House, R. J., and T. R. Mitchell. 1971. The path-goal theory of leadership. In *Perspectives in leadership effectiveness*, ed. P. Hersey and J. Stinson. Ohio University: The Center for Leadership Studies.

Hoy, W. K., and C. G. Miskel. 1987. *Educational administration.* New York: Random House.

Hoyle, J. R., F. W. English, and B. E. Steffy. 1985. *Skills for effective school leaders.* Arlington, VA: American Association of School Administrators.

Jago, A. G. 1982. Leadership: Perspectives in theory and research. *Management Science* 28: 315–336.

Kamm, R. 1982. *Leadership for leadership: Number one priority for presidents and other university administrators.* Washington, DC: University Press of America.

Kanter, R. 1977. *Men and women of the corporation.* New York: Basic Books.

Kanter, R. M. 1983. *The change masters.* New York: Simon and Schuster.

Keim, M. C. 1988. Two-year college faculty: A research description. Paper presented at the annual meeting of the Council of Universities and Colleges, Las Vegas, Nevada, April.

Kellerman, B. 1984. *Leadership: Multidisciplinary perspectives.* Englewood Cliffs, NJ: Prentice-Hall.

Keyser, J. S., ed. 1986. *Toward mastery leadership in student development services.* Summary report of a colloquium held in Traverse City, MI, July, 1985. Published by the American College Testing Program.

Kittay, E., and D. Meyers. 1987. *Women and moral theory.* Totowa, NJ: Rowman and Littlefield.

Klemp, G. O., M. T. Munger, and L. M. Spencer. 1977. *Analysis of leadership and management competencies of commissioned and noncommissioned naval officers in the Pacific and Atlantic fleets, final report.* Boston: McBer.

Klimoski, R. J., and N. J. Hayes. 1980. Leader behavior and subordinate motivation. *Personnel psychology* 33: 543–555.

Kohlberg, L. 1972. *Collected papers on moral development and moral education.* Harvard University: Moral Education Research Foundation.

Komarovsky, M. 1985. *Women in college: Shaping new feminine identities.* New York: Basic Books.

Koprowski, E. G. 1983. Cultural myths: Clues to effective management. *Organizational dynamics* 12(2): 30–51.

Kotter, J. 1988. *The leadership factor.* New York: Free Press.

Kuhn, R., and G. Geis. 1984. *The firm bond: Linking meaning and mission in business and religion.* New York: Praeger.

Lacoursiere, L.B. 1980. *The life cycle of groups: Group developmental stage theory.* New York: Human Services Press.

Lepper, M. R., D. Greene, and R. E. Nisbett. 1973. Undermining children's intrinsic interest with extrinsic rewards: A test of the "overjustification" hypothesis. *Journal of personality and social psychology* 28: 129–37.

Lewis, R., and Stewart, R. 1958. *The boss.* London: Phoenix House.

Lex, W J. 1984. "Motivational, attitudinal, and demographic correlates of two-year college chief executive officers' success." Ph.D. diss., University of Texas, Austin.

Lorsch, J. W., and P. R. Lawrence. 1970. *Studies in organizational design.* Homewood, IL: The Dorsey Press and Richard D. Irwin.

Lyons, N. 1983. Two perspectives on self, relationship and morality. *Harvard educational review* 53, 125–145.

Marascuilo, L. A. 1971. *Statistical methods for behavioral science research.* New York: McGraw-Hill.

Maslow, A. H. 1950. "Self actualizing people: A study of psychological health. Reprinted from *Personality symposium No. 1.,* ed. W. Wolff. New York: Grune & Stratton.

McClelland, D. C. (1978). *Guide to behavioral event interviewing.* Boston: McBer and Company.

McGregor, D. 1960. *The human side of enterprise.* New York: McGraw-Hill.

———. 1966. *Leadership and motivation.* Cambridge: The MIT Press.

McHolland, J. D. 1977. *Human potential seminar.* Evanston: National Center for Human Potential Seminars and Services.

Miller, J. 1976. *Toward a new psychology of women.* Boston: Beacon Press.

Miller, J. G. 1987. "An examination of women college presidents: Career paths, professional preparation, and leadership style." Ph.D. diss. George Peabody College for Teachers of Vanderbilt University.

Mintzberg. H. 1979. *The structure of organizations.* Englewood Cliffs, NJ: Prentice-Hall.

Mooney, C. J. 1988. The college president. *Chronicle of higher education* (March 30): 14–15.

Myran, G. 1983. *Strategic management in the community college.* New Directions for Community Colleges, no. 44. San Francisco: Jossey-Bass.

National Commission on Excellence in Education. 1983. *A nation at risk: The imperative for educational reform.* Washington, DC: U. S. Government Printing Office.

Noddings, N. 1984. *Caring: A feminine approach to ethics and moral education.* Berkeley, CA: University of California Press.

O'Banion, T., and J. E. Roueche. 1988a. Revitalizing leadership for community colleges. *Leadership abstracts* 1:1.

O'Banion, T. and J. E. Roueche. 1988b. Transformational leaders: An emerging national response. *Community, technical, and junior college journal* 58 (June/July): 40–41.

O'Neil, R. M. 1987. University presidents: Changing modes of leadership. *Liberal Education* 74: 39–40.

Ouchi, William G. 1981. *Theory Z.* Reading, MA: Addison-Wesley.

Parnell, D. 1985. *The neglected majority.* Washington, DC: The Community College Press.

———. 1988. Leadership is not tidy. *Leadership abstracts.* 1:4.

Peters, T., and N. Austin. 1985. *A passion for excellence.* New York: Random House.

Peters, T. J., and R. H. Waterman. 1982. *In search of excellence.* New York: Warner Books.

Pinder, C. 1984. *Work motivation: Theory, issues, and applications.* Glenview, IL: Scott, Foresman.

Quinn, R. E., and R. H. Hall. 1983. Environments, organizations, and policy makers: Toward an integrative framework. In *Organization theory and public policy: Contributions and limitations,* eds. R. H. Hall and R. E. Quinn. Beverly Hills, CA: Sage Publications.

Reddin, W. J. 1970. *Managerial effectiveness.* New York: McGraw-Hill.

Rich, A. 1977. *Of woman born.* New York: Bantam Books.

Rosenberg, R. 1982. *Beyond separate spheres: Intellectual roots of modern feminism.* New Haven: Yale University Press.

Roueche, J. E., and G. A. Baker. 1987. *Access and excellence: The open-door college.* Washington, DC: The Community College Press.

Roueche, J. E., G.A. Baker, and R. Rose. (1988). The community college president as transformational leader: A national study. *Community, technical, and junior college journal* (April/May): 48–52.

Schein, E. H. 1985. *Organizational culture and leadership.* San Francisco: Jossey-Bass.

Selznick, P. 1957. *Leadership in administration: A sociological interpretation.* Evanston: Row, Peterson and Company.

Shakeshaft, C. 1987. *Women in educational administration.* Newbury Park, CA: Sage Publications, Inc.

Simeone, A. 1987. *Academic women: Working toward equality.* South Hadley, MA: Bergin and Garvey Publishers.

Simmel, G. 1950. *The sociology of Georg Simmel.* New York: Free Press.

Simon, H. A. 1983. Discovery, invention and development: Human creative thinking. In *Proceedings of the national academy of science* 80 (July): 4569–4571.

Singer, M. S., and A. E. Singer. 1986. Relation between transformational vs. transactional leadership preference and subordinates' personality: An exploratory study. *Perceptual and motor skills* 62: 775–780.

Smith, W. E. 1974. "The effect of social and monetary rewards on intrinsic motivation." Ph.D. diss., Cornell University.

Solomon, B. 1985. *In the company of educated women: A history of women and higher education in America.* New Haven: Yale University.

Steers, R. M., and L. W. Porter. 1979. *Motivation and work behavior.* New York: McGraw-Hill.

Tannenbaum, R., and W. H. Schmidt. 1958. How to choose a leadership pattern. *Harvard business review* (March/April): 95–101.

Taylor, E. 1981. Women community college presidents. In *Women in community colleges*, ed. J. Eaton. New Directions for Community Colleges, No. 34. San Francisco: Jossey-Bass.

Tichy, N., and M. Devanna. 1986. *The transformational leader.* New York: John Wiley and Sons.

Tichy, N. M., and D. D. Ulrich. 1984. SMR Forum: The leadership challenge—A call for the transformational leader. *Sloan management review* 26(1): 59–68.

Tucker, A. 1984. *Chairing the academic department: Leadership among peers.* New York: American Council on Education/Macmillan.

Vaughan, G. B. 1986. *The community college president.* New York: American Council on Education/Macmillan.

Vough, C. F., and B. Asbell. 1979. *Productivity.* New York: American management associations.

Vroom, V. H. 1964. *Work and motivation.* New York: Wiley.

Walters, J. 1987. *The art of supportive leadership: A practical handbook for people in positions of responsibility.* Nevada City, CA: Crystal Clarity.

Watson, T. J. 1963. *A business and its beliefs: The ideas that helped build IBM.* New York: McGraw-Hill.

Woolf, V. 1938. *Three guineas.* New York: Harcourt Brace.

Zaleznik, A. 1977. Managers and leaders: Are they different? *Harvard business review* (May/June): 67–78.

APPENDICES

Appendix 1
Phase I Letter

September 4, 1987

≪full name≫
≪address≫

Dear ≪name≫:

Every recent study of higher education in America has pointed to the need for improved leadership as we move into an era of increased accountability and decreased resources. We have been examining leadership in American community colleges and have begun a new national research project to identify and study today's most effective community and technical college chief executive officers.

We especially want to recognize those leaders who have demonstrated the ability to influence, shape, and embed values, attitudes, beliefs, and behaviors consistent with increased staff and faculty commitment to the unique mission of the community college. In your view, which chief executive officers in your state have been most successful in building strong internal faculty and staff commitment to both access and excellence within the college that they lead?

On the enclosed self-addressed card, will you please identify up to five chief executive officers from your state who you think best meet the above criteria?

As always, we appreciate your assistance in helping us research and report new information regarding the community college movement. Thank you very much for your participation!

Sincerely,

John E. Roueche   George A. Baker
Professor and Director   Associate Professor and Co-Director

Appendix 1a
Phase I State Director Letter

October 13, 1987

≪full name≫
≪address≫

Dear ≪name≫:

Every recent study of higher education in America has pointed to the need for improved leadership as we move into an era of increased accountability and decreased resources. We have been examining leadership in American community colleges and have begun a new national research project to identify and study today's most effective community and technical college chief executive officers.

In Phase I, we sought nominations from over 900 public two-year CEOs in order to identify those leaders within a state who have demonstrated the ability to influence and shape behaviors consistent with increased staff and faculty commitment to the unique mission of the community/technical college. To date we have received a response from over 700 CEOs. Their nominations have generated a list of some 350 who received multiple nominations.

We recognize that if we ended our search with the present selections, we would have an exceptional group of community/technical college leaders. However, in order to strengthen our study, we wish to further identify an even more select group of individuals who have been recognized as strong leaders through personal observation by their peers and knowledgeable others such as yourself. We need your assistance in completing this important task.

Because of the significant role you play in your state and in the community college movement, we would appreciate your help in the second phase of our national research project. In your view, which CEOs in your state/nation have been most successful in building strong internal faculty and staff commitment to both access and excellence within the college they lead? Please share with us your nominations on the attached form.

We appreciate your assistance in helping us research and report this new information regarding the community college movement. Thank you very much for your participation.

Sincerely,

John E. Roueche
Professor and Director

George A. Baker
Associate Professor and Co-Director

Appendix 2
Phase I Response Card

My nominees for the most effective community college chief executive officers in this geographical region are:

Name:

College:

_____   _____

_____   _____

_____   _____

_____   _____

_____   _____

Your signature and state: _____

Your identification and selections will remain confidential.

Appendix 3
Phase II Letter

October 8, 1987

≪full name≫
≪address≫

Dear ≪name≫:

Congratulations! You have been recognized by your colleagues as an outstanding community college chief executive officer in ≪state≫. We trust that you will share this information with those in your college and community who have contributed to the recognition that you and your college so richly deserve.

In our initial letter, we sought nominations from over 900 public two-year CEOs in order to identify those leaders who have demonstrated the ability to influence and shape behaviors consistent with increased staff and faculty commitment to the unique mission of the community college. You have emerged as one of the CEOs in your state or region who has been successful in building strong internal faculty and staff commitment to both access and excellence in your college.

We recognize that if we ended our search with the present selections, we would have an exceptional group of community college leaders. However, in order to strengthen our study, we wish to further identify an even more select group of individuals who have been recognized as strong leaders through personal observation by their peers and knowledgeable others. We need your assistance in completing this important task.

Because of the significant role you play in the community college movement, we would appreciate your help in the second phase of our national research project. Will you please complete the following forms per the instructions provided?

(a) Presidential Information (orange form)
   PLEASE ATTACH A COPY OF YOUR VITA.
(b) Educational Leadership Philosophy (white form)
(c) Criteria for Selection—Exceptional CEOs (blue form)

We know this request will take some of your valued executive time; however, the information generated will be of great value to us and hopefully to you. We appreciate your assistance in helping us research and report this new information regarding the community college movement. Thank you very much for your participation.

Sincerely,

John E. Roueche   George A. Baker
Professor and Director   Associate Professor and Co-Director

Appendix 4
Educational Leadership Philosophy

In the space provided below, please share with us your personal philosophy regarding educational leadership. Feel free to cite examples of your thinking and your behavior that may help us to understand better the context in which you lead. (Please attach any artifacts developed by you that support your leadership philosophy.)

Appendix 5
Presidential Information Questionnaire (PIQ)

Directions: ANSWER ONLY THE QUESTIONS THAT ARE NOT CON-
TAINED IN YOUR ATTACHED VITA. Please circle the appropriate
answer to each question as it applies to you. In addition, please supply
information where blanks are provided and specific information is
requested.

Part 1—Biographical

1. Age   _____ yrs

2. Place of birth   City _____
                           State _____

3. Population where family lived at the time of your birth?

Rural (less than 2,500)	A
Town (2,500—10,000)	B
City (10,000—25,000)	C
City (25,000—100,000)	D
City (over 100,000)	E

4. Years that you have been a resident of your present state?

                _____ yrs

5. In what state were you residing immediately prior to now?
                State _____

6. Were you a resident of your present state immediately prior to your
   Presidential appointment?   Yes   No

Part 2—Background and Experience

1. What educational positions have you held prior to your present appointment and for how long?

		YRS
Teaching: elementary	A	_____
secondary	B	_____
community college	C	_____

college—university   D _____
Administration: elementary   E _____
secondary   F _____
community college   G _____
college—university   H _____
Occupation other than above   I _____

If "I," please identify occupation and give location:

_____

2. Years you have worked at your present position?   _____ yrs

3. Number of community colleges you have been associated with as an instructor and administrator: (Circle one for each)

	Instructor	Administrator
One	A	A
Two	B	B
Three	C	C
More than three	D	D

4. What was your first administrative position?

(Identify and give location) _____

5. At what age did you first become an educational administrator?
     _____ yrs

6. Have you been a founding president?   Yes   No

7. Please identify the position you held just prior to assuming your present position.

Position-title: _____

Organization: _____

Dates: From _____ To _____

Location: _____

8. Highest degree earned: Ph.D _____ Ed.D _____ Masters _____

Other (please specify) _____

Name of university _____

Location _____ Major _____ Minor _____

9. Identify the activity, topic, date, location and value of your last participation in a community college course, workshop, seminar, or institute.

Activity _____

Topic _____

Date: _____ Location: _____

Please estimate value: _____

Part 3—Time Utilization

1. On the average, how many hours per WEEK do you spend at your college (regular work hours)?   _____ hrs

2. On the average, how many hours per WEEK do you spend in college-related activities (outside of regular work)?   _____ hrs

3. Given a typical work WEEK, please estimate the number of hours spent in each location.

   At Home: _____ hrs   In Office: _____ hrs

   Out of Office but on Campus: _____ hrs

   Off Campus but in Service Area: _____ hrs

   Out of Service Area: _____ hrs

4. Given a typical work DAY, please estimate the number of hours you spend:

Alone ____ hrs   With one other person ____ hrs

With two or more people ____ hrs

5. Considering a typical work WEEK, how would you estimate that you divide your/time among the major roles listed below? (Please give approximate percentages.)

   I. Leading and influencing others ____ %

  II. Developing, disseminating, evaluating information ____ %

 III. Planning, making and evaluating decisions ____ %

6. In accomplishing each of the major roles identified in question five, please estimate the number of hours spent per WEEK with each of the following constituent groups.

Trustees ____ hrs	Administrative team ____ hrs
Faculty ____ hrs	Classified staff ____ hrs
Students ____ hrs	Outside individuals/agencies ____ hrs

Appendix 6
Criteria for Selection—Exceptional CEOs

The criteria for selection are as follows:

1. Nominate individual(s) who have demonstrated the ability to influence, shape, and embed values, attitudes, beliefs, and behaviors consistent with increased staff and faculty commitment to the unique mission of the community college (technical institute).

2. Nominate CEOs from anywhere in the nation with whom you have had direct personal and/or professional experience in the past five years. Direct experience would include working for or with this individual in a relationship where you have had an opportunity to observe leadership ability.

3. Your nominee(s) must have been an active CEO within the past twelve months.

Based on my professional first-hand experience, I wish to nominate the following individual(s) as effective community college (technical institute) chief executive officer(s) worthy of national recognition. (Your personal selections will remain confidential.)

NAME: COLLEGE:

_____   _____

_____   _____

Appendix 7
"Blue-Chip" Interview Format

This interview is focusing on Presidential Leadership. It seeks to point out the characteristics of effective leadership as exhibited by those who have been selected as excellent community college presidents throughout the nation. Our questions are aimed at demonstrating the characteristics of **transformational leadership: the ability to influence, shape, and embed values, attitudes, beliefs, and behaviors of the college family** (Roueche and Baker, 1987).

Would you please share your thoughts concerning your abilities as an effective leader? What do you bring to each of the following dimensions of transformational leadership that enables you to bring about change in your college environment?

1. In your role as President of a community college, what is it that you do that focuses upon the future direction of your college? Can you describe an incident that required you to (re)direct the focus of your college? Were you successful?

2. How would you explain or characterize your particular style of leadership? Can you tell me about a particular situation which demonstrates your leadership style? What happened? What was the outcome?

3. How would you describe your relationships to students and staff in your institution? Can you discuss a particular incident or situation which describes your orientation or relationship with students, faculty, administrators, or board members? What happened? What was the outcome?

4. Describe how you as College President motivate others around you? Tell me about an incident in which you inspired others.

5. How do your personal values impact your position as College President? Can you tell me about an incident in which your values were challenged? What happened?

6. If you could change education in any way, what would it be? How might you accomplish the change(s)?

Appendix 8

MULTIFACTOR COLLEGE LEADERSHIP QUESTIONNAIRE (MCLQ)

COMMUNITY COLLEGE VERSION

GEORGE BAKER
JOHN ROUECHE
BOB ROSE

FORM A: CHIEF EXECUTIVE OFFICER

March 1988
First Version

MULTIFACTOR COLLEGE LEADERSHIP QUESTIONNAIRE (MCLQ)

FORM A

PURPOSE: The intent of this instrument is to obtain your perceptions of the extent to which you are able to influence your executive leadership team as they perform their duties and responsibilities.

RATIONALE: Most experts agree that the leadership, more than any other component, is responsible for setting the tone for behavior within the college. Thus your self-appraisal will be extremely important in determining the perceived quality of your leadership as you influence others.

ASSUMPTION: We assume that you typically work through and
               with your executive leadership team to accomplish
               the supervision and direction of the college/district
               that you lead. "Leadership team" is defined as
               those who report directly to you either in a staff
               or line capacity.

INSTRUCTIONS: Please rate yourself on the leadership dimensions
               listed in the survey. <u>Circle the letter of the response</u>
               that best represents your perception or belief.

               Your responses are <u>ANONYMOUS</u> and individual
               responses will be kept <u>CONFIDENTIAL</u>. All origi-
               nal survey forms will be destroyed after responses
               have been analyzed. Your responses will be
               grouped, tabulated, and presented as normed data.
               No one will see your survey except the research
               personnel working on this project.

1. When interacting with the leadership team, I attempt to apply consistent ethical standards of professional behavior.

A	**B**	**C**	**D**	**E**
Frequently if not always	Fairly often	Sometimes	Once in a while	Not at all

2. I inspire my leadership team to extra effort through appropriate
praise and direction.

A	**B**	**C**	**D**	**E**
Frequently if not always	Fairly often	Sometimes	Once in a while	Not at all

3. I empower my leadership team by delegating appropriate authority
and responsibility.

A	**B**	**C**	**D**	**E**
Frequently if not always	Fairly often	Sometimes	Once in a while	Not at all

4. I take appropriate risks to bring about change.

A	B	C	D	E
Frequently if not always	Fairly often	Sometimes	Once in a while	Not at all

5. I seek and value the opinion of my leadership team.

A	B	C	D	E
Frequently if not always	Fairly often	Sometimes	Once in a while	Not at all

6. I am able to conceptualize a specific future for the college/district.

A	B	C	D	E
Frequently if not always	Fairly often	Sometimes	Once in a while	Not at all

7. I am able to enhance the development of my leadership team.

A	B	C	D	E
Frequently if not always	Fairly often	Sometimes	Once in a while	Not at all

8. Within my leadership team, I am able to accommodate individual needs.

A	B	C	D	E
Frequently if not always	Fairly often	Sometimes	Once in a while	Not at all

9. My values are influenced by my leadership team.

A	B	C	D	E
Frequently if not always	Fairly often	Sometimes	Once in a while	Not at all

10. I demonstrate a commitment to the quality development of the leadership team.

A	B	C	D	E
Frequently if not always	Fairly often	Sometimes	Once in a while	Not at all

11. When interacting with my leadership team, I am characterized by a bias for action.

A	**B**	**C**	**D**	**E**
Frequently if not always	Fairly often	Sometimes	Once in a while	Not at all

12. I understand the character, sentiment, and moral values of my leadership team.

A	**B**	**C**	**D**	**E**
Frequently if not always	Fairly often	Sometimes	Once in a while	Not at all

13. I influence my leadership team by setting a personal example of expected conduct.

A	**B**	**C**	**D**	**E**
Frequently if not always	Fairly often	Sometimes	Once in a while	Not at all

14. I motivate my leadership team through clarification of my expectations.

A	**B**	**C**	**D**	**E**
Frequently if not always	Fairly often	Sometimes	Once in a while	Not at all

15. I articulate a strong commitment to student access and success.

A	**B**	**C**	**D**	**E**
Frequently if not always	Fairly often	Sometimes	Once in a while	Not at all

16. I am able to involve my leadership team appropriately in decision-making.

A	**B**	**C**	**D**	**E**
Frequently if not always	Fairly often	Sometimes	Once in a while	Not at all

17. When interacting with the leadership team, I demonstrate consistent judgment.

A	B	C	D	E
Frequently if not always	Fairly often	Sometimes	Once in a while	Not at all

18. Above other concerns, I value students and consider their needs.

A	B	C	D	E
Frequently if not always	Fairly often	Sometimes	Once in a while	Not at all

19. I demonstrate a high need to be visible and to stay in touch with those I am attempting to influence.

A	B	C	D	E
Frequently if not always	Fairly often	Sometimes	Once in a while	Not at all

20. I am committed to specific courses of action in order to accomplish selected goals.

A	B	C	D	E
Frequently if not always	Fairly often	Sometimes	Once in a while	Not at all

21. When interacting with the leadership team, I build openness and trust.

A	B	C	D	E
Frequently if not always	Fairly often	Sometimes	Once in a while	Not at all

22. I cause my leadership team to feel powerful through tasking and consideration of their needs.

A	B	C	D	E
Frequently if not always	Fairly often	Sometimes	Once in a while	Not at all

23. I believe that I can shape the future as it applies to the college/district.

A	B	C	D	E
Frequently if not always	Fairly often	Sometimes	Once in a while	Not at all

24. I am able to motivate my leadership team to significant levels of commitment and action.

A	B	C	D	E
Frequently if not always	Fairly often	Sometimes	Once in a while	Not at all

25. I am able to facilitate high-level problem-solving within the leadership team.

A	B	C	D	E
Frequently if not always	Fairly often	Sometimes	Once in a while	Not at all

26. I demonstrate a commitment to the higher intellectual development of the leadership team.

A	B	C	D	E
Frequently if not always	Fairly often	Sometimes	Once in a while	Not at all

27. In responding to the needs of my leadership team, I demonstrate a respect for individual differences.

A	B	C	D	E
Frequently if not always	Fairly often	Sometimes	Once in a while	Not at all

28. I am able to cause my team to share in a vision of the future.

A	B	C	D	E
Frequently if not always	Fairly often	Sometimes	Once in a while	Not at all

29. In interacting with the leadership team, I am energetic when the situation demands action.

A	B	C	D	E
Frequently if not always	Fairly often	Sometimes	Once in a while	Not at all

30. I am able to motivate my leadership team to utilize their creative skills.

A	B	C	D	E
Frequently if not always	Fairly often	Sometimes	Once in a while	Not at all

31. I reward those within my leadership team contingent on their effort and performance.

A	B	C	D	E
Frequently if not always	Fairly often	Sometimes	Once in a while	Not at all

32. I am able to communicate to others a sense of mission.

A	B	C	D	E
Frequently if not always	Fairly often	Sometimes	Once in a while	Not at all

33. I am able to build an effective communication network within the leadership team.

A	B	C	D	E
Frequently if not always	Fairly often	Sometimes	Once in a while	Not at all

34. I employ humor appropriately to motivate and inspire the leadership team.

A	B	C	D	E
Frequently if not always	Fairly often	Sometimes	Once in a while	Not at all

Appendix 9

MULTIFACTOR COLLEGE LEADERSHIP QUESTIONNAIRE (MCLQ)

COMMUNITY COLLEGE VERSION

GEORGE BAKER
JOHN ROUECHE
BOB ROSE

FORM B: THE EXECUTIVE TEAM OF THE CHIEF EXECUTIVE OFFICER

March 1988
First Version

MULTIFACTOR COLLEGE LEADERSHIP QUESTIONNAIRE (MCLQ)

FORM B

PURPOSE: The intent of this instrument is to obtain your perceptions of the extent to which your CEO is able to influence the leadership team as you perform your administration duties.

RATIONALE: Most experts agree that the leadership, more than any other component, is responsible for setting the tone for behavior within the college. Thus your evaluation will be extremely important in determining the perceived quality of leadership of your CEO.

ASSUMPTION: We assume that the CEO typically works through and with the executive leadership team to accomplish the supervision and direction of the college/district. "Leadership team" is defined as those who report directly to the CEO either in a staff or line capacity.

INSTRUCTIONS: Please rate the CEO (President or Chancellor) listed below on the leadership qualities included in the survey. <u>Circle the letter of the response</u> that best represents your perception or opinion of the CEO's behavior when interacting with the leadership team.

The last question on the survey is an open-ended question. It seeks a written example of an incident where the CEO was involved in a critical situation requiring significant leadership skills to resolve a problem. Your thoughtful response is appreciated.

Your responses are <u>ANONYMOUS</u> and individual responses will be kept <u>CONFIDENTIAL</u>. All original survey forms will be destroyed after responses have been analyzed. Your responses will be grouped, tabulated, and presented as normed data. No one will see your survey except the research personnel working on this project.

Name and position of CEO to be rated: _____

1. When interacting with the leadership team, the CEO applies consistent ethical standards of professional behavior.

A	B	C	D	E
Frequently if not always	Fairly often	Sometimes	Once in a while	Not at all

2. The CEO inspires the leadership team to extra effort through appropriate praise and direction.

A	B	C	D	E
Frequently if not always	Fairly often	Sometimes	Once in a while	Not at all

3. The CEO empowers the leadership team by delegating appropriate authority and responsibility.

A	B	C	D	E
Frequently if not always	Fairly often	Sometimes	Once in a while	Not at all

4. The CEO takes appropriate risks to bring about change.

A	B	C	D	E
Frequently if not always	Fairly often	Sometimes	Once in a while	Not at all

5. The CEO seeks and values the opinion of the leadership team.

A	B	C	D	E
Frequently if not always	Fairly often	Sometimes	Once in a while	Not at all

6. The CEO is able to conceptualize a specific future for the college/district.

A	B	C	D	E
Frequently if not always	Fairly often	Sometimes	Once in a while	Not at all

7. The CEO is able to enhance the development of those within the leadership team.

A	B	C	D	E
Frequently if not always	Fairly often	Sometimes	Once in a while	Not at all

8. Within the leadership team, the CEO is able to accommodate individual needs.

A	B	C	D	E
Frequently if not always	Fairly often	Sometimes	Once in a while	Not at all

9. The CEO's values are influenced by the leadership team.

A	B	C	D	E
Frequently if not always	Fairly often	Sometimes	Once in a while	Not at all

10. The CEO demonstrates a commitment to the quality development of the leadership team.

A	B	C	D	E
Frequently if not always	Fairly often	Sometimes	Once in a while	Not at all

11. When interacting with the leadership team, the CEO is characterized by a bias for action.

A	B	C	D	E
Frequently if not always	Fairly often	Sometimes	Once in a while	Not at all

12. The CEO understands the character, sentiment, and moral values of the leadership team.

A	B	C	D	E
Frequently if not always	Fairly often	Sometimes	Once in a while	Not at all

13. The CEO influences the leadership team by setting a personal example of expected conduct.

A	B	C	D	E
Frequently if not always	Fairly often	Sometimes	Once in a while	Not at all

14. The CEO motivates the leadership team through clarification of expectations.

A	B	C	D	E
Frequently if not always	Fairly often	Sometimes	Once in a while	Not at all

15. The CEO articulates a strong commitment to student access and success.

A	B	C	D	E
Frequently if not always	Fairly often	Sometimes	Once in a while	Not at all

16. The CEO is able to involve the leadership team appropriately in decision-making.

A	B	C	D	E
Frequently if not always	Fairly often	Sometimes	Once in a while	Not at all

17. When interacting with the leadership team, the CEO demonstrates consistent judgment.

A	B	C	D	E
Frequently if not always	Fairly often	Sometimes	Once in a while	Not at all

18. Above other concerns, the CEO values students and considers their needs.

A	B	C	D	E
Frequently if not always	Fairly often	Sometimes	Once in a while	Not at all

19. The CEO demonstrates a high need to be visible and to stay in touch with those that the CEO is attempting to influence.

A	B	C	D	E
Frequently if not always	Fairly often	Sometimes	Once in a while	Not at all

20. The CEO is committed to specific courses of action in order to accomplish selected goals.

A	B	C	D	E
Frequently if not always	Fairly often	Sometimes	Once in a while	Not at all

21. When interacting with the leadership team, the CEO builds openness and trust.

A	B	C	D	E
Frequently if not always	Fairly often	Sometimes	Once in a while	Not at all

22. The CEO causes the leadership team to feel powerful through tasking and consideration of their needs.

A	B	C	D	E
Frequently if not always	Fairly often	Sometimes	Once in a while	Not at all

23. The CEO believes that he/she can shape the future as it applies to
the college/district.

A	B	C	D	E
Frequently if not always	Fairly often	Sometimes	Once in a while	Not at all

24. The CEO is able to motivate the leadership team to significant levels
of commitment and action.

A	B	C	D	E
Frequently if not always	Fairly often	Sometimes	Once in a while	Not at all

25. The CEO is able to facilitate high-level problem-solving within the
leadership team.

A	B	C	D	E
Frequently if not always	Fairly often	Sometimes	Once in a while	Not at all

26. The CEO demonstrates commitment to the higher intellectual development of the leadership team.

A	B	C	D	E
Frequently if not always	Fairly often	Sometimes	Once in a while	Not at all

27. In responding to the needs of the leadership team, the CEO demonstrates a respect for individual differences.

A	B	C	D	E
Frequently if not always	Fairly often	Sometimes	Once in a while	Not at all

28. The CEO is able to cause the leadership team to share in a vision of the future.

A	B	C	D	E
Frequently if not always	Fairly often	Sometimes	Once in a while	Not at all

29. In interacting with the leadership team, the CEO is energetic when the situation demands action.

A	B	C	D	E
Frequently if not always	Fairly often	Sometimes	Once in a while	Not at all

30. The CEO motivates the leadership team to utilize their creative skills.

A	B	C	D	E
Frequently if not always	Fairly often	Sometimes	Once in a while	Not at all

31. The CEO rewards the leadership team contingent on their effort and performance.

A	B	C	D	E
Frequently if not always	Fairly often	Sometimes	Once in a while	Not at all

32. The CEO communicates to the leadership team a sense of mission.

A	B	C	D	E
Frequently if not always	Fairly often	Sometimes	Once in a while	Not at all

33. The CEO is able to build an effective communication network within the leadership team.

A	B	C	D	E
Frequently if not always	Fairly often	Sometimes	Once in a while	Not at all

34. The CEO employs humor appropriately to motivate and inspire the leadership team.

A	B	C	D	E
Frequently if not always	Fairly often	Sometimes	Once in a while	Not at all

35. Consider your responses to the previous questions. Please relate
    to us an important incident where you believe that your CEO was
    highly successful or unsuccessful in influencing the leadership team.

The situation: _____

_____

_____

_____

The circumstances: _____

_____

_____

_____

What the CEO did: _____

_____

_____

_____

_____

What the results were: _____

_____

_____

_____

_____

Appendix 10
Leadership Team Members

Jefferson State Junior College (AL)
Robert Drennen, Dean of Finance and Development
Joe Morris, Dean of Instruction
Jerry Farquahar, Dean of Administrative Services
Martha Markus, Business Manager/Treasurer
Grace Kelly, Director of Community Relations

John C. Calhoun State Community College (AL)
Sandra K. Martin, Vice President
Robert D. Searcy, Academic Dean
Jo N. Beene, Dean of Students
Robert Rose, Dean of the Technical College
Catherine Hansberry, Director of Development/Title III Coordinator
Roy G. Childers, Business Manager

Maricopa County Community College District (AZ)
Nancy Jordan, Executive Assistant Chancellor
Alfredo De Los Santos, Vice Chancellor for Educational Development
William Waechter, Vice Chancellor for Human Resources
Dan Whittemore, Vice Chancellor for Business Services
Rea Drennen, Executive Director of Maricopa Foundation
Ron Bleed, Chief Information Officer
Jan Baltzer, Director of Telecommunications
Myrna Harrison, President of Gateway Community College
John Waltrip, President of Glendale Community College
Bill Berry, President of Phoenix College

Phillips County Community College (AR)
Steven Jones, Vice President for Administration
Gene Weber, Vice President for Instruction
John Baker, Dean of Occupational Education
Jerald Barber, Chief Fiscal Officer
Daniel Rusak, Dean of Students

De Anza College (CA)
Don Perata, Vice President for Student Services
Barbara Reid, Vice President for Instruction
Oscar Ramirez, Dean of Instructional Development

Dick Wright, Dean of Administrative Services
Jorge Guevarra, Dean of Technical Education
Ralph Steinke, Dean of Learning Resources
Jim Lucas, Director of Institutional Research

Foothill-De Anza Community College District (CA)
  Tom Clements, President of Foothill College
  Bob DeHart, President of De Anza College
  Miriam Rosenthal, President of Foothill College Academic
    Senate
  Paul Setziol, President of De Anza College Academic Senate
  Jack Mason, Director of Business Services
  Sharon Keyworth, General Counsel
  Gerry Kaspar, Director of Human Resources & Affirmative Action
  Peggy Moore, President of Foothill-De Anza Faculty Association
  Carol Clawson, President of CSEA Chapter 416
  Jim Ayers, President of CSEA Chapter 96

Los Rios Community College District (CA)
  Marc Hall, President of Cosumnes River College
  Robert Harris, President of Sacramento City College
  Queen Randall, President of American River College
  Douglas Burris, Vice Chancellor
  Ann Reed, Director of Community and Media Relations
  Sue Shelley, Director of Legal Services
  Janis Coffey, Director of Planning and Research
  Diane Carey, Director of Community and Economic Development
  Jeanie Lee, Executive Secretary to the Chancellor

Rancho Santiago College (CA)
  Carter Doran, Vice Chancellor of Instruction
  Grace Mitchell, Vice Chancellor of Student & Community
    Services
  Bob Matthew, Vice Chancellor of Business
  Peter Parra, Director of Personnel
  Ray Giles, Executive Assistant for Public Affairs & Development
  Julie Slark, Director of Research & Planning

Santa Barbara City College (CA)
  John Romo, Vice President for Academic Affairs
  Martin Bobqan, Vice President for Continuing Education
  Lynda Fairly, Vice President for Student Affairs

Dan Oroz, Director of Personnel
Charles Hanson, Business Manager
Burt Miller, Administrative Assistant to the President
James Minow, Executive Director, The Foundation of SBCC
Jim Williams, Director of Public Information
Rob Reilly, Director of Publications

Yosemite Community College District (CA)
Berdette Cofer, Vice Chancellor of Business Services
W. Dean Cunningham, President of Columbia College
Pamila Fisher, Assistant Chancellor of Educational Services
Stanley Hodges, President of Modesto Junior College
Richard Peralta, Assistant Chancellor of Personnel Services
Dorothy Swartwood, Administrative Assistant to the Chancellor
Delores Adair, Executive Secretary to the Chancellor

Community College of Denver (CO)
Mary Kelly O'Donnell, Director-Public Information &
    Community Relations
Marlene Hall, Vice President for Instruction
Martin Van deVisse, Vice President for Student Services
Steve Hunter, Vice President for Administrative Services
Sally Conway, Director of Development and Special Projects
Tim Griffin, Director of Institutional Research

Quinebaug Valley Community College (CT)
John T. Boland, Dean of Administration
Ellis A. Hagstrom, Academic Dean
Beverly Hounsell, Dean of Students

Delaware Technical and Community College (DE)
Henry J. Decker, Coordinator of Computer Services and
    Information Systems
Raymond R. Dotts, Fiscal Coordinator
James L. Ford, Jr., Assistant to the President for College Relations
William C. Pfeifer, Acting Director of Development
John H. Jones, Vice President & Campus Director-Stanton/
    Wilmington Campuses
Orlando J. George, Jr., Assistant Campus Director-Stanton/
    Wilmington Campuses
Anthony S. Digenakis, Assistant to President-Technical Services/
    Specialized Training

Jack F. Owens, Vice President and Campus Director-Southern
Campus
Wayne N. Dabson, Assistant Campus Director-Terry Campus
Linda C. Jolly, Acting Vice President and Campus Director-Terry
Campus

Brevard Community College (FL)
Joseph M. Keller, Vice President of Instructional Advancement
Stephen J. Megregian, Vice President for Business Affairs
Robert Anderson, Associate Vice President, Collegewide Student
Services
Leon E. Stearns, Provost, Facility Planning
Harold Creel, Director of Plant Maintenance and Operations
Patrick D. Smith, Director of College Relations
Walter L. Gilfilen, Assistant to the President/Federal Programs Office
Barbara Kirk, Director of BCC Foundation

Gulf Coast Community College (FL)
Linda B. Adair, Dean of Academic Affairs
Lewis Baber, Dean of Career Education
Ian C. Barker, Assistant to the President
Ivie R. Burch, Director of Planning and Development
Anne McCullen, Dean of Student Development
Robert L. McSpadden, Acting President
Carole Mancinelli, Coordinator of Public Information
Charles Mitchell, Comptroller
John Morris, Dean of Business Affairs
Pamela L. Whitelock, Dean of Lifelong Learning

Miami-Dade Community College (FL)
William Stokes, Vice President for South Campus
J. T. Kelly, Vice President for North Campus
Karen Dillman, President of Faculty Senate Consortium
Eduardo Padron, Vice President for Wolfson Campus
Roy Phillips, Vice President for Public Affairs
Lester Brockner, Vice President for Business Affairs
Piedad Robertson, Vice President for Education
Duane Hansen, Vice President for Administration
Horace Traylor, Vice President for Advancement

Dalton Junior College (GA)
Wayne E. Bell, Academic Dean

Harlan L. Chapman, Registrar and Director of Admissions
Patricia Fornash, Director of Continuing Education
R. Larry Little, Chairperson, Division of Vocational/Technical
  Education
Jacqueline Stanley, Associate Comptroller

College of DuPage (IL)
  Theodore Tilton, Provost of Central Campus
  Carol J. Viola, Provost at Open Campus
  Richard Petrizzo, Vice President of External Affairs
  Kenneth Kolbet, Vice President of Administration
  Ronald Lemme, Vice President of Planning and Information

Danville Area Community College (IL)
  Wilbur J. Dickson, Vice President for Instruction
  Sue I. Murphey, Dean of Student Services
  David Kietzmann, Dean of Community Services
  Rebecca Schlecht, Director of Personnel
  Ann Abel, Director of Job Training Partnership Program

North Iowa Area Community College (IA)
  Homer Bienfang, Dean of Student Services
  Robert Church, Business Manager
  Noreen Coyan, Director of Personnel
  Mark Evers, Director of Community Relations
  Alfred Hecht, Assistant Superintendent for Academic Affairs
  Roger Holcomb, Dean of Community Services
  Don Kamps, Director of Learning Services
  Robert Peterson, Director of Operational Services

Johnson County Community College (KS)
  Jerry Baird, Vice President for Administration
  Dan Radakovich, Vice President for Academic Affairs
  Linda Dayton, Dean of Student Services
  Mary Lou Taylor, Dean of Instruction
  Glen Gabert, Dean of Institutional Planning and Advancement
  Dane Lonborg, Dean of Community Services
  Bob Burdick, Director of College Information and Publications
  Al Barton, Director of Development

Jefferson Community College (KY)
  Diane Calhoun-French, Dean of Academic Affairs-Southwest Campus

Norma Gaskey, Dean of Academic Affairs-Downtown Campus
Larry Clardy, Budget/Personnel Officer
Peggy Mull, Assistant to the President
Charles Ainsworth, Dean of Student Services-Downtown Campus
Mary Abrams, Dean of Student Services-Southwest Campus
Steve Yeager, Coordinator of Technical Resources
Kevin Engler, Coordinator of Public Relations
Jim Meeks, Supervisor of Maintenance and Operations-
   Downtown Campus
Katy Varner, Coordinator of Faculty/Staff Development

Montgomery College (MD)
   Frederick J. Walsh, Academic Vice President
   Charlene Nunley, Vice President for Planning & Advancement
   Vergil Dykstra, Administrative Vice President
   Antoinette Hastings, Provost-Rockville Campus
   O. Robert Brown, Provost-Takoma Park Campus
   Noreen Lyne, Provost, Continuing Education
   Robert Watson, Assistant to the President
   Frank Tusa, Director of Employee Relations
   Joan Gordon, General Counsel
   William Campbell, Director of Institutional Research

Bristol Community College (MA)
   David Feeney, Academic Dean
   Jack Warner, Dean of Students
   Janice Motta, Dean of Continuing Education
   John Fonseca, Dean of Administration
   Richard Sobel, Assistant to the President
   Jack Wiberg, Director of Personnel
   Mary Fitton, Administrative Assistant

Macomb Community College (MI)
   Helen Liebgott, Assistant to the President
   James J. Blanzy, Senior Vice President for Academic Affairs
   Karl J. Wagner, Senior Vice President for Student and
      Community Services
   Robert A. Shankie, Senior Vice President for Business
   William J. MacQueen, Vice President for Employee Relations
   Catherine B. Ahles, Vice President for College Relations

Schoolcraft College (MI)
    Saundra P. Florek, Director of Institutional Research
    Barbara Geil, Vice President for Business Services
    Conway Jeffress, Vice President for Instruction
    Gerald W. Munro, Manager of Personnel Services
    Adelard H. Raby, III, Vice President for Business Services

Washtenaw Community College (MI)
    Harry Konschub, Vice President for Administration and Finance
    Guy Altieri, Vice President for Instruction and Student Services
    Catherine Arcure, Executive Director for College Advancement
    John Lynch, Executive Director for Business and Industry
      Services

Meridian Community College (MS)
    Clarence Roberts, Vice President of Instruction
    John A. Johnson, Business Manager
    Anne Donolr, Director of Development
    Aljean Young, Dean of Student Services
    Tommy McDonald, Director of Admissions/Records
    John M. Turner, Director of Vocational/Technical Education

St. Louis Community College (MO)
    James E. Billings, Vice Chancellor for Administration
    Gwendolyn Stephenson, Vice Chancellor for Educational
      Development
    Larry Patten, Vice Chancellor-Information Technology/
      Telecommunications
    Vernon Crawley, President of Forest Park Campus
    Ralph Doty, President of Meramec Campus
    Michael Murphy, President of Florissant Valley Campus
    Robert Gaffner, Executive Director-Foundation/Assistant to
      Chancellor
    Gary Mohr, Executive Director-St. Louis Business/Industry/Labor
      Center
    Ray Taylor, Executive Director-Resource Development

Metropolitan Technical Community College (NE)
    Dick Baer, Vice President of Finance & Administrative Services
    Burrell Beck, Vice President of Marketing & Public Relations
    Kathryn Brailer, Vice President of College Support Services
    Karen Wells, Vice President of Educational Services

Walt Kujawa, Assistant to the President
Jody Addison, Executive Secretary to the President

San Juan College (NM)
Marjorie Black, Assistant to the President
Bob Hokom, Dean of Instruction
Karl Zaffke, Dean of Student Services
Dennis Marquez, Dean of Fiscal Affairs
Donna Ogilvie, Director of Public Relations
Pete Rahn, Director of the San Juan College Foundation
Mary Jo Clark, Director of Institutional Research

Monroe Community College (NY)
Frank Milligan, Vice President for Academic Affairs
Jerry Ryan, Vice President for Institutional Advancement
Thomas Murphy, Vice President for Administration
Thomas Flynn, Vice President for Student Services
Robert Brown, Assistant to the President

Westchester Community College (NY)
John F. Flynn, Jr., Vice President of Academic Affairs
Julius C. Ford, Jr., Vice President of Student Services
Fred Boyar, Vice President of Administrative Services
Leonard Harper, Vice President of Educational Opportunity
    Center
Mark Gesoff, Director of Management Information Services
Betsy Weiner, Director of College/Community Relations

Central Piedmont Community College (NC)
Gayle Simmons, Executive Vice President for Education
Bill McIntosh, Vice President for Planning and Development
John Harper, Vice President for Business and College Services
Mike Myers, Executive Director for Community Relations
Worth Campbell, Assistant to the President

Sandhills Community College (NC)
Don Scott, Vice President for Business
James C. Halstead, Vice President for Instructional Programs
Inza Abernathy, Administrative Assistant
Sharon Shaw, Assistant for Communications
Larry Allen, Assistant for Public Relations and Fundraising

Cuyahoga Community College District (OH)
   Carol Scheid, Assistant to the President
   Joseph Nolan, Executive Vice President
   Paul Shumaker, Vice President of Telecommunications/
      Computer Resources
   Curtis Jefferson, Vice President of Academic Affairs
   Marshall Moore, Treasurer
   Alan Hoffman, Vice President for Facility Service
   Bud Weidenthal, Vice President for Public Affairs & Information
   William Murphy, Acting Vice President for Personnel & Legal
      Counsel
   Ronald Sobel, Provost/Vice President for Western Campus
   Ronald Zambetti, Provost/Vice President for Metro Campus
   Grace Brown, Provost/Vice President for Eastern Campus
   Michael Taggart, Executive Director of Unified Technologies Center

Sinclair Community College (OH)
   Barry Blacklidge, Vice President for Business Operations
   Ned Sifferlen, Vice President for Instruction
   Steve Jonas, Vice President for Administration

Tulsa Junior College (OK)
   Dean Van Trease, Executive Vice President
   Herman Robbins, Vice President of Business & Auxiliary Services
   Robert Melott, Vice President of Computer Services & Data Systems

Clackamas Community College (OR)
   Jim Roberts, Dean of Students
   Lyle Reese, Dean of Instruction
   Bill Ryan, Dean of Administration
   David Dickson, Assistant to the President
   Jeff Molatore, President of Faculty Association
   Neale Frothingham, President of Student Association
   Paul Kyllo, President of Classified Association
   Chuck Adams, Director of Information and Planning
   Bill Symes, Director of Public Information

Community College of Rhode Island (RI)
   Rosemary Zins, Director of Development-Flanagan Campus
   Nancy Abood, Assistant to the President-Knight Campus
   Raymond Ferland, Vice President for Student Affairs-Knight
      Campus

Robert Henderson, Vice President for Business Affairs-Knight
Campus
Robert Silvestie, Vice President for Academic Affairs-Knight
Campus
John White, Jr., Director-Affirmative Action Pgms/Minority
Student Affairs

Greenville Technical College (SC)
Kay Grastie, Vice President for Education
Doug Brister, Vice President for Administration
Marty Herbert, Associate Vice President for Education
Jerry Campbell, Associate Vice President for Education
Lola McDonald, Finance Officer
Robert Clanton, Auditor
Walt Brannon, Director of Physical Plant
Aurelia Morrow, Public Relations Assistant
Brenda Purvines, Administrative Assistant

Midlands Technical College (SC)
Lester Reed, Senior Vice President for Resource Management
Reid Holland, Vice President for Educational Affairs
Leroy Brown, Vice President for Student Development Services
Starnell Williams, Director of Marketing
Linda Mast, Executive Assistant
Becky Price, Executive Secretary

Chattanooga State Technical Community College (TN)
Sherry Hoppe, Dean of the College
Doris Evans, Dean of Financial and Computer Services
Daryl Gilley, Executive Assistant to the President
Jack McEwen, Dean of Arts and Sciences
David Duvall, Acting Dean of Technology
Connie Brooks, Director of Student Services

Kilgore College (TX)
Wade Kirk, Executive Vice President/Chief Academic Officer
Bert Woodruff, Vice President/Business and Finance
Jim Campbell, Associate Vice President/Student Services
Melvin Marshall, Associate Vice President/Institutional Advancement
Charles Florio, Dean of Arts and Sciences
Beryl McKinnerney, Dean of Occupational Education
Joe Hendrix, Dean of Longview Center

Gerald Pinson, Dean of Continuing Education
Joe Cruseturner, Director of Admissions/Registrar
Archie Whitfield, Director of College Relations

Midland College (TX)
Raymond Yell, Vice President for Instruction
Bob Phillips, Vice President for Business and Finance
Camal Dakil, Dean of Students
Deana Lush, Dean of Community Services
Hosni Nabi, Dean of Transfer and General Education
Will Morris, Division Chair-Cultural Studies

Tyler Junior College (TX)
Raymond Van Cleef, Vice President for Educational/Student Services
Ken Dance, Vice President for Financial & Administrative Services
C. C. Baker, Jr., Vice President for Development of College Relations

Northern Virginia Community College (VA)
Max L. Bassett, Dean of Academic and Student Services
Barbara D. Holmes, Provost-Annandale Campus
Wilfred B. Howsman, Jr., Provost-Manassas Campus
Jean C. Netherton, Provost-Alexandria Campus
Cecil W. Shuler, Dean of Financial & Administrative Services
Lionel B. Sylvas, Provost-Woodbridge Campus
M. Charlotte Wilhelmi, Director-College Relations & Development

Piedmont Virginia Community College (VA)
Brent A. Cool, Dean of Administrative Services
James R. Perkins, Dean of Instruction and Student Services
Patricia Buck, Executive Secretary Senior
Ronald B. Head, Director of Institutional Research and Planning
Rose Shultz, Coordinator of College Relations

Grays Harbor College (WA)
Gene Schermer, Vice President of Instruction
Bill Becker, Vice President of Business Services
John Smith, Associate Dean of Admissions
Jon Krug, Associate Dean of Vocational Education
Craig Wellington, Associate Dean of Student Services
Susan Moore, Director of Library Services
Madonna Faunce, Assistant Dean
Jim Fenton, Director of Financial Aid

Appendix 11

Gender Differences—Presidential Participants

Alabama
James Chasteen, John C. Calhoun State Community College,
 Decatur
Yvonne Kennedy, S. D. Bishop State Junior College, Mobile
Judy Merritt, Jefferson State Junior College, Birmingham

Arkansas
John Easley, Phillips County Community College, Helena

California
Marjorie Blaha, Solano Community College, Suisun
Lois Callahan, San Mateo County College District
Virginia Holton, Lassen Community College, Susanville
Peter MacDougall, Santa Barbara City College, Santa Barbara

Connecticut
Robert Miller, Quinebaug Valley Community College, Danielson

Florida
Catherine Cornelius, South Florida Community College, Avon Park

Georgia
Derrell Roberts, Dalton Junior College, Dalton City

Iowa
David Buettner, North Iowa Area Community College, Mason City

Kansas
Chuck Carlsen, Johnson County Community College, Overland
 Park

Kentucky
Ronald Horvath, Jefferson Community College, Louisville

Maryland
Robert Parilla, Montgomery College, Rockville

Massachusetts
Eileen Farley, Bristol Community College, Fall River
Brunetta Wolfman, Roxbury Community College, Boston

Michigan
Anne Mulder, Lake Michigan College, Benton Harbor
Marilyn Schlack, Kalamazoo Valley Community College, Kalamazoo

Minnesota
Geraldine Evans, Rochester Community College, Rochester
Jerry Owens, Lakewood Community College, White Bear Lake

Mississipi
William Skaggs, Meridian Junior College, Meridian

Nebraska
Richard Gilliland, Metropolitan Technical Community College,
  Omaha

New Jersey
Flora Mancuso Edwards, Middlesex County College, Edison

New York
Peter Spina, Monroe Community College, Rochester

North Carolina
Ruth Shaw, Central Piedmont Community College, Charlotte
Raymond Stone, Sandhills Community College, Pinehurst

Oklahoma
Al Philips, Tulsa Junior College, Tulsa

Oregon
John Keyser, Clackamas Community College, Oregon City

Pennsylvania
Judith Eaton, Community College of Philadelphia, Philadelphia

Rhode Island
Ed Liston, Community College of Rhode Island, Warwick

Tennessee
Karen Bowyer, Dyersburg State Community College, Dyersburg
Harry Wagner, Chattanooga State Technical Community College,
  Chattanooga

Texas
Patsy Fulton, Brookhaven College, Farmer's Branch
Stewart McLaurin, Kilgore College, Kilgore
Nellie Thorogood, North Harris College, Houston

Virginia
Richard Ernst, Northern Virginia Community College, Annandale

Washington
Shirley Gordon, Highline Community College, Des Moines
Joseph Malik, Grays Harbor College, Aberdeen

West Virginia
Barbara Guthrie-Morse, West Virginia Northern Community College, Wheeling

Wisconsin
Beverly Simone, Milwaukee Area Technical College-North, Mequon

COLLEGE AND PROPER NAME INDEX